WHEREVᴇʀ ɪ ʜᴀɴɢ
MY LEAD

Havoc Bathard

An autobiography of a little dog's life and travels, including his 5,000 mile walk around the coastline of Great Britain

To Bertie
Love from
Havoc
x x x

I

Havoc Bathard

ISBN 9781718010635

Published in 2018

Acknowledgements

I would like to thank the following people too numerous to name individually, who, with their help made my 5,000 mile walk around the coast of Great Britain just that little bit easier:

Members of the Guide Dogs for the Blind local committees, Guide Dog owners and Puppy Walkers who came out and supported us, walked with us and kindly put us up in their homes.

The Royal National Lifeboat Institution crew members who made us welcome and let us sleep the night in their Lifeboat stations.

Slimming World members, family members and the general public who had never met us before, but with unquestioning generosity invited us unto their houses to sleep and gave us food.

Also, everyone who kindly donated towards the £50,000 we raised for Guide Dogs and RNLI on our walk. Then of course the Hash House Harrier network who helped, supported and walked with us, and have been such a huge influence on my life.

Lastly I would like to thank Ian, for his patience and support while composing this book, Mum for helping me write it and Auntie Sally for proof reading it.

Havoc Bathard

Contents

Havoc Bathard

Preface

Those of you that have ever owned a dog will appreciate the strong bond that develops between us and our owners. Those of you that haven't, will hopefully understand when you have finished reading this book.

We grow together and become part of each other – like the fur on your back and the claws on your paws. When a sign reads 'NO DOGS' it might just as well say 'You can come in but leave your head outside!' Or, 'You are welcome but your husband isn't!'

Once you have an owner, you are an item; you go together, like salt and pepper, needle and thread or Jack and Jill.

I recognise that sometimes, it may not be the right place for a dog to be, for example: – well, I can't actually think of one at the moment. But, if all our owners were responsible, then why shouldn't we enjoy a football match, the theatre or even THE BEACH heaven forbid.

Years ago, so I'm told, pubs were places where old men could go in the evenings for a bit of peace and quiet away from the kids, take the dog and sit for a few hours by the bar – No children allowed.

Nowadays, pubs seem to be play areas with restaurants for families of noisy children – No dogs allowed. But, I don't run about screaming or have a 'paddy' when I can't get my own way, or spill my drink or stick the salt cellar up my nose. I just like to sit and relax, enjoy the ambience or curl up small and just sleep under the table.

If the manager tries to look apologetic, shrugs his shoulders and says, "Sorry, health and safety", that really gets my goat. Perhaps, if it is about dog hairs and germs, then what about Guide Dogs? After all, they are also still 'just dogs'.

When I did my eleven month walk around the coast of Great Britain, I was treated as somewhat of a celebrity, just because I was wearing a fluorescent jacket and raising money for charity. I was allowed into almost (I repeat almost) everywhere: castles, stately homes, fire stations and even into the offices of Parliament. Now though, by people that don't know me, I am treated as 'a nobody' again; an ordinary dog of little or no importance. A second class citizen even.

But, I am not an ordinary dog. I may not be able to speak the English language, but I have human thoughts and feelings. I can communicate with sounds and body language, and of course telepathy through my mum (who was a big help in writing this book) and, by the time you have finished reading it, you too will realise that I am not just an ordinary dog… Or, maybe I am, but as my vet said once, "A very lucky dog."

Introduction

I first suspected something out of the ordinary was going to happen to me, when people we met said things like, "Have you told him yet?", and "Do you think he will make it?" Being quite a nervous little dog my immediate thought was a visit to the vet – maybe I'd contracted some serious illness and they'd not told me, but I was only four years old. I thought I was right with my intuitive suspicions when a few weeks later I was rushed to the vets – luckily I wasn't dying, just broken my leg, but I still ended up in a plaster cast for four weeks. Concern really set in though when I heard Mum saying to the vet, "Will he still be able to walk?" Was she worried I would never walk again? I could just picture myself strapped in to one of those trolley gadgets that you sometimes see dogs trundling around the park in. How humiliating.

My over-protective mum is called Wendy and I've lived with her since I was eight weeks old. She's not my real mum I know. I'm an orphan. Both of my birth parents were shot, so I've overheard it whispered, for worrying sheep; yet another thing that concerns me - because, try as I might, sheep are so tempting to chase.

Preparation for my big walk

Whilst I was nursing my broken leg, I noticed other abnormalities were happening at home. Ornaments were being wrapped in newspaper, packed into boxes and taken up to the shed, (which unsettled me). Mum was packing all her clothes into big, black, plastic bags and taking them to another house down the road. While most items were leaving the house, different things were arriving, like a new tent, sleeping bags and rucksacks. That was OK, because I liked camping, I could cope with that and anyway I was getting really fed up with being indoors resting all the time. I needed to get out, get some proper exercise, get this plaster cast off my leg and run again.

My plaster was eventually removed and suddenly I was of interest to the newspapers. Paparazzi were turning up and taking pictures of me walking down the street. Was a dog recovering from a broken leg that unusual?

My beloved Hashing routine changed too. (Hashing is a cross country running club I belong to) but instead of running with the rest of the group, we walked at the back with huge rucksacks on. I say we – because even I had to wear one! Panniers that were strapped on my back and got caught on everything that I passed. Not my idea of fun anymore.

I thought I'd finally discovered the big secret when a few weeks later I was packed off to Grandpa's house in Bath for three weeks. Mum had gone on a Hashing holiday to Thailand and she couldn't take me because of aeroplanes and elephants. I didn't mind too much because I loved Grandpa. He looks a lot like me, with his white beard and whiskers, although his ears don't flap up and down like mine when he walks. Nanny is nice too - she gives me treats in the kitchen when she thinks Grandpa isn't looking.

As usual, I had a great time - so why had people been asking, if I would make it? Grandpa only takes me around the block because he's waiting for a new knee... Oh no! Perhaps I'd got it wrong. What if they meant would it be too much for Grandpa? Or even worse, would **he** make it through his operation! Anyway, we both survived the three weeks, and all too soon it was time for me to be taken home, back to Devon.

Mum didn't go back to work after her holiday. Rucksacks were packed and unpacked and packed again. Maps were put into shoeboxes and the postman, instead of bringing us post, came and took them away. New boots and coats were tried on - yes, I had coats as well! And shoes - the most ridiculous things you ever saw which even had Vibram soles. When they arrived the enclosed note said, "Do not laugh at your dog" Yeah right! - When Mum put them on my paws she and Hannah (my human sister) could not stop laughing at me. I tried shaking them off, I tried jumping round the room and I even tried standing on only two legs at a time. They were hideous and so uncomfortable but Mum said that the special 'Search and Rescue' dogs wear them to protect their paws, so that made me feel better, important even, but I still hated wearing them.

We went Hashing that week and people were saying goodbye and wishing us well.

More reporters took photos.

What was I about to do that was so special?

It was mid-November 2006, dark and cold outside. The radiators had just clicked on and I could feel the warmth slowly seeping through my body. I was dreaming of lying on a soft sandy beach relaxing in the hot sand, but was aware of a strange distant noise. It was a Saturday so why on earth was Mum clattering about in the kitchen so early in the morning? I was still bleary eyed when she called me down stairs and practically force-fed me breakfast. I was just in the middle of licking my bowl for the third time, when our neighbour arrived and our newly acquired luggage was put into his car. I clambered in the front onto Mum's lap and we were all driven to the railway station. I was most surprised to see Nanny and Grandpa on the platform, as I knew they lived miles away. Lots of other people seemed to be waiting for us and calling my name. Guide Dogs and puppies were coming up to me, sniffing and poking; but amongst the excitement and bedlam I sensed there was an air of apprehension.

The next moment a noisy train came into the station, hissing and snorting and we were quickly ushered aboard. Nanny, Grandpa and the group were frantically waving as the train slowly rumbled out of the station. Mum put all our luggage in the wire racks at the end of the carriage, then flopped down into the nearest seat. I climbed up onto her lap and gazed in bewilderment out of the window and watched as the people left behind on the platform became just tiny specks.

I sat on Mum's lap, I sat on the floor, I sat under the table, I had a look up and down the carriage, I sat under the table again and I sat on her lap again. How long were we going to be on this train? I gazed out of the window. The countryside was whizzing by: open meadows, wooded valleys, trickling streams, herds of cows, flocks of sheep, rows of houses, bustling streets and deserted beaches.

How I wanted to be out there enjoying it all. I crawled back under the table again, and drifted off into a deep nostalgic sleep. I was dreaming of my puppyhood.

A Pub Dog

I was born on March 11th 2002, in an outside shed of a little house in a small village on the edge of Dartmoor, called Ilsington, not far from where I live now.

My biological mum was a small, quiet, wire haired Jack Russell Terrier and my biological dad was a Rough Collie/ German Shepherd, but I never really knew him. I had six brothers and sisters and our mum looked after us as best she could. We were quite big puppies and I was the biggest, so her milk was rationed and I had to fight to get my share, but often still felt hungry.

I don't really know what I look like, a long-legged Jack Russell I guess. I know I'm tri coloured because it is written on my health card, but what three colours I don't know, as I only see shades of black and white. When I look in a mirror I can see the black and white and try to work out my other colour, maybe red, maybe blue? I'm not sure. Mum has never told me but I fancy blue. I have scruffy fur and whiskers from my chin which makes me look older than I am. I have a long pointy nose and my ears stick up but then fold down at the top and bounce when I walk. This makes me look cute – so I am forever being told.

The lady that looked after us all was called Philippa and was very kind, her two children named me Biscuit and came to play with us every day. I didn't like the scary shed and hated it when the children went off to bed and we were left in the cold. I would try and snuggle closer to mum, bury my head in her soft fur and hide my ears from the creaking wood and noises outside. I was frightened of the dark and longed for morning when the sun came up and the children would come back in to play. "Diddle diddle diddle" they would call out to us and I knew I was safe again. We slept in the shed with our mum at night and played with the children in the day while we ate, played rough and tumble and doubled in size. I only ever remember my dad coming to see us once.

One afternoon, when I was just eight weeks old but about the same size as my biological mum, I was carried up to the local pub where I met two new children, called Hannah and Scott, who lived there and were to become my new family. I liked them instantly. A few days later I met Wendy (my mum now). I moved in, changed my name to Havoc, and became the pub dog.

Pub life was noisy and I didn't like it much. Mum's partner (now ex), who reminded me of an English Bulldog with his big squashed nose and stance, would make me sleep outside in another shed where I often cried myself to sleep. I shared this shed with Mum's two old cats, Tara who was terribly thin and Alex who was fat with tabby markings. They also hated the shed, but the ex-partner (whom I will refer to from now on as, The English Bulldog or TEB) wouldn't let us sleep inside. Poor Tara, who was the eldest, really needed the warmth of a fire, but we snuggled up together and got through the chilly nights. I couldn't wait till the morning when Mum would come and let us out and I could play on the grass and charge around the churchyard next door. "Busy busy" Mum would say to encourage me to have a wee. It's what she would say to the Guide Dog puppies that she used to walk, in order to get them house trained and wee on command. I soon got the hang of this and had less and less accidents indoors. (Although, I did have an occasional wee on the pub floor if I got desperate and thought nobody was looking.)

Mum had lived at the pub for just a short while and only worked there in the evenings and at weekends. During the day, she worked at a school for 'naughty boys'. I would go with her in the car and curl up on the front seat until break time. Then she would come and let me out and I played happily in the car park with the boys, they were great fun but break times were soon over. During lunchtimes we would go for a walk around the lanes and often a couple of the boys would come with us, taking it in turns to hold my lead. By 3.30pm I was fed up with sitting in the car, but it was home time, and as I was still quite tiny Mum would let me sit on her lap while she drove. As I got bigger, I was allowed to spend the day in the small fenced school garden and the children would come and visit me at break times. Sometimes I would bark at them through the long glass windows in their Art lessons. I enjoyed going to the naughty boys' school and regularly joined in their outdoor education lessons, especially if they went walking on Dartmoor, or anywhere exciting in the school minibus.

Mum hated working in the pub. I knew it was too much for her doing two jobs, so I would snuggle in and comfort her when she got upset. We only lived at the pub for a couple of months, then TEB had a huge disagreement with the Landlady and she asked us to move out. We left that night and moved back to Mum's house in town where I spent the next ten years of my life. I was happier there and Tara and Alex loved being home again. Hannah and Scott moved back into their old bedrooms and life was less stressed for everyone, for a while. Unfortunately, during the following summer, Tara who was now 19 became very ill, and then one morning she just didn't wake up. Mum cried a lot and said that she had died, I didn't know what that meant but I didn't like it because I never saw her again. Tara never said much but I missed her frail little body tottering past me in the mornings. Alex and I became firm friends and would cuddle up on the sofa when no one was home. We knew how each other was feeling and were support for each other when arguments were occurring between TEB and Mum. Unfortunately, the following year, Alex who was now 17 became very poorly. I could see in his eyes that he was struggling, (and he kept wetting his bed) he stopped eating and wouldn't come out of the bathroom. I went in to see him a few times but he wouldn't even look at me. Mum made him a comfy corner in there for the night and the following morning took him to the vets, but he didn't come home. I presume that he too had died, because Mum cried again like she did when Tara died, and I never saw Alex again. I think dying is something that happens when you get old, I don't know where you go but you have to leave your family behind and I don't like the thought of that, so I hope I never get old.

An Educated Dog

Mum changed her day job and TEB joined her as Outdoor Education Instructors for 'naughty boys and girls' and could take me to work with them. We were first based at a training centre in the middle of Dartmoor, I loved the drive there each morning across the open grassland. I would sit in the front seat of the car looking out the window and try to spot the sheep, cows and ponies that roamed freely on the moor. The children that came to the centre were all teenagers from troubled backgrounds and had been removed from mainstream schools for bad behaviour. At the centre, they had to learn to do as they were told, learn to share, take turns and trust other people, not to swear and how to behave in public. I was a very important part in helping them to adjust and trust other people. Sometimes they would come in in the mornings in a bad mood because they had had a rough time at home with their family. Mum would send me out with them for a walk around the block to calm down (they usually had a quick puff on a crafty cigarette), then return to the centre more relaxed and able to cope with the day. The children were educated using the outdoors as a tool, canoeing, kayaking, rock climbing, abseiling, moorland walking, cooking indoors and out, bivouac building and overnight camping. I loved being with them, every day we did something exciting and new. I would sit on their laps in the kayaks and jump into the canal whenever I fancied a change, then climb into another child's boat and shake all over them till they laughed and we both fell in. One time we were walking by a lake and one 'cocky' little lad leaned over the water to collect tadpoles in a jar. I pushed past him to take a closer look but accidently knocked him into the water. Oh dear! I thought he was going to explode with rage but luckily, he managed to see the funny side and forgave me. He got his own back another day by strapping me into a harness and lowering me over the abseil wall, I didn't mind as Mum was watching and I trusted him. I knew they all adored me, and I loved them. In the afternoons, if they were doing book writing or project work inside, I would just curl up by one of the children's feet and let them run their fingers through my fur, it was calming for them and so relaxing for me.

TEB was far less tolerant with the naughty children than Mum. He couldn't cope with their disruptive behaviour and eventually he left work. He wanted Mum and me to resign as well but we loved the job and didn't want to leave, so he did everything in his power to make our life miserable for the remaining time we worked there. During this time, our work colleagues realised that things were 'far from perfect' at home and the Domestic Violence team were involved. They came to our house and requested TEB to leave straight away. He left, and after sleeping in his car and then living in his tent for a while, he bought a little cottage just up the road. But, as the weeks went by he slowly wormed his way back into our lives, which is where this story started.

Just thinking about those times made me twitch and squeak, then suddenly I woke with a start – the train jolted and… I needed another a wee! I still had quite a few more uncomfortable hours trying to sleep. Eventually the train stopped and I could get off. "Busy Busy" Mum said, and with total relief I piddled on the platform. I was just squeezing out the last dribble when she yanked the lead and pulled me back onto the train again. Then off it rumbled heading even further North. At least I was more comfortable and slept the remainder of the journey.

By the time we arrived at Edinburgh it was dark. Mum strapped my panniers on my back and I walked cautiously out of the station straight into the hustle and bustle of a busy city. Buses, cars, people dodging left and right and even an urban fox darted across the road. I was scared, everything was taller, brighter and noisier than it was in Devon. People were pushing and shoving past saying incredulously, "Look at that dog!" and "Look he's carrying his own bags".

We walked a few blocks away until it became quieter and we reached Hoggy's house. He is an Edinburgh Hasher. He wasn't there but a friend let us in and we had tea. Despite the fact I'd been asleep most of the day on the train, I just crashed out that night.

Early next morning we walked briskly back to Waverly Station, ready to leave Edinburgh and head even further north, changing trains at Inverness, with just enough time for another quick wee. I settled myself under the table by Mum's feet and was rocked back to sleep again by the rhythmical movement of the train. It had been warm and cosy at Hoggy's house which made me reminisce about my other Hashing friends back home.

A Hash Hound

On Mondays and Wednesdays, we all went Hashing. I would look forward all week to these evenings, and would get myself more and more excited as the time drew closer. Mum would put on her trainers and get out her kit bag. That was the sign and I knew it was the night.

A group of humans called 'The Hounds', meet, (usually outside a pub) then run through the countryside looking for and following a trail of dots and signs made in flour or sawdust that someone else, 'The Hare', has laid earlier. Hashing is enjoyed by thousands of like-minded people all over the world. Everyone is given a silly nickname or 'handle', Mum is called Soapy. I don't have a silly nickname; I can't think why. Lots of my human Hashing friends are mentioned throughout this book, their names may sound peculiar but I honestly don't know them by any other name. It seems strange I know, but its great fun and there is always lots of excitement and noise – people talking and laughing. Some of my best doggy friends go too: -There is KC the Jack Russell, (well he's a bit of a pain really), forever jumping on my back, which I hate. Bill the collie is great company and Charlie the Springer Spaniel will turn up occasionally if his mum will let him out. Then there was Crusher the old vice president of our Hash, he was a Staffie and had been Hashing for years. I always looked up to him, (well down because he was smaller than me) but sadly he stopped coming, Mum says he Hashes in heaven now. At the following Annual General Meeting, I was officially made the new vice president – an important position, which I take very seriously.

At the beginning of the Hash people gather in a circle, I get so excited that my legs shake with anticipation and my heart pounds so hard it nearly jumps out of my chest. Once we start running I bark and bark with excitement and if I'm on my lead I pull so hard my tongue goes grey. (Mum bought me a harness but it didn't make much difference.)

A Hash trail usually covers between three and six miles through fields, woods, rivers and mud, ending an hour or so later, back at the pub where, more often than not, I fall fast asleep under a table, exhausted. The Hashers (or Hash House Harriers - their proper title) will then eat, drink and sing. Sometimes if I'm not too tired, just to make people laugh I'll join in the singing. Sometimes there is a fancy-dress theme to the run. Mum loves dressing up and has a whole room of costumes that she's made. I have numerous fancy dress outfits as well but I'm not quite as keen to wear them as her, but I go along with it to keep her happy. I love my Hashing, friends, fresh air and countryside - Sadly none of this could be done when my leg was in plaster.

So how did I break my leg? – Well…

During the house clearing in preparation for our walk, Mum was out and TEB was left in charge of looking after me. The front door of his cottage was open which led straight onto a busy road, so he tied me to a heavy builder's wooden work bench. As he went out of the front door I tried to follow, pulling the workbench over making it clatter. It frightened me so much, I ran through the kitchen and down the little step into the lounge. The workbench followed on the end of the lead but as I jumped down the step, it came down crack on the back of my left leg. "Howling Shih-tzus!" The pain shot through my body and I yelped in fright. TEB shouted loudly at me, so I hobbled upstairs and hid under the bed in the spare room. This was my safe space, I always hid there if I heard shouting and arguing or loud noises like thunder or fireworks.

When Mum came home I was in dreadful pain and could hardly walk on my injured leg. She was very upset and gently tried to look for the damage. I did my best to be brave and not whimper but was hiding the pain so she wouldn't fret.

Next morning, I still couldn't walk on my leg, so off to the vets I went on the other three. Again, I tried to be brave as the vet pulled and pushed the limb. I was screaming inside but didn't want him to think I was a sissy. He gave me pain killing anti-inflammatory tablets and told Mum that I should rest it for a week. I did – no Hashing for a whole week and only along the road for a quick wee, not allowed upstairs and confined to sleeping in a cage. I hated it and was going crazy, cabin fever was setting in. A week later I was still limping with pain, so off I went to the vets again. This time Mum insisted on me having an x-ray. I had to be put to sleep for this so that I couldn't move whilst they took a photo of the bones inside my leg. I was scared and thought of Alex not coming home when he went to the vets, but the nurse was kind and talked gently to me as I drifted off. The next thing I knew I was awake with my leg in a plaster cast, they had found a hairline fracture in my hock. The cast was so heavy it took a lot of getting used to. I could walk with it on, but if it was raining or wet when I went out for a wee Mum would wrap it in a plastic bag held on by an elastic band to keep it dry. I was house bound again. Mum still went Hashing without me and went on lots of long walks, I just had to stay home and rest. I was angry and so bored, I slept a lot and looked longingly out of the window at people passing in the street. At last, four weeks later, the time had come for me to have the cast taken off, so Mum dropped me off at the vets on her way to work. I was already anxious of being left and suddenly the nurse came towards my leg with a noisy spinning saw. I was terrified and thought she was going to hurt me, so I got in first, turned around quickly and bit her on the arm! This was not a good plan as I was severely reprimanded and then put to sleep again. When I woke up I felt dreadfully sick and wobbly. I couldn't stand up properly and my leg that had been in plaster was completely useless, it gave way whenever I tried to stand, and boy did it hurt!

Gradually over the next few weeks I got stronger and did more and more exercise to try and strengthen my leg. I tired quickly though, and it really hurt towards the end of long walks, so I would just lift it up and continue my journey on the other three. What's more, to add insult to injury, Mum made me carry my panniers on my back. I thought I looked silly but she wore hers, so we walked and Hashed looking silly together.

Only 5,000 miles to go.

Hours had passed by when I woke again on the train, my legs were stiff and my back ached, I needed to stretch and was desperate for another wee. The train was stopping and the few people that were still left in the carriage were preparing to get off. Mum picked up our bags and strapped my panniers on my back, we then followed the others through the station to where a bus was waiting. The railway track was being repaired, and the last few miles had to be done by road. I just managed to get a quick wee out before we were all squeezed onto the already steamed up bus. I sat on Mum's lap while our bags went in the storage area underneath. Although not that late, it was already dark outside and scary. The bus was hot and smelly and twisted and turned as it sped along the narrow roads, throwing us from left to right in our seats. I was just beginning to think I was going to throw up when we pulled into the dimly lit streets of the little Scottish town of Thurso. It was too dark to try and find somewhere to put the tent up, so we found a little Bed and Breakfast for the night. Although we still hadn't done any walking, it had been a long day and all that travelling had exhausted us, so we went straight to bed. I curled up on the floor beside Mum and wondered what tomorrow would bring.

I awoke to the smell of bacon cooking and my tummy

rumbled. I could hear the rain pattering on the window and Mum was checking that she had packed everything back into our bags. We ate breakfast, put on our rain coats (yes, I had a silly raincoat too – with proper sleeves for my front arms, ridiculous. I only wore it once but it was too tight, so Mum posted it back home with the first lot of finished maps – thank goodness) then, traced our way back to the bus stop. The next bus to leave Thurso got us to John O'Groats by lunchtime.

It was deserted there. Pouring with rain, cold and not very welcoming. Mum found the pub that keeps a book to write in if you are travelling from John O'Groats to Land's End, so she added our names and the date, then wrote that we were walking the whole way around the coast and back again. She took a photo of the first and last shop and that was it…

We were off, on our eleven-month adventure, to walk clockwise around the entire coastline of Scotland, England and Wales. Not only was this an adventure, but we were raising money for two charities, Guide Dogs for the Blind and The Royal National Lifeboat Institution.

We soon left the pavements behind and walked across open heathland. I came off my lead for the first time in days and ran around in silly circles chasing imaginary rabbits, completely oblivious of the rain. The heather was high and the ground underneath was uneven as we rounded the first corner at Duncansby Head, and started our long journey south. Despite the wind whistling around my ears I could clearly hear some people shouting from over the cliffs. We all stopped and listened, thinking that perhaps someone had fallen over the edge onto the jagged rocks hundreds of feet below. Quickly Mum grabbed my collar so that I couldn't follow. Imagining we might have to do a cliff rescue, we cautiously went to the edge and peered over – "Woah" what a long way down! I dug my claws into the ground as my head spun. Sprawled happily on the beach below us was a large colony of seals barking and growling to each other. I was so relieved, I really didn't fancy an abseiling experience on my first day!

I found it quite tiring jumping the heather and Mum stumbled a few times as we continued along a narrow boggy animal track, trying to catch up with TEB who was way out in front. Scotland has very few signed footpaths as walkers have the 'Right to Roam', so we just followed the cliff top as near to the edge as we safely could. We had only been walking a couple of hours and the sun was already starting to go down as we arrived at the little fishing village of Keiss. Mum found a local man and asked him if he knew of any grass we could camp on. He kindly offered us his net store for the night to save putting the tent up, which was great; dry but smelly. Fishing nets and lobster pots hung all around over big chest freezers which contained frozen lobsters and crabs. Mum cooked sausages and savoury noodles on the little methylated spirit stove for their tea. I carried some dry complete dog food in my panniers which I ate, along with some bits of sausage. A big dog food company had given Mum £300 to pay for my food on our walk. Sometimes I ate the dry food but most evenings if we passed a shop, Mum would buy a big tin of dog meat for me. I would eat half the tin for supper and the other half for breakfast in my little plastic bowl that I also carried in my pannier. Mum uncurled her foam roll-mat and laid her sleeping bag on top, then with most of her clothes still on, wriggled down inside. I sneaked onto the end and curled up by her feet thinking of my adventure so far and drifted off into a restless sleep.

The next morning, as like most mornings to follow for the next eleven months, Mum boiled water and dried milk powder on the little stove and made instant porridge for their breakfast whilst I ate my dry food (and licked clean the saucepan). Everything was packed meticulously back into our bags and off we set, albeit a bit stiffly at first, around Sinclair Bay.

All around the coast of Britain, rivers flow out to join the sea and somehow we had to cross them. Some were shallow enough for me to wade through, some I had to swim, others I was carried. If they were very wide and deep, we either had to find the first bridge or a boat with a friendly skipper. Lo and behold, within a few miles we came to the first river crossing where I had to be carried. I didn't like it much and still paddled my feet as if I was swimming. Glad to be safe on the other side I rolled in the sand waiting for Mum to put her boots back on.

We stopped frequently for bag rests, Mum's rucksack was very heavy, weighing about forty pounds. I also looked forward to the break from my panniers so that I could wriggle and scratch my back in the sand; one of my favourite activities - and it still is. Whilst rummaging amongst the debris at the far end of the beach, I came across a baby seal and ran over to investigate, but Mum called me away in case its mother came back. It was quite sweet though, not much bigger than me and covered in a pale fur, but I didn't want to frighten it.

By early afternoon we were getting tired and started looking for a flat area of grass on which to put the tent up for the first time. We had used it just once before on a practice camping weekend and it had been erected several times in the garden, but this was the first time to sleep in

on our walk. Mum and TEB had it off to a fine art, as the carbon poles slid easily through the loops in the canvas and within minutes I was crawling inside onto Mum's bed. Mum lit the meths stove and cooked tea, but she had to wake me up to eat mine, as I was already fast asleep.

The next morning, we reached a largish town called Wick. Here I saw my first of many Lifeboats, the 'RNLB Roy Barker II', which looked impressive floating in the water. A crew member met us and chatted for a while, politely interested in our adventure but it was still early days and not much to tell, so time to get walking again before our joints seized up.

The open cliff tops were an enormous playground. Miles of crispy dead heather crunched as I walked and bewildered rabbits appearing from everywhere, scattered in all directions as soon as they saw me. I had never had so much freedom and fun. I charged around in huge decreasing circles chasing everything that moved, coming back frequently to check on Mum's slow progress across this uneven terrain. Negotiating the deep geos (Scottish name for a gully) took ages as we descended the safest way down, then climbed back up the other side, Mum carrying her enormous rucksack. At the top of each geo were barbed wire fences that the farmer had 'kindly' put in our way to hinder our right to roam. Each fence crossing took careful planning. First the rucksacks would have to come off, then TEB would scramble over, then Mum would pass the rucksacks to him, then I would be bundled indignantly over the fence, lastly Mum would climb over and rucksacks were put back on again. In all it would take about ten minutes to cross each fence.

Our next night's stop was a bit of a mystery and hard to find. TEB had read John Merrill's book 'Turn Right at Land's End', the first recorded trip of walking the coastline of Great Britain. John had walked 6,824 miles clockwise in 1978 and had slept at the Mains of Ulbster, so we were now trying to find it.

We were all very tired, it had been a full day of hard walking, my legs ached and the bottom of my paws were beginning to burn. We wearily walked down a very long driveway which on the map showed as a farm. When we eventually reached the building, we found that it was deserted and beginning to fall into disrepair. We wandered around the grounds obviously looking for something, although I wasn't sure what but looked anyway. Then, beyond the outbuildings tucked around the back of the farm, I saw a little stone crypt with wooden shutters and roof. At the top of a small flight of steps was a tiny wooden door. It was empty inside, except for an open fire place with the remains of a burnt-out fire, so we dumped our rucksacks and all searched around the farm for some pieces of wood to burn. TEB then built a wonderful fire in the grate to keep us warm. The crypt was only about ten feet square so Mum pushed the tent canvas in around the door cracks to keep out the draught and we slept cosy and warm on the floor. I curled up on the bottom of her sleeping bag and within seconds was fast asleep - completely oblivious to the dead bodies that were buried beneath me.

The next morning, we were up early and I eagerly finished off the other half of my large tin of dog meat that Mum had bought the day before. Rucksacks were repacked and we keenly strolled out into the morning sun back up the long drive to the main road, heading south again. Negotiating the barbed wire fences and geos had been slow going, so we decided to walk down the main A99, which was not too busy and had plenty of grass verge. We were only a few metres from the sea and at times the road ran right along the water's edge. As we passed through the village of Ulbster, a lovely gentleman got talking to us outside his bungalow about our walk. It was still only midmorning but he invited us in to meet his wife who offered Salmon sandwiches, "Say yes say yes" I thought. Luckily, Mum never refuses free food so in we went for a rest and an opportunity for me to have a quick nap as my injured leg was already aching. Mum slid her hand under the table and fed me her juicy fish tasting crusts whilst the resident cat licked his lips in anticipation – "No chance of that mate."

Re-fuelled we continued, stopping again quite soon, in my view to pointlessly descend Whaligoe Steps. This is a manmade stairway with 365 stone steps built in the 19th century for fisherwomen to haul up the fish that had been landed at the harbour beneath. They would gut the Herring, cod and Haddock then carry them in baskets back up the steps to be taken off on foot to be sold in Wick. My legs were killing me by the time I got back to the top and I never even saw a tiddler.

Rain continually threatened as we painstakingly made our way south over already sodden heathland. We were trying to reach Helmsdale before it got completely dark but by the time we reached the dimly lit streets it was lashing down, had turned to sleet and was biting into our faces. Despite wearing one of my silly coats, I was soaked through, bitterly cold and trying to shelter behind Mum's legs. She was already using the torch, but it was too dark to find a piece of grass to put the tent on, so reluctantly she decided to use some of her savings to pay for Bed and Breakfast (Not a good start as we had only been walking a few days – although I was all for it.) A slightly scary, but kind lady put us up for the night and dried Mum and TEB's clothes around her Range, whilst I wriggled dry on her antiquated thread bare carpet. Later, TEB went out and bought fish and chips which we were allowed to eat in the lounge in front of the huge roaring fire. They were scrummy and a real treat. After breakfast next morning, we had a stroll around the village and went into a general store to replenish supplies, only to find the owner had herself once walked the coast of Britain. Vera Andrews, or Granny Vera as she was known, had visited all the British Gas showrooms on her way as she walked 3,524 miles anticlockwise in 1984.

Our journey south was much flatter now and we took a small road which ran along next to the sea shore, stopping regularly for Mum and TEB to have their rucksack breaks. At the start of the walk, I very rarely rested when Mum did. I loved sniffing all the new smells and investigating the rocks and driftwood on the beach, I didn't want to miss anything. I never ventured far from them though and always returned when the sandwiches came out, ever hopeful of a spare crust of bread. The early days of our walk were relatively short as by 3pm it was already beginning to get dark.

We passed the outskirts of a village called Lothmore and walked hopefully through a small caravan park right on the coast, looking for somewhere to pitch the tent. The old caravans were undoubtedly privately owned and obviously well loved by local families, but none of them were inhabited and there was no one around so Mum jokingly said "I wonder if any of them are open?" They hesitantly tried a few doors and quickly found one unlocked. Relieved to get out of the cold, unquestioningly I climbed in. Mum got our stove going and cooked their tea, which quickly warmed up the van, then laid their sleeping bags out on the caravan beds whilst I snuggled down under the table. I could smell that another dog had been there before but was too tired to care and soon drifted off dreaming of chasing bunny rabbits.

When the first glints of sunlight shone through the caravan's faded curtains I got up and had a good look around. It was full of family holiday memorabilia and children's seaside playthings. We didn't do any harm and left the caravan exactly as we found it, so I'm sure the owners wouldn't have minded us staying... If only caravans could talk.

I spent most of the next day playing along a long straight sandy beach which took us to Brora. The soft sand under my feet was lovely providing respite from the hard tarmac. I paddled in the shallow water at the edge of the sea, chased pebbles that Mum kicked along as she walked and checked out the flotsam and jetsam on the beach, ever hopeful that I would find something disgusting to eat. The day went quite quickly, as by early afternoon we were already on the outskirts of Brora, the next biggish town down the coast. The first pub we reached in the high street was The Sutherland Arms, so we popped in for a rest and after Mum got chatting to the cheery Landlord he offered us a room for the night. (Surely our luck couldn't keep going like this - somebody up there was definitely looking after us.) Then, he let Mum and TEB have a cheap evening meal, (ham, egg and chips if I remember rightly) and after begging for scraps, I was soon ready for bed.

Although not for us, Sunday is a day of rest in rural Scotland, so no shops open, nobody works at all, not even to hang the washing out. Only the poor vicar works. Now, although I'm not religious, I think Mum may be, as she says "Oh my God" at least four times a day! So, to keep in the Lord's good books, we attended the local chapel. It was, I imagine, like stepping back fifty years in time. Everyone was in their Sunday best and all the ladies wore hats. There was no music, and people stood up to pray and sat down when they sang, not what I have seen before on the odd occasion that I have been to church. When at last the service was over everyone was extremely friendly and quite surprised to see me in chapel as I had been so quiet. They all came over and chatted, taking it in turns to make a fuss of me and wanting to find out more about our walk.

Our sins forgiven, we followed the narrow coastal path

from Brora along the sea edge and past the spectacular Dunrobin Castle. A strong chilly breeze blew across the bay encouraging little waves to lap at our feet and seagulls circled overhead as if dancing in the wind, making white patterns against the stormy skies. I wore my ridiculous all-in-one fleece that had been specially made for me and shipped over from America. I didn't like wearing it at first but soon realised that it kept me warm, however silly I looked.

We picked up the A9 again, which runs along the coast through the small village of Golspie, then headed inland to make our way around Loch Fleet. Walking on the unforgiving tarmac made my front right leg hurt, causing me to limp. I think I twisted it whilst chasing rabbits the day before. We crossed the River Fleet at 'The Mound' and stopped at a convenient picnic bench for a lunch break. This usually consisted of sandwiches made from out-of-date bread bought at the end of the day before and something savoury like cheese or meat. Mum always shared hers with me and I got TEB's crusts if I was lucky. Mum looked at my leg and felt all around my toes. They didn't hurt at all, it was further up that was painful. I rested for a while and it eased, but as we crossed the Royal Durnoch golf course and headed back to the coast I was limping more with each mile. I tried to hide it as best I could but walking on the road was agony. I was soaked to my skin from the freezing rain and feeling utterly miserable. Suddenly through the drizzle, like an oasis, appeared a whisky distillery. On the door a big sign read, 'NO DOGS ALLOWED', however the two ladies inside were lovely. They felt sorry for me and let me warm up on their tartan rug in front of the roaring open fire, then gave me a shortbread biscuit and bowl of water, while Mum and TEB sampled the single malt whisky to warm themselves.

By the time we reached Tain, I was really struggling;

limping on my strained front leg and trying not to use the back one that I broke only a few weeks ago, which still ached at the end of a long day walking. Mum managed to get me an appointment at the local vets who was quite concerned about what I had been expected to do. He gave Mum some tablets which I had to take daily and was told that I MUST rest for a few days!

Mum and TEB discussed all the options of how we could continue the walk:

a) Pull me in a shopping trolley?…... Nope.
b) Push me in a wheel barrow?……..Nope.
c) Carry me in a rucksack?………… Nope.
d) Get someone to look after me for a week?……. Maybe.

Mum went through her list of people that had offered to put us up for a night and the next one on the list was Chris, at Forres, ninety miles away! (He was a fund raiser for Guide Dogs for the Blind and had offered us a bed for the night over a year ago when Mum had been doing all the planning.) She gave him a ring and fantastic news, he agreed to drive all the way to Tain to collect me. He would then take me back to his house, look after me and give me my medication, while she and TEB carried on walking round the coast to meet up with me a few days later.

What utter Bliss... A ride in a car and then the best B&B ever, with a few days of rest and relaxation being spoilt rotten by Chris and his lovely wife. Mum phoned every night to check how I was, and Chris would jokingly respond "You're not having him back, I'm keeping him." This did concern me just a little, because although it was comfy at Chris's, I really missed my Mum. They made me a comfortable bed in their kitchen and we had just a slow short walk every day which gradually made me stronger and stronger. All too soon Mum and TEB came to pick me up, although I have to admit I was relieved to see them. They stayed the night with me at Chris's cottage and told us of their journey without me around Durnoch Firth to Tarbat Ness lighthouse, then on down the coast to Nigg, where they had crossed in a little boat to Cromarty. They then Headed south across a bridge into Inverness, staying in a hostel which didn't allow dogs (luckily, I wasn't with them). Next, they walked eastwards along the Moray Firth Past Nairn, to Forres to meet me.

Forres to Edinburgh

With all four legs rested and back working properly, we continued along the Moray Firth past Covesea lighthouse to Lossiemouth, which homes one of the largest and busiest fast-jet stations in the Royal Air Force. The planes screamed over head as we walked along the beach. I didn't like it and cowered down when they passed so low overhead. We crossed the river Lossie via a long wonky wooden footbridge which made my legs shake, onto a beautiful sandy beach that went on for miles with sand so soft that I felt the need to roll in it at every opportunity. Continuing eastwards we passed many deserted caravan parks, travelling through the town of Buckie and on to Cullen with its little fishing harbour, split in half by the two impressive Victorian viaducts. Here we had our next pre-planned overnight stay with Skye a sweet little black and white Collie. Despite feeling exhausted from walking all day, I still found enough energy to play in the garden with her. Standing on our hind legs we 'boxed' like a couple of hares in springtime, till Mum called us in for bed.

As I left Skye the next morning still licking Cullen skink (creamy haddock soup) from my whiskers, I stopped in the pet cemetery and contemplated the tiny headstones covered in flowers, immaculately tended little graves and stone plaques placed either side of the twisting narrow paths which led up the hillside. Back on the coastal path I noticed a dead mouse. He seemed perfectly intact with no apparent reason for dying. This was the first of many I saw on my journey and I wondered what made him expire right in the middle of the footpath? Mum took off my panniers so I could run, but I walked quietly beside her deep in thought.

The landscape around Aberdeenshire varied greatly as we journeyed along its jagged coastline, across high rocky cliff tops, along never ending sandy beaches, over immaculately mown golf courses, around more empty caravan parks, past North Sea gas terminals and sometimes right next to the main road. I was off my lead for the majority of the time, so that I could investigate every rabbit hole and ditch, just taking my time sniffing and checking who had been there before me. Whenever I got left behind, Mum would just whistle and I would run and catch up but more often I would be on ahead, clearing the way of bunnies before Mum's arrival. My favourite place of all was the open sandy beach; miles and miles of it all to ourselves with not another person or dog in sight. The occasional helicopter would fly low overhead on its way out to the North Sea oil rigs, disturbing the serenity. I didn't like them at first and would bark and chase them as they interrupted my thinking time, but eventually I got used to them. Sometimes they would catch Mum out if she was trying to have a discreet wee, as there was nowhere for her to hide – but it never bothered me.

I was exhausted by the time we got to Gardenstown and the light was getting dimpsy. I was intrigued by the Macduff Lifeboat which had arrived back from a call out and watched it from the quay wall. Someone had reported seeing a body floating in Banff bay and I waited eagerly to see it hauled ashore but boringly, it just turned out to be a huge floating log.

In the small town of Rosehearty, further along the

coast, we needed somewhere to sleep the night and an elderly lady, whom I could hardly understand due to her broad Scottish accent, directed us to a small village hall, suggesting we might stay there. The local playgroup were just finishing their afternoon session and the children were skipping around the room singing their farewell song. It reminded me of Hashing, so I joined in, barking and running around the room with them excitedly, making them laugh. Afterwards, I was on my best behaviour and allowed them to pet and make a fuss of me, they were all very good. Every child handled me gently and kept clear of my tired feet.

I stayed on my lead the next morning, which I hated, as we walked even further east beside the busy B9031, hugging the coast to Fraserburgh. The cars came far too close and made me jump each time one passed. It was a miserable, overcast day, but we were greeted by a jolly group of Lifeboat men sheltering in their cramped, temporary porta-cabin station. They were so pleased to see us and managed to make tea while I rested under their make-shift table. After recuperating, we left Fraserburgh behind and rounded the corner at last heading south again, crossing the Inverallochy golf links and onto the soft sand dunes around Rattray Head. We were following a narrow sandy track through the tufts of spiky grass which passed The Rattray Head Eco Hostel, but despite piles of rubbish dumped outside, it seemed completely deserted. I felt that sense that things didn't seem quite what they ought to be and couldn't understand why there were so many dead rabbits scattered everywhere! It felt sinister and sent a shiver up my spine, so I kept close to Mum and passed by quickly, avoiding the skulls, backbones and rib cages, thankful that we weren't staying there for the night! Relieved, I caught sight of the top of the Rattray Head lighthouse which guided us safely back towards the coast. The dunes were enormous. We walked for ages up and down but I could see nothing but sand. I imagined it must be like walking through a desert. When we did eventually reach the sea, it was lapping around the bottom of the dunes, so I had to carefully dodge each wave as the loose sand fell away into the water from underneath my paws and scamper quickly around the water's edge.

We skirted the fence of one of the UK's main gas terminals at St Fergus, which looked like a scene from a sci-fi movie, then followed more golf links trimmed with precision which led us into the big fishing town of Peterhead. Here we had a guided tour of the 'Misses Robertson of Kintail'; a Tamar class Lifeboat which was the first one in Scotland. We stayed the night with Dennis, his Polish wife and the tiniest baby I've ever seen. Dennis was a pest controller and had access to explosives to scare birds. He had been having a problem with intruders in his garden, so made himself a burglar deterrent to frighten them away. Unfortunately someone had informed the police that he was making bombs in his house! The next thing he knew he was being arrested, the streets were cleared and the local school was evacuated. His story hit the national newspapers! Luckily for us he had been released and not charged.

The beautiful soft sands of Cruden Bay were a doddle, before the winds blew us along the top of very high, steep cliffs, where we passed memorials to people that had fallen to their deaths near Slain Castle. It was nearly dark when we got there and it looked quite spooky silhouetted against the stormy sky. Mum kept me on a short lead so I didn't get blown over the edge, but nevertheless I tucked in tight behind her to be on the safe side.

During daylight hours, farmers' grassy fields and open cliff tops gave me the prime opportunity to chase anything that moved. My legs were feeling strong and I was ready for any bunny that dared to pop his head out.

Our arrival in Newburgh on 7th December gave me

my first insight of Christmas 2006. We entered the Udney Arms Hotel to find the landlady and landlord in fits of laughter, wrapping themselves and their Christmas tree with festive lights. After untying themselves and then decorating their tree correctly under my watchful eye, they offered us complimentary bed and breakfast. Many a cold night we had been sleeping in our tent, so I was glad that this was another night when we didn't have to, (plus Mum gave me the fatty rind from her bacon and two pieces of sausage in the morning)

Beautiful sandy beaches and mile after mile of easy to walk undulating golf links, steered us to Aberdeen, where we were met outside a busy central shopping mall by a Hasher called Olymprick. 'NO DOGS ALLOWED' were the words written clearly on the glass doors. I smugly ignored the black lettering, held my head high and strutted through the bewildered shoppers wearing my fluorescent charity jacket. Olymprick took us to his house so that we could sleep the night in comfort, then, while the humans stayed up late chatting, I sneaked up to the bedrooms and had a much needed early night.

The following morning, we were dropped off, by car back at the coast, where we circumnavigated the harbour wall and climbed up the hill out of town. As I glanced back to watch Olymprick disappearing in the distance I saw two dolphins playing in the harbour, breaking the surface of the water as if waving goodbye. It was a cold, damp start to the morning and I was glad to be wearing my full body fleece, but as the day continued, the weather deteriorated and by early evening it was absolutely lashing down, stinging my eyes and dripping off the whiskers under my chin. Our route took us up the side of a steep hill next to the A90; a very busy main road into Stonehaven. It was almost dark and the car lights looked like the eyes of angry animals, screaming past and covering me with filthy spray. I was scared and cowered down, squeezing in tightly behind Mum's legs, almost tripping her up. We were trying to reach a caravan park a few miles on, where we had been promised a bed for the night. Suddenly a blue flashing light sparkled amongst the raindrops. A police car pulled onto the grass in front of us and two burly police men insisted we got in.

Dripping wet we slid onto the back seat of the car and Mum explained why we were walking up the side of a dangerous main road at night in the rain. They were very sympathetic and took us right to the door of our caravan. (This was very exciting, albeit a couple of miles of our round Britain walk that we didn't actually walk!)

The next day I presumed was Sunday, as Mum was up but I was having a lovely lie in. As I stretched each leg in turn on the thread-bare caravan carpet, easing the stiffness from my body, I was rudely aroused by a sharp knocking at the door. A lady had arrived to give us a lift in her car to meet up with Aberdeen Hash House Harriers for their morning run. I instantly knew by the trainers and shorts that she was a Hasher. I didn't even stop to eat my breakfast and just jumped straight into her car. I love Hashing so much that although my legs were aching, my body refused to say no.

I shook from head to toe with anticipation as we stood amongst the circle of Hashers. As soon as I heard the familiar sound of a horn blowing and everyone set off running and shouting, I instinctively joined in the chase, charging across the open fields following the other runners, dragging Mum on the end of my lead. In the distance I could hear loud gun fire which I normally hate, but my mind was so focussed on Hashing that my little legs just kept running without hesitation.

After the run, we circled up again in the car park and ate warm stovies, a delicious mix of potatoes and steak in Gravy, which Olymprick had brought for everyone. Of course, Mum shared hers with me which was just what I needed on a cold winter's morning, especially as I had been in too much of a hurry to eat breakfast. The Hashers then bid us farewell and we were driven back to our caravan, where the rucksacks were packed once again and by early afternoon we were back on our walk across a lovely sandy beach, along the edge of St Cyrus nature reserve.

Although I usually loved to paddle and cool my feet, on this occasion I allowed Mum to carry me across the mouth of the river Esk, so that I wouldn't still be damp at bed time when I curled up on her bed. By late afternoon we arrived in Montrose where I introduced myself to a Norwegian sea dog called Bamse; a World War II lifesaving Hero and crew member in the Royal Norwegian Navy. He was only a statue but I was still humbled by his bravery. Alas, he died in 1944 and is buried somewhere in Montrose. Now on automatic pilot, I trotted wearily along the soft sands of Lunan Bay and before the sun set completely we wove our way through the narrow streets around the eerie ruins of Arbroath Abbey. In the gloaming, waiting to meet us was Margaret, a lovely lady who put us up in her cosy little house for the night. I must have slept well because before I knew it, the smell of bacon cooking in the kitchen was wafting through the house and it was the start of yet another day.

A gentleman friend of Margaret came to pick us up in his car and drove us to the Lifeboat station where we were due to meet the local crew members and a small group of Guide Dog supporters, including a large black Labrador dog in his white harness. I didn't communicate with him as Mum tells me I shouldn't distract a working Guide Dog. I stood politely as we had our photos taken for the local newspaper, then said our goodbyes before disappearing around the corner. My nose was beginning to twitch as I detected a smell in the air that made me drool. On the edge of the harbour was a 'Smokey House' selling traditional hot Arbroath Smokies; haddock, trout, mackerel and herring. It was only 11 o'clock in the morning but we had to taste this local delicacy. I was only allowed a taster but it was heavenly, I could still taste it on my whiskers hours later when I was curled up on the rug in the sitting room of Gill and Sandy, our hosts for the night in Carnoustie.

I experienced quite a restless sleep that night, as I was keeping one eye on the row of musical Christmas characters staring at me from lined up on the hearth, in case they burst into festive song and needed to be curtailed. Sandy was a keen golfer and met us again later the next day as we walked across Carnoustie golf course. I became quite an expert at finding golf balls and Mum often had to retrieve one from my mouth on our many golf link crossings. After rounding Broughty Castle our route took us into the bustling city of Dundee, famous for the making of jam and of course cakes. We sauntered through the high street taking the opportunity to collect money from the shoppers and stopped for a quick photo by a large bronze statue of Desperate Dan and his friends from the Beano magazine, before continuing down to the harbour to see an old wooden sailing ship called 'The Discovery'.

We stayed the night with a lovely family in their little

flat. They knew we were arriving as Mum had made contact with them a year before, (as with everybody that had offered us lodgings in advance) then a week before, then the day before, but when we eventually got to the flat they had to find us somewhere to sleep! Their poor son had to give up his bed for Mum to sleep in (even the same sheets I think!) Still, despite all the toys and muddle, they were very friendly and cooked an amazing smelling curry roasted vegetables. Mum took the recipe and still cooks this occasionally now. The following morning, our hosts took us in their car to the top of Law Hill, a local land mark, so that we could experience a panoramic view right across Dundee. In the distance, I could just make out the Tay Bridge, which we walked over later that morning into Tayport, but for me, the pungent smells in the long grass around the old park bench were far more interesting.

It was very cold first thing in the morning and I was glad of my fleece as we fought our way through the trees to the beach around Tentsmuir Point. There was a peculiar feeling beneath my paws. The top layer of the sand was frozen and cracked as I stood on it, which reminded me of the sound of Mum biting into the thick chocolate of a choc ice, making me feel even chillier. However, the sun was beginning to rise and gradually warmed me up as I walked across yet another golf course and into the old castle town of St Andrews. Here we stayed the night with two special dogs, a retired Guide Dog and a Guide Dog puppy. Their owner cooked toast in the evening and they were both allowed a piece before they went to bed and I was allowed a piece too. I liked this idea and think Mum should keep up this naughty habit when we get home.

Christmas was fast approaching and so was Edinburgh. We were now over a month into our walk and I was getting fitter, muscles were developing where I never had muscles before, my legs were aching less each day and I was beginning to really enjoy my adventure. I had now come to realize that I wasn't going home sometime soon and learnt that when Mum stopped for a rest then so must I, a quick nap here and there was enough to recharge my batteries.

We were striding out across the cliff tops in the December sunshine when suddenly Mum stopped by a sign on the edge that read,

'WARNING – THIS UNIQUE COASTAL SCRAMBLE WILL TAKE YOU ACROSS HAZARDOUS TERRAIN. BEWARE OF THE RISKS TO YOURSELF AND OTHERS WITH YOU!'

Mum and TEB did a lot of talking and I heard my name mentioned along with chains, cliffs and rucksacks! "What on earth were they planning now?" I was soon to find out.

They took off their rucksacks and tied me to them so I couldn't move. Then they said goodbye and walked off without me! Normally I would bark in protest, but the sun was warm and I was tired, I knew Mum wouldn't leave me for long, so I watched them disappear out of sight and settled down for a nap. I woke with a shiver as the wind was blowing across my fur. I don't know how long I had been asleep but it must have been an hour or so. I sat up to look for them but no one was in sight. Just as I was about to panic, TEB's head popped up over the cliff right in front of me. He heaved himself over the edge and Mum was close behind. I was so glad to see them. Then suddenly he grabbed my lead and dragged me towards the edge of the cliff. I protested and dug my claws into the ground. I'd never trusted him. He snatched me up, squeezed me under his arm and took a couple of steps down the cliff hanging onto a thick chain with one hand. I was shaking from ear to paw. I thought he was going to drop me onto the rocks below and I looked to Mum for help, but she picked the camera up, took a photo and said, "That's one for the album to make people think that Havoc did the Elie chain walk as well." When TEB put me back on the cliff top I instantly weed with relief, narrowly missing his rucksack, then wriggled on my back in the grass, safely back on terra firma again.

The next few days passed quickly as we walked easily down the coast around Largo Bay, along more links golf courses and as rapidly as we could past the shabby towns of Buckhaven and Kirkaldy. Then, in the distance as the sun was setting, through the haze I could make out the unusual shape of the Forth rail bridge. At last Edinburgh was in sight. Still a long way off, but I knew we were going to spend Christmas there and enjoy a much needed break.

There was a beautiful sunset and it was almost dark as we walked on hard tarmac and trudged past rows of tired terraced houses with their curtains all pulled closed for the night. It was weirdly silent except for the loose gravel, which crunched beneath Mum's boots. The bottom of my paws hurt as we crossed a carpark strewn with deflated rubber balloons, (well, they looked like deflated rubber balloons to me!) and into the streets of Inverkeithing. We had met a man a few days earlier who promised us a night's stay in a pub overlooking the bay. We eventually found the pub and hesitantly walked up the steps to the bar. He wasn't there, but true to his word this guy had paid for us to stay the night. It certainly wasn't four star but it was warm and after my half a large tin of dog food, I slept soundly on the well-worn smelly carpet.

The next morning was Christmas Eve, and I eagerly finished the second half of my tin of meat while Mum and TEB tucked into their complimentary full Scottish breakfast. Mum usually slipped me a piece of bacon or sausage under the table, so I waited expectantly and sure enough I was rewarded.

With my panniers strapped firmly to my back and under a clear crisp winter sky we boldly walked over the

Forth road bridge. It is quite a long way across and not many people or dogs walk it. Cars zoomed past us and the murky water of the Firth of Forth estuary rushed below me, so I was glad when we reached the other side and into Queensferry. It was still about ten more miles to Edinburgh and the last few were all on road.

Edinburgh to Scarborough

It was early evening and I was exhausted from our long days walk. I dragged my aching legs the last few miles into the city and we still had nowhere to sleep the night. Mum had arranged for us to stay with some people over Christmas in their house, but unfortunately the husband had been taken ill and they were unable to accommodate us. I can empathize with Mary and Joseph now, walking into Bethlehem with nowhere to stay. However, after a few frantic phone calls, Olymprick from Aberdeen Hash offered us his holiday flat which overlooked the city. He explained that an Edinburgh Hasher called Mr. Nuisance had a spare key and luckily, we managed to locate him at his office where he duly handed it over. Another couple from Edinburgh Hash came along to meet us and loaned us their spare TV, then took Mum to a supermarket to buy food for Christmas. As it was 5pm everything was reduced dramatically and she managed to buy a great feast for only a couple of pounds. Olymprick's flat was lovely; on the third floor, overlooking Edinburgh's Christmas ice rink with all the twinkling lights of the city reflecting on the ice, I could even hear the excited shouting of people in the street below.

I was just licking my bowl for the umpteenth time to

check if I'd missed any supper and thinking about settling down in front of the TV for the evening, when my lead was clipped back on to my collar and out of the door I was pulled. The air was cold and I could see my breath, but I had a feeling that something unusual was going to happen. The Christmas lights were still shining but the streets had gone quiet, so I knew it was late. We walked briskly along the paved streets of the Royal Mile until we met a few more people heading up some wide stone steps. We followed, and entered through the doorway of a huge, dimly candle-lit church. I immediately felt excited by the presence of all these persons, but somehow knew it wasn't a Hash and I must behave and not bark. Inside the church were hundreds of seated people but we had to stay at the back with the hundreds more that were standing, whilst Midnight Mass took place. I curled up tight on the cold stone floor listening to mumbling that I couldn't understand and the singing of Christmas carols that seem to go on forever. By the time we eventually got back to Olymprick's flat I was cold, stiff and exhausted. The thick pile carpets beckoned and I drifted into a long deep sleep dreaming of an old man, with a big white beard flying through the sky on a sleigh pulled by reindeer.

When I eventually stirred the next morning, I was surprised that Mum was still in bed – why weren't we up and out walking? I stretched out a leg and something squeaked. It made me jump and retract. I gingerly moved my paws again and nudged something round and hard. I sat up and sniffed the air, could I smell a hide chew somewhere? "Yippee!" Santa had remembered me again. He had left a hide chew and a squeaky Christmas pudding by my bed. I soon forgot about the walking and settled down to enjoy my presents.

I was still gnawing on my chew when Mum appeared and wished me a Happy Christmas. She put the television on and went to the kitchen area to start preparing lunch. Not the usual soggy sandwiches, but turkey pieces, vegetables and roast potatoes. The smell was wafting through the flat and I was feeling very hungry. I had already consumed my breakfast but always ready to eat again. Downstairs in the apartment block was a communal laundry area, so Mum made the most of this and put almost all of their clothes in for washing; so it was in their vests and pants with crackers and paper hats that they ate their Christmas lunch. I also had a big bowl full and was adorned with the traditional paper hat – (I will do anything to eat a meal like that, it was delicious). In the evening, we walked down the hill and into the city. There were lots of people bustling about and I seemed to be under everyone's feet. I didn't like the noise, the dark evening or the flashing lights. I wanted to return to the flat and kept pulling to go back, but Mum insisted we stayed to watch the festivities in the streets. We hung around for a while and wandered aimlessly around. "Grr" I hate just walking without a purpose. We watched the skaters on the ice rink for a while, then made our way back up the hill to the flat. It had been a strange day – I wasn't used to doing nothing. I liked being out on the cliff tops walking somewhere or playing on the sandy beaches, chasing pebbles. I lay down on the plush carpet again and was soon asleep dreaming, – maybe tomorrow…

Tomorrow soon came and we were out of the door again quite early, but something wasn't quite right. Half of our stuff was still at the flat – had they forgotten to pack everything? It was very cold and I had been made to wear my thicker all-in-one fleece under my fluorescent charity jacket. I didn't like it, as it was a bit tight and uncomfortable. We walked down the hill once again, over the bridge and past Waverley train station, from which we had departed just over a month ago on our way north at the start our adventure. I was trying to sniff the lamp posts to reminisce, but TEB dragged me on past and into the shopping area. It was Boxing Day, named either because of all the empty boxes that get thrown out after presents are opened, or because families fight the day after Christmas. Anyway, apparently, it's when people love to go shopping and spend their Christmas money in the Sales. We set ourselves up outside the shops and stood there for what seemed hours with our collecting tins and bucket. A man in a skirt – (Mum says kilt) was stood on the opposite corner, driving me mad blowing an instrument called bagpipes and making a noise that made my ears hurt. I was so bored and hated wearing my thick fleece. I lowered my head, put on my most depressed look and gave that watery stare in my eyes to let everyone know how I was feeling. So many people stopped and felt sorry for me, but when they read the print on my charity jacket that said I was walking around the coastline of Britain, they just smiled in empathy and generously put money in my tin.

We stayed in Olymprick's flat for three more nights. However, during the days we carried on eastwards along the coast, walking in the rain, working our way around towards Musselburgh, Prestonpans, Cockensie and Port Seton. When I got to the sandy beaches I bounced along off my lead. I didn't mind getting cold and wet, as each night we caught the bus back to the warmth of our Edinburgh 'home'. It seemed a bit strange catching the bus back again from where we had walked the day before but I never refused the opportunity of a lie down and quick nap for the duration of the ride.

We stayed the next couple of nights with a nice lady called Anne who lived on the outskirts of Edinburgh in her lovely cosy house and relaxing garden. I could have stayed there forever because she was so kind. After Anne's we stayed across the other side of Edinburgh in a tenement block of flats for the night, with a completely blind lady called Roz and her German Shepherd Guide Dog, Lilly.

Roz was very enthusiastic when we arrived and couldn't do enough for us. She even gave up her own bed for Mum and TEB, while she slept in her clothes on a plastic sofa in the kitchen and would not take no for an answer. She was an amazing lady and told us some incredible stories of her life and travels with her Guide Dogs. I was a little bit taken aback though, when she showed us the pelt of one of her previously departed Guide Dogs that she couldn't bear to be parted from. She kept it draped over a chair in the lounge cupboard and smoothed it whenever she felt sad! I just hope Mum doesn't get any ideas. It made me feel very uneasy and I didn't want to look.

After a rushed tea, (that I'm sure contained a pill which I tried avoiding, but was so hungry I downed it by mistake) Mum and TEB changed their clothes. "Yippee!" I thought, "We're leaving," but, I then was left in Roz's bedroom and the door firmly shut in my face. I barked to be let out a couple of times but Mum came back in and told me off, so I was quiet. Then I heard the big front door close and I knew they had sneaked out and left me. I barked and barked and scratched at the door but began to feel very peculiar. My legs had gone wobbly, which made me panic all the more. Roz came to the door and was talking to me calmly through the key hole, but she wouldn't let me out. I heard the big clock in her hallway chiming, then suddenly, 'BANG!' The whole room shook and lit up for a second, then 'BANG!' again. I was absolutely petrified. I started to bark louder and scratch at the carpet. Little pieces were coming up and getting stuck in my claws, so I started again on the door. 'BANG!' again. "Oh no!" I thought it sounded just like gunfire! The room filled with flashing lights, and whizzing sounds were coming from outside. My legs wanted to collapse but I was determined to keep on my feet. "Where's my Mum?" I howled loudly. Eventually Roz got fed up with me scratching and barking so she reluctantly let me out. I rushed into the hallway, almost knocking her flying and managed to squeeze myself in between the wall and her sideboard. I could still

hear the noises but at least I felt safer and was supported so that I couldn't fall over. She knelt down to comfort me and said that she had phoned for Mum to come back. It was Hogmanay and they had gone back to Olymprick's flat for a party, thinking that I would be safer at Roz's because of the fireworks. They had given me a pill to make me sleepy but I was determined to fight it and kept awake. When eventually they returned – slightly annoyed to say the least, the firework noises were beginning to fade. I relaxed immediately, gave in and fell into a deep sleep.

What seemed like only minutes later, it was the morning. I felt dreadful, my legs still shook like jelly and my head was pounding. We said our goodbyes, apologies to Roz and Lilly and returned once more to the streets of Edinburgh, this time heading through the main street up towards the castle. A circle of people were gathering and I could tell by their clothes that they were Hashers. It was New Year's Day and traditionally a run. I could barely 'barking' walk, let alone run! The other Hashers were looking at me, asking if I was drunk? I certainly felt like I was. My eyes were sore and my legs wouldn't go in the direction I wanted them to. Uncharacteristically, I was glad when the run had ended and the reality of normal walking had returned.

We only did a short walk later that afternoon as the weather had deteriorated. We skirted around the edge of a golf course, as a bitter gale force wind blew straight into my face. It was lashing down with rain, and I couldn't believe that men were still actually playing golf. They could hardly stand upright, let alone direct a ball, but yet still gave us a cheery wave and dug deep into their soggy pockets for loose change.

Sandy golf links and beaches hug the coast all the way past Bass Rock towards North Berwick. It was late afternoon by the time we arrived and almost dark. The streets were deserted except for a small unobtrusive group of people huddled in the doorway of a pub. The smoking ban had just become law in Scotland and they had to puff their cigarettes outside, so stayed crammed in the doorway to keep warm. They saw our flags and banners and enticed us into the glowing atmosphere of the pub. Wow! What a welcome we got. Most of the customers were either Lifeboat men, or families of Lifeboat men. Mum and TEB were given beer and I was given a bowl of much needed water. After being bombarded with questions about our walk and charities we were whisked off in a car to the Lifeboat Station to see their Blue Peter Lifeboat, which they were very proud of. Then we were taken to the tiniest of flats and invited to stay in the home of a lovely couple. The promise of game pie was too much for anyone to resist. Here I met Sheba and Bumble, a huge German Shepherd dog and a minute grey kitten that simultaneously raised their heads, glared at me, then continued their sleep curled up together in the same bed. The man of the house, who was a little inebriated, looked how I felt that morning and was stumbling all over the place. He even fell into the television when trying to turn it on. Our bedroom was the lounge floor, but at least we were warm and dry and spent another night not having to sleep in the tent.

At Tantallon castle, just outside North Berwick, Mum and TEB had their first big row of the walk. Mum was in charge of the map (because she didn't need glasses to read) but TEB was adamant he knew a better way, past a sign that read 'PRIVATE LAND, NO ENTRY'. He did the normal shouting at Mum before she gave in and we walked across the forbidden ground. It upset me and made the walk even more uncomfortable than it already was. The next stretch of our journey was an arduous trek and took us around St Abb's head, where giant folds of rock covered in short wet grass made the unnecessary, circular yomp around the light house and back hard going. There were millions of rabbits teasing and taunting me to chase them. I resisted for as long as I could, until I could contain myself no longer and suddenly I charged after them, disappearing into the gnarled branches of a hibernating gorse bush. I was wearing my charity jacket at the time but came out minus the Guide Dog badge which Mum had carefully sewn on. I can just imagine the rabbits now laughing and admiring it hanging on the wall in their burrow as a trophy.

I was exhausted both mentally and physically by the time we reached the little harbour town of St Abbs. My back leg that I'd broken a couple of months ago was really hurting and I hobbled the last few yards on three legs. This occasionally happened on a long day's walk, but I soon recover after a good rest. We slept that night on the kitchen floor of the little church hall, which was greasy and sweaty, so Mum wiped it with paper towels before putting the bedding down. I gobbled down my tinned food, eagerly waited to clear up any remnants of theirs, then climbed onto Mum's sleeping bag and was oblivious of the filthy, slippery floor in seconds.

The next day we got up at the normal time but had an hour or so to look around the area. I checked out the best smelling lampposts before making our way slowly to the next fishing village of Eyemouth. TEB was starting to cough and sniffle and was grumpier than usual, but I was excited and wanted to walk faster because we were due to meet Spud in Eyemouth. Spud was a girl who had walked the coast of Great Britain with her dog Tess about ten years before us and had written a book about it, called 'Two Feet Four Paws'. Reading her book, had given Mum the inspiration to follow in their footsteps.

Next to the fishing boats moored in the harbour, Spud greeted us and took us in her car back to their house to meet her husband Rob, children Barnie and JP and her old brown horse called Ben. Ben had taken her and Barnie, when he was only sixteen months old, along all the drove roads of Scotland whilst she had been recovering from cancer. Unfortunately, Tess had passed away a few years earlier but we saw her grave in the garden and I paid my respects to this doggy legend. We stayed with Spud an extra day for TEB to recover from his full blown 'man flu' and my legs enjoyed the good rest. We were taken by car back to Eyemouth and set off again across the little harbour bridge. I ran up the grassy hill the other side and gazed out over the cliff; I swear I could see England. We kept as near to the cliff edge as possible, walking on the litter strewn grass, next to the busy road and main train line into Scotland which ran along beside us. We were heading towards Berwick upon Tweed but stopped abruptly in the middle of nowhere and out came the camera. Mum took a celebratory picture of me with a signpost on the railway behind. We had made it to the borders and crossed triumphantly into England. On the grass was a little mouse. I poked him with my nose but there was no movement. That's two dead mice I had noticed now, with no obvious reason for their death. How odd.

We made it to Berwick by sunset and managed to find a flat piece of grass to put the tent on near the castle ruins. Mum always carried the poles and TEB carried the canvas and although not many nights so far had been spent in the tent, it was a precise military operation putting it up. I had watched the procedure many times and reckon I could probably do it by myself now. Self-inflating mattresses and thick sleeping bags slid inside without an inch to spare and as soon as they were inside I would wriggle in on top, curl up tight and snuggle down for the night. Although it was only small inside, it had a big flysheet over the top to keep wet coats and rucksacks under, Mum also cooked in this area when it was cold or raining.

The following morning was warmer and I woke refreshed and eager to start the day. Licking my bowl again for the fourth time, I waited patiently while the tent and its contents were packed away neatly in the rucksacks, with just as much precision as when unpacking. We set off at last down the coast towards the Holy Island of Lindisfarne. I was off my lead so I could stop and sniff at my leisure, running to catch up each time I got left behind. We stopped for a lunch break on the soft sand dunes at the beginning of a tarmac causeway, which connects Lindisfarne to the mainland at low tide twice a day. After begging for crusts and a quick hunt for rabbits, it was time to start the long journey along the sand covered causeway. TEB said, as this was not actually part of the coast of Britain, it was OK to hitch for a lift. However, as their clothes were muddy, they were laden with bursting rucksacks and escorted by me, a scruffy looking traveller's dog, nobody stopped for us. An hour later and sore footed we eventually reached the island. It was late afternoon mid-January and everything except one tea shop was closed for the winter. Although dogs were not normally allowed in, the kind lady relented and took pity on me. After two cups of tea and a bowl of water, we were escorted to a Roman Catholic Youth Hostel. This too was closed for the winter, but we were invited to sleep inside as no camping is permitted on the island. I quickly ate my half a tin of meat for tea but just as I was about to curl up for the night, I was summoned outside again to see the abbey and castle. Why they couldn't have just left me asleep I'll never know. I was so tired and not interested in another 'barking' castle, so I dragged on my lead and piddled on every available gate post just to annoy them.

Back on the mainland again continuing south, I could clearly see the Farne islands off to my left. Little did I know that ten years later, I would be bobbing about in a little boat viewing nesting puffins on them. We stayed that night with a friend of Spuds called Anna and her two dogs; a young black Labrador called Ruin and what seemed like a really old dog of fourteen, called Puppy. I never imagined that the next time I visited Banburgh, I would also be a really old dog of the same age!

The next piece of coast was quite easy walking, mainly soft, sandy sea shores and in January there were only our footprints on the beach. I loved chasing away the seagulls and making patterns with my paw prints in the virgin sand. It was now my beach and I was reclaiming it from them. We passed more castles at Dunstanburgh and Warkworth, standing lonely, cold and empty. They made me shudder and remember home and my warm little house with Hannah and Scott. I wondered then, if we were ever going home or were we now walking forever - and where were we actually going? I quickly forgot my own home when we reached Amble and were welcomed into the home of a lady called Shelly, who looked after a visually impaired boy called Kurt every day. When he came home from school he played with me on the carpet and tickled my tummy, so I soon recovered from my homesickness. Then, just a few miles on down the North Northumberland Heritage coast, through the not so beautiful sandy bay of Druridge, we arrived at Newbiggin-by-the-sea. I thought it sounded a lovely seaside town, but it was actually run down and shabby. The pavements were littered with rubbish and most of the shops were closed and empty, so I just added my wee to the already highly scented doorways. We stayed that night with a blind lady called Jo who welcomed us warmly, although her black Labrador Guide Dog, Grace, kept staring at me from across the room, making me feel very uneasy. Jo's mum had kindly cooked shepherd's pie for tea. It smelt delicious and I drooled in anticipation, but I wasn't offered any! Just the usual half a tin of dog meat. "Come on, I'm not a Guide Dog!"

Passing St Mary's lighthouse, sat gleaming white on its headland, we met Dawn and Roger on our way to Whitley Bay. After putting us up for the night in their house, they walked with us the next day down to the town of Cullercoats. Here I sat and watched the inshore Lifeboat being launched from its ironwork cradle that was pushed down the beach and into the sea by a reversing tractor. I could sense everyone's excitement and barked loudly until Mum told me to keep quiet. Dawn and Roger left us that evening in Tynemouth and waved us off as we boarded the North to South Shields ferry.

Now on the Sunderland coast the scenery changed dramatically. It was much more industrious with dirty black sand and collieries to avoid as we navigated our way inland around Easington. We climbed the steep cliffs back into the winter sunshine and the cold air hit us making my skin tingle as the wind blew. We were getting higher but I couldn't quite make out the hazy grey shapes moving in the distance. As we got closer, I could see derelict buildings with their rusty corrugated roofs flapping in the wind. They were the remains of old magnesium factories on the outskirts of Hartlepool; the redundant chimneys, twisted metal roofs and tumble down buildings were literally being held together by strands of rusty barbed wire fencing and crumbling concrete posts. I stood and stared in horror at the eyesore. It reminded me of a bombsite, like those I'd seen on TV.

It was Mum's birthday and not a very nice place to spend it, but at least the Marina had been revamped a little and I'm sure the Hartlepool monkey sitting on a plinth granted her wish and gave me a wink as I piddled on the bottom of his column.

To cross the wide river Tees, we made our way inland towards Middlesbrough. I had left the seaside way behind and was walking all day on tarmac, on either pavement or dirty grass verges alongside the main road. The huge lorries scared me when they came too close, hissing and spraying me with oily smelly water from the stagnant puddles. Everything in sight was grey; the road, sky, vehicles and even the enormous industrial buildings belched out grey clouds. To my immediate right was the river Tees. I was amazed to see a large gathering of seals resting happily on the mud flats and sea birds fishing in what seemed such a polluted chemical industrial area, but I suppose the water was warmed by the factory outlets and no predators would dare venture into such an inhospitable area. We followed the lines of power cables and pylons overhead up the Tees to the transporter swing-bridge, where we squeezed in between the cars and lorries onto the deck of the bridge. It hung on wires from giant metal towers and hovered just above the water as it slowly slung us over to Middlesbrough. It was so exhilarating, that when I got to the other side I wanted to do it again but Mum insisted we were pressed for time, although she did say that there was one other transporter bridge like this in Britain, in

Newport Wales, that I could ride on in a few months' time.

Trying to follow signs back to the coastal path took us onto the Teesdale Way, which unfortunately started badly by squeezing us tightly along a filthy narrow path between the railway line and concrete factory fencing. I was tired and fed up with being on my lead, and we were passing some amazing urban doggie smells that needed reading, but I was dragged on, unable to interpret them quickly enough. By Redcar, the beaches were beginning to reappear and we climbed the cliffs once more to join the Cleveland Way into Yorkshire. Although an overcast evening, the old fishing port of Staithes looked so quaint nestled at the base of the cliffs in its tight little valley. As usual, by the end of the day my leg was aching and I hopped on the other three down the steep hill to the Lifeboat Station, hoping for a well-earned rest. To my disappointment though, it was all shut up. Not a soul was about, so we wearily crossed the little footbridge and on into the narrow cobbled streets of the town and made a beeline for the pub, where I collapsed in a heap in front of the fire. One of the customers who had been chatting with Mum, kindly offered to put us up in her cottage with her black and white Collie called Tiff and despite being exhausted, I found enough energy to roll and play on the carpet with Tiff until it was time for everyone to go to bed.

On our way to Whitby, with the rain lashing into my face I encountered the 'Hob Holes'; fast flowing, dirty brown water rushing down the cliff gullies as we clambered up in the opposite direction. Rope handrails had been put in to assist humans, but of course I didn't need them, with 'four paw drive' I nimbly jumped from boulder to boulder working my way easily up the steep cliffs. Once I reached the top, goodness it was a different story! I was stopped abruptly in my tracks, and almost blown back down the cliff again, as the wind literally took my breath away. I could hardly breathe as it was howling directly into my face. I was so frightened that I cowered in again behind Mum's legs as we kept as close as we could to the wire fence, which gave little or no protection. With her rucksack on, Mum was top heavy and found it difficult to remain upright. At least I was lower and had four anchor points, so despite the jarring to my joints I breathed a sigh of relief when eventually they decided it would be safer to come in from the coast and walk the adjacent road.

Whitby is traditionally known for its links with Dracula. The whole town was Dracula mad; pubs, clubs, coffee shops and gift shops all selling Dracula trash. Yorkshire Hash House Harriers had arranged for us to be put up for the night in a Dracula themed Bed and Breakfast, which I thought was going to be tacky but was actually quite scary. It even had a life size statue of the man himself outside the front door! In the dark, narrow hallway was a real coffin and ghosts hung menacingly from the ceiling. All the bedrooms were given spooky names and contained spiders, dragons and cobwebs draped around the four poster beds. I slept with one eye open, just in case something should crawl over me in the night. In the morning, I was a tad tired and grumpy but tried not to show it as we climbed the huge flight of stone steps to the ruins of Whitby Abbey. I waited at the top for TEB to catch up and looked back over the harbour to watch a big yacht in full sail slip slowly out to sea. The morning was dry and I soon forgot my bad mood, as I chased rabbits along the cliff tops and strolled down the hill into Robin Hood's Bay. It was a tiny village, and must have been built for very thin people, as the streets were so narrow. We stopped in a bar so that Mum and TEB could have a rest and got talking to the barman who introduced us to a guy called Phil, who coincidentally, apparently was also walking the coast of Britain. He was dressed in a dark woolly pulley and said he was a Royal Marine doing a challenge with a friend who was walking in the opposite direction. He explained they walked only on roads and these could be up to twenty miles from the sea. He said they were also raising money for the RNLI. Well, he couldn't have looked more different from Mum and TEB! He was smart and tidy, with shiny black boots and didn't have dried mud up to the knees of his trousers. I was instantly suspicious and couldn't stop staring at him. His eyes were too close together, making him look shifty and he wasn't keen to chat too much about what he was doing. He hastily said goodbye and left the bar. Weeks later, we were informed by the RNLI that he was a rogue, trying to 'diddle' people out of their money and not walking the coast at all! Apparently, he had even been in prison for assaulting a woman! I hoped we wouldn't bump into him again.

Scarborough to London

Big rolling hills with short grass meant easy going to Ravenscar. I could run backwards and forward chasing bunnies to my heart's content. Suddenly, over the hill from between the bushes, a lone figure of a man came walking towards us. I started barking at the man, in case it was 'Phil the Rogue', but as he got closer he nervously introduced himself as Stumpy, from Yorkshire Hash, who had come out to meet us. Relieved that I wasn't going to attack him (and visa-versa), he walked with us across the cliffs to Raven Hall Hotel, where Anne and Clive, members of the local Guide Dog committee had arranged for us all to have afternoon tea.

Doolittle and Talking Pussy, from Scarborough Hash House Harriers, had offered to put us up for a night and met us later as we rounded the corner on the steep cliff tops above Scalby Mills. With the help of Anne and Clive, they had also arranged for lots of other Hashers, puppy walkers and Guide Dogs with owners, to meet and join us for our walk along Scarborough seafront, collecting money in our tins and buckets as we went. I was excited and felt very important. It was a lovely sunny day and despite being in the middle of winter, lots of people were out enjoying the beach. Mum kept stopping and talking to them about our walk as they dug deep into their pockets for money. I was wearing my fluorescent charity jacket to help attract attention but was far more interested in hoovering my way along the promenade sucking up chips, candy floss and anything else I could find to eat. Halfway along the promenade was the Lifeboat station where Guide Dog supporters had organised a tea and cake reception before Doolittle presented us with a cheque for our charities from Scarborough Hash House Harriers. I ate lots of cake and posed for numerous photos. It had been a long tiring day and I was looking forward to curling up in front of the fire, as our hosts drove us back to their house. To my dismay, I was shown the cold draughty porch. Admittedly there was a nice soft bed to sleep on but no roaring fire! Talking Pussy was allergic to dog's fur, therefore, I wasn't allowed in the house. Mum put my fleece on me for extra warmth and as I was so tired I didn't try to protest and slept right through till morning.

Leaving the excitement of Scarborough far behind, we kept to the sea shore, walking through thick white spume. It was as if the sea had become a giant washing machine and someone had overdone the soap powder which was overflowing out onto the beach. I found it amusing and chased little pieces as they blew into the air. Rummaging amongst the pebbles, I found a delicacy called pipe fish, they were so addictive, a bit salty but I still ate quite a few! It was a long steep climb to the flat topped grassy cliffs at Bempton, with its perilous sheer drops to the sea, where huge groups of black backed and herring gulls had found a safe haven to rest and build their nests. At the top was a bird watching centre with café, complete with a big sign that unsurprisingly read, 'NO DOGS'. As we were about to walk away a sympathetic lady popped her head out of the door and said, "It's OK you can come in." Mum and TEB were given a free cup of tea and I quickly gulped down a whole bowl of water. Within minutes, I started to feel a bit queasy and my tummy lurched, the next minute I regurgitated all my pipe fish and water across the floor!

Mum apologised profusely and we made a hasty exit. I don't suppose the kind lady let any other dogs in after that. Feeling embarrassed, I walked quietly on my lead till we rounded Flamborough Head with its gleaming white lighthouse. On the horizon, the sun was setting and lit up the evening sky like fire over Bridlington in the distance.

Between Hornsea and Withernsea, we walked along a very narrow beach below eroding clay cliffs. For miles loose boulders, caravans, and houses clung for dear life on to the cliff edge, ready to let go at any minute. Whilst keeping one eye on falling objects from above, I had to watch where I put my paws, as littered along the beach were bombs, yes real bombs! Over the cliff above us was a military firing range and these were shells that had never quite reached their targets out to sea. A bit further on we came upon a sign that read,

'DO NOT TOUCH ANY MILITARY
DEBRIS IT MAY EXPLODE AND KILL
YOU!'

I'm glad we had walked the beach before I saw the sign.

We slept the night in Withernsea Lifeboat station, I always felt important being left to guard a million pound boat. I woke the following morning to a beautiful sunrise. It was a dry day but with a biting wind, so Mum put my smart, newly acquired proper wax dog-coat on me before we continued south along the cliff tops. We reached the legs of the giant wind turbines near Holmpton. Their arms spun noisily overhead as we stopped for a lunch break. Usually I hovered for crusts and scraps, but the going had been really tough and muddy, I was absolutely exhausted so I curled up tight in the dry grass. I had learnt my lesson that when Mum and TEB stopped for a break I must have a quick nap too, but I fell fast asleep and completely missed lunch. The long walk down the narrow spit of land to Spurn Head was painful on my joints. We had to keep to the tarmac road as either side was a bird sanctuary and of course, 'NO DOGS ALLOWED.' At the end of the spit was the Lifeboat Station and a few houses where the crew lived. It seemed deserted. There was no one about and we had been hoping to grab a lift in a pilot boat over to Grimsby. I sniffed around the empty buildings while TEB made some phone calls. After about an hour, we noticed Sue, chugging across the water in her little pilot boat to pick us up. Cheerfully she invited us aboard and even let me sit in the co-pilot's seat to look out of the front window, as we slowly made our way back across the River Humber.

No red flags were flying, so, avoiding any more unexploded military debris we walked along the shore via Mablethorpe to Skegness. We entered the town and were met by a newspaper reporter with a camera who crouched down to take a photo of us walking down the street. As he was now at my level, I took the opportunity to lunge in for a kiss! I knocked him flat to the floor and proceeded to lick his face all over, which made him laugh so much he couldn't get up - so I kept on licking till Mum dragged me away. After a bundle of boring questions, asking if there were any down sides to our walk or if anything had gone wrong, we negotiated our way around the harbour to their Lifeboat Station, where we were greeted by the crew and three golden retriever Guide Dogs. Once inside the building, we boarded the boat for yet another group photograph. Unfortunately one of the Guide Dogs tried to push past me to take my lime light, barking cheek! So, I chanced a quick nip and caught him on the nose making it bleed. It was a shame really and I did feel a bit guilty afterwards as he meant no harm. I got a sharp reprimand from Mum and was kept well away from the others, but even from a distance I still gave them 'The Look', so that they knew I was top dog. Well, at least it gave something for the reporter to write about.

We rounded the head of Gibraltar point, but I was disappointed not to see any Barbary Apes eating bananas on the rocks. Then we followed muddy footpaths around the edges of the flat fields of Lincolnshire, famous for growing vegetables. Very few hedges border the fields, so I could watch the lorries being loaded and driven away to market. I was also fascinated by the people bent over all day long, planting new seedlings and I admired the slender sprout stalks laden with crisp little Brussel sprouts just waiting to be picked. (Naughty Mum obliged and picked a couple, slipping them into her pocket for her supper!) From the dirty farm tracks, we continued along country lanes that smelt of rotten vegetables and covered the miles quickly to the outskirts of Boston. We had a couple of hours to spare, so made our way to their Cathedral, nick-named 'The Stump'. It was a huge building and people's voices echoed around inside. One of the vergers escorted us up a steep, narrow, stone staircase to get a panoramic view out over the rooftops. I don't think many dogs have been up there, but it was a fantastic feeling to be up as high as the birds. We stayed in Boston with Mary, her very obliging husband and her three Guide Dogs, Heidi, Ben and Pedro (one working and two now retired). They also had a budgie, whom I found most fascinating. I had never seen a bird in a cage before and wondered if he really liked being imprisoned, or should I give him the taste of freedom to fly like the pigeons around the Stump? (I decided not to release him). We were looked after impeccably, we couldn't ask for more, although I did feel a little sorry for Mary's husband, who hardly ever sat down to rest. I managed to behave myself with the Guide Dogs and not bite any of them, and felt even more respect when I saw Heidi in her harness the next day, skilfully Guiding Mary across the roads towards the outskirts of Boston, where we said our goodbyes.

We continued on the hard tarmac main road to the pretty village of Fosdyke, in order that we could cross the river Welland, where, despite the very cold weather, I saw the first signs of Spring with carpets of snowdrops hanging their little white heads. We ventured back towards the coast, and the going got easier under paw, as we walked for miles on the soft grassy dykes around the flat reclaimed land around the Wash towards Kings Lynn. Huge swarms of little birds made patterns in the sky as they played in the thermals overhead, it made my neck ache trying to watch them. At the mouth of the river Nene was a lighthouse. Just a couple of yards away on the opposite bank was another lighthouse which we needed to get to, but the river was just too wide and deep for us to wade across and the banks had steep muddy sides. Unusually, there were no boats around for us to hitch a ride in, so we had to walk nearly four miles inland to Sutton Bridge, and then four exasperating miles back again to the coast. Despite soft grassy paths on the dykes, it had still been a long day walking in heavy rain, my shoulder joints ached and my back leg was hurting again. I was so relieved to find that there was a little passenger ferry to take us across the Great River Ouse to King's Lynn, where I met Dorothy and her Golden Labrador Guide Dog, Honey, who had made a special journey to come out in the rain and meet us.

By the time we reached Hunstanton, Mum and I were both limping quite badly. She had blisters and my back leg was killing me. We were met by Denise and Rob with their two Golden Retrievers at the Lifeboat Station and posed for yet more press photos. I was so tired I couldn't be bothered to argue with them about who was top dog, so was on my best behaviour as I was hoping to stay in their house that night. Denise and Rob felt sorry for me and let me stay an extra day to rest and recover there while

Mum and TEB carried on walking around the Norfolk coastal path. During the morning Rob took me out for a gentle stroll along the grassy seafront to keep my joints from totally stiffening up, but most of the day I just slept on the sofa, totally oblivious to the other two dogs playing around me.

I re-joined Mum and TEB again the following day. By Wells Next the Sea, I was totally revived and bounded off across the salt marshes to chase birds. The sky was clear and it was a beautiful crisp day. A gaggle of geese flew overhead honking directions to each other as they passed, while hundreds of smaller birds were feeding on the mud flats of the Moston Marshes in the distance. We fought our way through dry teasels and grasses much taller than me, trying to find the Pedars Way footpath over the cliffs to Sheringham, then around the coast to Cromer, where to my horror, I saw a dead dog!

Bored and uninterested, I was dragging my paws around Cromer Lifeboat museum, when to my surprise, I saw a completely motionless man and his dog standing next to a beach hut. I blinked twice and barked but they didn't flinch. As I stared harder, I realised that Monty was a real, stuffed, dead dog! He looked a bit like a St Bernard, but he was a bit moth-eaten so it was difficult to tell. Apparently, he had been the faithful companion of Henry Blogg, the man by his side, (who wasn't a real stuffed man) who had founded the Royal National Lifeboat Institution. That was it; I didn't want to see anymore, in case there was something else dead or stuffed, so I put on a pained expression, pretended I needed a wee and pulled Mum quickly out of the door.

Endless soft sandy beaches ran from Cromer to Caister so walking was easy, but the recent rough sea and high tides had thrown an awful lot of sand from the beach across the promenade, making it difficult to see where one ended and the other began. At Happisburgh, the sea was lashing right up to the sea wall as we walked along the top. I didn't like the sound of the waves crashing against the concrete and covering me with spray. I imagined each wave was an angry hand reaching out to grab me and pull me back into the ocean. I cowered down and didn't want to walk past, so Mum put me on my lead and with 'gentle encouragement' I made it safely to the end of the wall.

Sometimes I got fed up of being with just Mum and TEB, especially when they weren't talking to each other, so I enjoyed it when we had company. A lady called Valerie walked with us from Winterton-on-Sea. She had kindly given us a bed for the night and joined us for a few miles the next day. She also gave us a donation for our walk which Mum popped into the bucket; that 'chink chink' sound always excited me as it fell on the other coins. I thought then, that when I got home I wanted to get a job so that I could count my money every night like Mum and TEB did, and take delight in the chinking sound that it makes.

Our fund raising was going quite well, I had it down to a fine art. If I saw people on the footpath I would run on ahead of Mum and greet them, then as they bent down to smooth me they read the words on my fluorescent jacket:

"I AM WALKING 5,000 MILES
AROUND THE COASTLINE OF
GREAT BRITAIN TO RAISE MONEY
FOR GUIDE DOGS FOR THE BLIND
AND RNLI".

By the time Mum caught me up, they had their money out, ready to pop in the collecting bucket. As the tins and buckets became fuller they got heavier, so were emptied almost daily. Our 'Charity walk' had its own Post Office and bank deposit accounts, so if we were in a village or town we stopped and paid money in, which had to be counted and bagged the previous evening. If there was nowhere to deposit all the coins, then TEB would ask either a shop keeper or a pub landlord if they could exchange it for notes, which were lighter to carry.

We reached Caister and I smiled to myself as we passed the first pub. Its sign read, 'NEVER TURN BACK', which was the Lifeboat crew's motto. I decided then and there, that this would also be my motto in life; however far I was asked to go, I would make it to the end and never turn back.

Caister's Lifeboat was called C.L.B. Bernard Mathews and was sponsored by the man on TV that breeds turkeys for Sunday dinner. It made my tummy rumble just thinking about it and I couldn't wait for lunchtime. We sat on the beach and Mum threw me a couple of her left-over sandwich crusts - but they were 'bootiful'.

It was early February and still pretty chilly. Although not raining, the wind tore at my panniers trying to rip them off my sides. I lowered my head to try and stop any loose sand blowing in my eyes and kept in close behind Mum's legs for shelter, as we rounded the fast-eroding easterly coast of Norfolk.

In front of Great Yarmouth Pier I met Kim, whom I believe, at the time, was the only Leonburger ever to pass the strict training to be a Guide Dog. She was with her owner Kay and her husband who treated Mum and TEB to lunch in a 'NO DOGS' café; which luckily, I was allowed in as I was with a working Guide Dog - It certainly helps to have friends with benefits.

After continuing along Great Yarmouth's Sea Front, past the second Nelson's column in Britain, we joined the Norfolk Hash House Harriers in the countryside for their Sunday run. No matter how tired I am or how much my legs ache, somewhere within me I can always find enough energy to run with the Hash. At least I didn't have to carry my panniers and we ended up at one of the Hasher's house for a barbeque, where I did very well scrounging for scraps.

The coastal erosion was even more significant down the Suffolk Heritage Coast towards Southwold. Trees and turf hung over the edges of the cliffs, fearfully waiting for the next high tide to grab them and pull them into the sea. I liked Southwold, it had a lovely clean, sandy beach with a row of neatly painted beach huts; like many others that I passed on my walk. It also had an interesting pier, full of bizarre slot machines, invented by a man called Tim Hunkin. One of them was called 'RENT A DOG', inviting people to walk a dog on a rolling road. It was not a real dog of course, but he had that look of embarrassment in his eyes that made me feel quite sorry for him.

As we left boats bobbing on the pretty river inlet of Walberswick, we carefully picked our way through snowdrop carpeted woods, heading for Aldeburgh, where we were due to spend the night at the Lifeboat Station. It was beginning to drizzle as we squeezed along a narrow path between Sizewell Power station and the beach. The building towered above me and was as grey as the sea and the sky. Every building and piece of metal merged together, apart from a strange looking, enormous, white 'half of a golf ball' sticking out of the top. I felt very out of place amongst this unnatural sci-fi habitat and hurried past as quickly as I could, dragging Mum behind me. I loved sleeping at Lifeboat Stations, we crashed at many during our eleven-month adventure and they were always warm and cosy. Mum would just lay the sleeping bags out on the floor of their mess room so I could curl up comfortably wherever we were. Most of the buildings were ultramodern, with good kitchen facilities, a drying room for wet clothes and rucksacks, showers and usually a TV. Before we started our walk, Mum had contacted the RNLI, but Head Office had said we wouldn't be allowed to stay - 'Health and Safety' no doubt "Grr!" Nevertheless, most of the crews at the stations were only too pleased to help us and were so grateful for what we were doing for them.

Crossing the river Alde the next morning could have been a problem if it hadn't been for Johnny and his little old wooden fishing boat. He gave us a lift part way, then transferred us, rather wobbly at sea, into his little dinghy and then rowed us right onto Sudbourne marshes. Quite a manoeuvre. Back on dry land and a bit shaky on my feet, we entered an Avian Influenza (bird flu) control measure restricted area. I was trying not to look too much like a chicken, as I was finding it painful to walk on the pebbly beaches around Hollesley Bay.

As I said before, I am not a religious dog, but I found the churches to be most accommodating, allowing us to sleep in their halls, vicarages or even on the floor of the church itself. All denominations were so welcoming. I found out later, that apparently if someone on a pilgrimage asks a vicar for a place to sleep, it is his duty to provide shelter. We were on a kind of pilgrimage and they certainly did their duty. Anyway, on this stretch of coast we were invited into the vicarage of Geoff. He was a campanologist and had to go out that evening for hand bell practice. He told us to "Make yourself at home, and help yourself to food and drink". I was just as surprised as Mum when she opened one cupboard to find a 'barking' great shot gun! Well, it takes all sorts to make a world and who am I to judge. He seemed a pleasant enough bloke, and kept plenty of biscuits.

My paws were feeling less sore by the time we reached the river Deben, but I never refuse a kind gesture. A man called John offered to take us across to Felixstowe in his newly-painted little fishing boat and there we were duly met by a bundle of Guide Dogs and puppies in training, causing chaos outside a seafront tearooms. They then joined us for a short walk along the promenade before a noisy send-off as we boarded our pilot boat to take us across Harwich Harbour. It was another dry day as we marched around Pennyhole Bay and I was feeling good. The daily routine of getting up early and walking all day was becoming easier, my legs were strong and only gave me pain in my back leg if I walked too long on tarmac pavements. That afternoon, a slightly better behaved group of Guide Dogs and puppies greeted us, along with the crew at Clacton-on-Sea Lifeboat Station and joined us briefly along a stretch of concrete sea wall, where I saw my first Napoleonic lookout Mortello tower. We seemed to be faced with one obstacle after another as we squelched our way round a very boggy coastline before trying to negotiate the river Colne. Luckily the Harbour Master, Ian, came to our rescue and kindly offered us a ride in his boat. I was just enjoying a quick 'forty winks' on the deck, lulled by the gentle 'chug chug' of the boat, when I was startled by the loud roar of an engine, and the Mersea inshore Lifeboat pulled up alongside us. To my amazement, we were ushered aboard over the sides, and then, with Mum holding on to me and me holding on to my stomach, we were bounced at top speed over to Mersea Island.

It was Shrove Tuesday when we arrived at Bradwell-on-Sea and we stayed at Othona, a Christian retreat, but as it was still only February we were the only ones visiting. The lady vicar of the village invited us to her house for the evening for a pancake supper with her parishioners. Well, I didn't have to be asked twice. I was definitely the centre of attention, so as well as trying to beg as much as I could from people's plates, it was a good opportunity to promote our walk and collect money. We were also cordially invited to join them the following morning at St Peters-on-the-Wall church, for an early Ash Wednesday service. It was a good job we turned up, as we actually doubled the congregation number in the bare stone church, which only contained a few tiny benches and an altar. At the end of the short service, the six of us, which included the vicar and me, were all then duly anointed with Ash on our heads.

Feeling now rather grubby, we made our way across the Dengie Peninsula, which was not quite as dingy as I thought it sounded. Despite being very barren and marshy, it was a safe haven for migratory birds. We kept to the road which passed through pretty villages heading towards Burnham-on-Crouch. The last few yards along a footpath were so overgrown that even I had to crawl to pass under the wet branches. A couple of friendly donkeys leaning over their fence found it highly amusing to witness the three of us entering their village on all fours.

To cross the River Crouch a lady called Lizzie and her young son, Arthur, gave us a ride in their little old wooden boat. It was quite a wide choppy crossing and the water was leaking in rapidly. I held my breath as the water steadily rose up my legs and I wished I was wearing a life jacket like Arthur. I was relieved when we moored safely at the other side and was the first one to jump out onto solid ground. Thankfully we were now on our way to Southend-on-Sea, where we were put up for the night by Hashers, Windsock and Tops.

As one of the charities we were collecting for was RNLI, our ambition was to visit all of the Lifeboat Stations around the coast that we passed. Southend-on-Sea hosts its Lifeboat Station at the end of its pier. Unfortunately, the pier is not dog friendly and neither is the little train that runs the length of what claims to be the longest pier in Britain. No matter how much Mum begged and pleaded, even offered to carry me the whole way, Mr 'Jobsworth' at the entrance of the pier would not be swayed into changing his mind. Disgruntled, I tried to put it out of my mind and trek on. I had a very important meeting in London and no time to waste.

We briefly hopped on and off Canvey Island just to say we'd been there, then trudged around Tilbury docks to Grays. The pads on my paws were burning from all the tarmac walking, and I missed the muddy salt flats and soft grassy footpaths of Suffolk. Instead, huge concrete industrial buildings flanked both sides of the River Thames. Towering chimneys puffed out smoke in the distance, huge metal cranes hung menacingly overhead and graffiti covered concrete walls with grey steel handrails guided us along the river bank. The suburb town of Grays was welcoming, with its neat little terraced houses and their pocket handkerchief gardens. We stayed with Hashers Digger and The Duchess and ate our tea in their warm, homely kitchen. I left the others chatting and wandered off to check out the best place to sleep. I popped my head around the lounge door but was instantly startled by hundreds of little black faces with beady white eyes all staring down at me from the sofa, grinning mischievous smiles. I barked loudly at them but nobody moved. This brought Mum running in "Oh I see you've met The Duchess' Golly collection", she laughed.

I would have loved to have slept on that comfy sofa but there were far more of them than me, so I took second best and curled up on the carpet. However, every time I looked up they were watching me, watching them, watching me, the Gollies didn't want to blink first and I certainly wasn't going to.

London to The Jurassic Coast

We crossed under the Greenwich Tunnel and continued along hard pavements towards the city, now on the south bank of the Thames. I was lingering to read a particularly interesting urban dog's calling card, when I was interrupted by a group of pirates laughing and joking. Not wanting to miss out on a tin shaking opportunity we joined them on their pub crawl. Great fun, until I made an exhibition of myself by barking loudly at a moving light reflection on the ceiling and jumped up onto a startled unsuspecting man's lap. We made a hasty retreat and continued up the Thames Embankment towards the centre of London.

I was in absolute awe of the place. Not many dogs travel to the Capital of England. I felt like Dick Whittington. I gave up sniffing lampposts and street corners and walked proudly with my nose in the air as I strolled across the grand Tower Bridge. But, like that famous Dick, I too was quickly disillusioned by London. It was very noisy and huge lorries and buses drove past so close, almost pulling me off the pavement; their exhaust pipes belching stinking fumes in my face. The dirty grey buildings towered above making me feel ant-like, then legs, hundreds of legs, scurrying past at top speed trying to stamp on me. I froze on the pavement too scared to move, when suddenly Mum scooped me up, tucked me under her arm and we disappeared down a hole in the

ground on a moving staircase, with hundreds of other people, all in a hurry. The air was thin and I found it difficult to breath. It was hot and there was a peculiar smell. We were in a tunnel waiting on what seemed like an underground railway station. A rush of cold air sent a shiver down my spine, then a deafening rumble came from within the dark tunnel and a train roared towards me. I almost jumped back into Mum's arms before she had chance to pick me up and whisk me onto the train. I lay panting on her lap, looking about me as hundreds of people jiggled up and down in their seats while the train swayed and shook its way back into the dark tunnel. Within a few minutes, my terrifying experience of imitating a mole was over and we were back in the daylight, walking through narrow streets of terraced houses above ground. A Hasher called Call Girl was letting us sleep in her house for the night, but before we could sleep… "Yippee!" Trainers were going on. It was City of London Hash House Harrier's run night. It was not quite in the areas of London you would like to walk on your own at night though. We ran through poverty stricken housing areas, back lanes and car parking areas of tenement flats, across rubbish strewn wasteland and past more grey concrete tower blocks, but it was still Hashing. The calling of "On on" was just the same and the welcome from the other Hashers was friendly. I was exhausted when I eventually got to bed, it had certainly been a day like no other.

After a good night's sleep, the next morning we had time to see some of the sights of London. St Paul's Cathedral, Nelson's Column (the original one.) The London Eye, which I would have loved to have had a ride on to get a bird's eye view of the city, but yes, you've guessed – 'NO DOGS'. We continued along the Embankment until we found the Thames RNLI. Apparently, it is the busiest Lifeboat Station in Britain and floats on pontoons on the river. We were welcomed aboard and proudly shown around. I was even allowed to sit in the coxswain's seat of their boat, but I was far too excited to concentrate because today was an important day. I was going to meet a very special dog.

We arrived at Westminster Abbey and Big Ben towered above me, making me feel so small and insignificant, but as I crossed the road I knew I was about to go where only very special doggies go.

Portcullis House is the offices for Members of Parliament and I was going in.

The whole front of the building had tinted windows and I could only see inside if I pressed my nose up hard against the glass. As I peered in, I could see men in uniform standing with big machine guns. Following close behind Mum, I walked boldly through the door and into the foyer, before being confronted by the security men asking whether we had an appointment. Which we did.

In front of me, smartly dressed ladies and gentlemen were putting their briefcases onto a conveyer belt, which carried them through a machine that takes a photo of the contents before they were allowed further into the building. Likewise, we did the same with our rucksacks and panniers, pushing and shoving them to fit through, so that the security men could view our tent poles, cooking stove, pots and pans etc.

Eventually we were shown up a staircase and into a room to meet David Blunkett, a visually impaired Member of Parliament with a very important job or so I'm told and curled up in a basket at the side of the room fast asleep, there she was; a shiny black, curly coated bitch called Sadie. I knew Guide Dogs did a very important job leading visually impaired people, but to work in London and go into Parliament you had to be an extra special dog. She lifted her head and we gently touched noses. I could feel my heart beating hard inside my chest and I suddenly felt all weak and tingly. Mum and TEB were offered a seat, so I curled up tidily by Mum's feet keeping one eye on Sadie, as they chatted to Mr Blunkett about our walk so far. After about twenty minutes conversation he gave his cheque book to Mum and asked her to write one out for £100, which he promptly signed.

A press photographer then came into the room to take a group photograph, but as soon as Sadie stepped out of her basket to join us, stupidly, I flew at her growling and barking, I wasn't prepared to share the limelight again. Mum apologised profusely and yanked me back, picking me up quickly so I couldn't bite her but I was still writhing and grumbling as the reporter took the pictures. I can just imagine the headlines of the papers 'Havoc in Parliament'. "Ha ha", I wasn't thrown out but we made a hasty retreat.

Still on a high, I literally bounced along the pavements of London, forgetting how hard they felt under my paws. We admired the huge, shiny Thames barrier straddled across the river, where the Gravesend Lifeboat gave us a lift beyond suburbia and dropped us on the banks of the Isle of Grain; which isn't an island but still had to be walked around. As I was trotting along a shop fronted pavement, I started to get that weird feeling of being followed and kept looking over my shoulder. Narrowly missing a couple of lampposts, I eventually caught a glimpse of a tatty looking Collie. He was walking close behind and playing 'grandmother's footsteps'. When I walked he walked, but if I turned around to look, he stopped. He was a very nervous dog and had a nasty mark around his neck that had once bore a chain. Mum tried to coax him towards us. He wanted to come but backed off at the last minute and almost ran into the road a couple of times. He followed us for miles, but then one time I turned around and he had gone. I was a bit disappointed. It would have been nice to have a companion on my walk, but then again, I wouldn't have wanted to share any of my food.

All three of us and our bags managed to squeeze into the spare seat of a van that gave us a lift through the pedestrian free tunnel under the river Medway to Chatham, avoiding the chaotic dockyard of Rochester. In Gillingham, we were put up for the night in a vicarage where two 'Show' English Bull Terriers lived. I have always considered them to be quite handsome with their long roman noses, (not to be confused with the English Bull Dog and their squashed in faces) but after meeting these two, I completely changed my mind. Well, I say meet; I couldn't even get close. They hated me at first sight! They barked and growled so much I had to be shut in the office. They had scabby skin which stunk to high heaven and thick horny toenails so long I could hear them clicking up and down the hallway as they patrolled outside the office door. They scared me and I couldn't wait to leave.

In contrast, the pretty village of Halstow welcomed me, as the daffodils merrily bobbed their heads in the gentle breeze. It was the first real signs of spring. After the Isle of Sheppey, I stayed on my lead along the Saxon Shore Way, through fields of sheep protecting their tiny new born lambs towards Swalecliffe beach, where a notice said

'NATURISM IS NOT CONDONED'.

However, the sea was so far out, you would be covered in thick mud anyway, and therefore no one would notice if you had any clothes on or not. Herne Bay looked cheery, with its long row of multi-coloured beach huts and optimistic sign post that told me I was only 2675 miles from the North Pole! I guessed that was as the crow flies, not the way I had just come.

Since London I had been walking east towards

Margate, which in Victorian times had been a popular holiday retreat for the people from the city. Now the sad, shabby looking buildings were mostly filled with people on benefits, overflowing from London. We quickly rounded the corner at North Foreland, so now, with the wind in my face and grey skies above, I was headed south once more. We continued on, through the almost deserted seaside towns of Broadstairs and Ramsgate into Pegwell Bay, where a replica wooden Viking ship was floating on a sea of daffodils and next to it, laid peacefully in the grass, was another dead mouse.

Following the narrow chalky paths, through the mist in the distance, I could see the famous white cliffs of Dover. We turned right at South Foreland and heading west passed Dover lighthouse, I kept a close look out for any blue birds flying overhead. Then, with the wind in my face, I strutted out across the top of the open white cliffs. From the car park at the end, straining to look over the edge, I could see the hundreds of cars and lorries being loaded and unloaded onto the cross-channel ferries below me and wondered if it would be possible to sneak on board and sail off in the sunset to France. Just a few miles further along the grassy cliff tops, I passed by the top of Samphire Hoe, which is where the Channel tunnel leaves England. It wasn't at all as I had imagined and I was slightly disappointed that I didn't see a train full of people splashing into the sea.

The North Downs Way took us into Folkestone, with its long concrete sea front and brightly painted double cliff railway. I would have loved to ride up and down but TEB marched right on past, so I had to run to keep up. Then, keeping the Romney, Hythe and Dymchurch railway line on my right, it led us out onto the gravel spit of Dungeness. A peculiar mix of quaint wooden chalets, a black and white painted lighthouse, a bird sanctuary and an ugly power station all rivalling for the best spot amongst the wilderness of pebbles. The terrain was flat but my feet were beginning to burn, as I hobbled along the shingle beach to Camber, and the little stones made my toes splay out making it so painful to walk. I thought it strange to see rusty, abandoned tanks trying to disguise themselves in the dry grasslands and imagined myself as a soldier crawling along the stony sandy track. Then all of a sudden, loud gun fire resounded in the distance and I jumped out of my skin. I hate loud bangs and dug my paws into the ground refusing to walk. Realising we were not far from a military training area, I concluded that I didn't want to be a brave soldier anymore. Mum tried to 'encourage' me by subtle quick drags along the pavement, but it doesn't look good in front of people when you're supposed to be walking 5,000 miles for charity. - I ended up being carried.

During their ceasefire, I was glad of our lunchtime rest, which we took on an abandoned old Pontin's train carriage. It had also been left to rust on an inland stretch of grassy wasteland, towards the pretty town of Rye, with its pebbled streets and black and white buildings. We crossed the river Rother, then headed back down the other side to Rye Harbour and along the never-ending sea wall to Cliff End. Always a popular place for day trippers, the warmer weather was beginning to bring the brave early holiday makers out, so I put on my cutest look as I approached and coerced them into parting with their money.

It was March 11th and my fifth Birthday. We were due to meet up with Richard and Shally Hunt, who had walked Britain's coast in 1995, just over a year after Spud and Tess. They were difficult to find as it was Hastings' half Marathon and the sea front was full of brightly coloured lycra vested runners, so, Mum and I went in search of some lunch. We were queueing at a hog roast stall when I had my first realisation that I don't like Boxer dogs. The poor chap hadn't done anything but I just turned on him for no reason, growling and baring my teeth. Mum dragged me away quickly and hence – I didn't get any hog roast! I still don't like Boxer dogs to this day.

We eventually found Shally and Richard near the tall, wooden huts used for drying fishing nets and they joined us walking and chatting for a mile or so along the promenade. We posed for photos, then bid them farewell. Suddenly, through a sea of lily-white legs out for their first exposure to British sunshine, I saw four black legs, a shiny black curly coat and slender body of a Curly Coat Retriever. My heart missed a beat and for one moment, I thought it was Sadie walking towards me. I was just about to apologise for my behaviour in London when I realised it wasn't her. The dog's owner saw that I was smitten and introduced us. She was called Myrtle and had been shown at Crufts that year. Unfortunately, she stuck her nose in the air and I got the message that we weren't in the same league - so I never bothered to keep in touch. As a consolation, later that afternoon, I met Avril and Richard at Bexhill Coastguard Station. They took us back to their cosy terraced house to sleep the night and presented me with a birthday cake complete with candle, which I did manage to share.

It was another cold, grey, drizzly day as we walked via Pevernsy Bay into Eastbourne; to a civilized Guide Dog reception. One cream and two black Labrador dogs with their owners turned out to greet us, plus one elderly gentleman dressed in a fundraising 'pretend' Lifeboat man's outfit. We joined them in a coffee shop and I managed to behave myself as I lay nose to nose with the other dogs under the table. After our rest, they then walked with us slowly along the seafront, but only the Lifeboat man accompanied us up the steep hill climb to Beachy Head. As we were walking, he was chatting to Mum about recently losing his wife, (I think he meant she'd died, not that he'd mislaid her) and said that fund raising for the RNLI kept him from being lonely. The cliffs are very high at Beachy Head and some people, if they are very sad, go there to jump off. We said goodbye to the Lifeboat man at the top and left him to walk back on his own as we continued along the South Downs Way over the Seven Sisters – I just hope he made it down OK.

The weather was improving as we walked over the Downs (which were confusingly 'ups'). The spring sun was getting warmer and the gulls were swooping overhead. A line of imitation wooden beach huts and another Mortello tower welcomed our arrival to Seaford, and on the skyline I could see the huge Dieppe cross channel ferry coming in to Newhaven. It was almost a run over the cliff tops as the grass was short and the soil was sandy, making it easy going on my paws and we covered quite a few miles in a short time. The sun was beating down on my back and I was getting hot, so we stopped for a much needed drink on the cliff tops. There was a shimmering heat haze along the jagged coast but I could clearly make out the outline of Brighton in the distance, with its famous pier jutting out to sea. As soon as I stepped onto the hard pavements of this 'liberal' seaside town my pace instantly slowed again, as every step jarred my shoulder joints. It was a long, hot, dirty sea front, and lots of noisy people stopped to read my jacket and put money in our cans, which slowed us further. I wanted to go on the pier and sit and watch the rides for a rest but another prejudicial notice read,

'NO DOGS ALLOWED'.

Totally fed up with this segregation, I couldn't wait to pass through "Hove actually" and onto Shoreham-by-Sea, where we were warmly welcomed into yet another Lifeboat Station. After checking out their Tyne class boat, I managed to grab a quick forty winks while Mum drank tea.

The concrete promenades and tall Victorian buildings of Worthing came and went, with a few more holiday makers beginning to emerge. We sped through Littlehampton, then on to Bognor which was far nicer than it sounded, as I found half a meat pasty in front of a row of newly painted little wooden beach huts and gobbled it up quickly before Mum could grab my collar. This cheered me up no end and boosted my energy levels, helping me across the tiny pebbles on the beaches which dug in painfully between my toes. I cooled my feet in the sea as we reached Pagham Harbour, which was wadeable if you are over three foot tall - but as I'm not, I was carried to save me getting soaking wet before bedtime. We rounded Selsy Bill and started heading towards Portsmouth, where a unanimous decision was made that we would catch a ferry over the Solent and walk around the coast of the Isle of Wight, to avoid traipsing through the depressing dock yard area of Southampton.

The relationship between Mum and TEB had been up and down for most of the walk and by the time we reached the outskirts of Portsmouth it was unbearable. They were arguing again and Mum had decided that she couldn't continue the walk with TEB and wanted to go home. Again, he apologised for his aggressive behaviour and persuaded her to give the Isle of Wight a chance, and make a final decision in a week's time. (Knowing he would get her to change her mind)

It was late afternoon and a choppy crossing on the hovercraft. (Another first for me) I was undignifiedly shoved between two seats with the baggage where I couldn't see a blooming thing, and after a very noisy and bumpy ride was glad when we reached the port of Ryde. We stayed with a Hasher called 'P Rick' and his Labrador dog Boykie, in their quaint cottage called Little Mouse Farm for the night. However, this was one of the only days I hadn't actually seen a dead one. I was far too excited to sleep that night, as I had heard a rumour that in the morning we would be joining the Isle of Wight Hash for a run. Boykie was a proper Hash Hound as well and loved it. We were both off our leads and tore around freely along the narrow paths, chasing each other through the woodland, checking out all the trails and trying to keep everyone together as a pack. It was so hot that day, that after an hour and a half of continuous running I just crashed and fell fast asleep in the middle of the road, totally exhausted. (Luckily, it was a very quiet road)

Our journey continued clockwise around the Isle of Wight. On another grey day that looked like it had never begun. The route to Benbridge Harbour took us over a rickety wooden jetty that tightly hugged the coast. Angry waves made a scary noise as they crashed onto the rocks beneath me, so Mum picked me up, but my feet kept paddling in the air just in case she accidentally dropped me into the water. Passing Benbridge Lifeboat Station, precariously perched out to sea at the end of its own narrow jetty, I had just enough time to quickly explore the rock pools before we upped the Downs of Benbridge and descended onto the beautiful sandy beaches of Sandown and Shanklin. We wove our way through the hilly streets with their chocolate box thatched cottages, to Ventnor. (They look nothing like chocolate boxes but that's what Mum called them, and being a chocoholic, she should know) The enormous landslip around St Lawrence, called The Undercliffe, had me innocently searching for fossils one minute then frantically hiding from dinosaurs the next! Breathless, I headed back through the trees onto the high, open, grassy coast path and past St Catherine's Lighthouse, the Isle of Wight's most southerly point. Tightly secured at the end of my lead, I tried to avoid walking on the cracks in the dry ground, just in case my weight was too much for the fragile cliff tops and sent us all tumbling over the sheer edge to the beach below. The wild unspoiled beaches are continually eroding along the south coast of the island and we ascended and descended many of the steep sided gullies called Chines. Eventually, we were joined by a Hasher called Bilbo who, at the end of an exhausting day, put us up for the night in his house. (In the morning, he gave me a whole sausage which Mum chopped up in my breakfast.)

With this added protein, I bounced my way happily across sheep-nibbled grass along the chalky white cliff top peninsula, towards the landmark Needles lighthouse, balanced dangerously on the tip, Mum continually warning me to keep away from the dangerous steep edges. As we sat eating lunch looking north across the Solent water, I could clearly see Lymington, where I would be heading by ferry the following day, but just a stone's throw away around the corner was the famous Alum Bay. The multi-coloured sandy cliffs (which all looked pretty similar to me) are a big tourist attraction - thus full of holiday makers. I carefully wove my way between their legs, encouraging them to read my jacket and part with their hard earned cash, which 'chink chinked' with satisfaction into the bucket, resulting in quite a profitable afternoon. Typically, I wasn't allowed on the chair lift "Grr" but we walked down the metal steps to the beach so I could enjoy a well-deserved paddle in the sea.

TEB had been on his best behaviour all week, so Mum and I didn't go home and continued our clockwise walk back on the mainland, where Guide Dog supporter Barbara and her black Labrador, Jeff, escorted us through the deserted sandy dunes around Christchurch. They then left us to fend for ourselves through the tantalizing squirrel infested parks of Bournemouth, which drove me crazy. Poole Harbour was massive and full of boats, hence it is the Home and Headquarters of the RNLI. They have a purpose-built training centre, which I was permitted to tour, and saw the huge deep swimming pool where crew members practice their capsize drill from an upturned Lifeboat. It was so exciting and I felt very important being allowed in there. Next door was their big modern hotel where Lifeboat crew and their families stay during training. Claire, the Devon area Fund Raising Manager came out to meet us. She was so proud of the hotel and the fact that she had managed to get us a room for the night. I was shattered, (probably still recovering from Hashing on the Isle of Wight) and my legs were quite stiff, so couldn't believe my floppy ears, when she then looked down at me and said, "You can't bring the dog in - but he can sleep in the boot of my car".

"I beg your pardon! Did I hear that right? You have got to be joking, I have walked about 2,000 miles and helped raise thousands of pounds for your charity - and I can't come in?"

I knew Mum wouldn't let me stay in a car without her and tried to bargain with Claire, putting forward my case, but she wouldn't change her mind or go inside and ask anybody. "No dogs allowed, in the hotel, those are the rules", Claire retorted.

"Those are the rules? - Huh, my paw".

Mum didn't want to stay in the hotel if I wasn't allowed, but TEB was desperate for a shower, meal and bed for the night, so 'persuaded' Mum that I would be OK in the car. It was quite a comfy car and yes, I was OK, but I was absolutely livid. After all that I had done for the RNLI they could have easily let me in, and none of the crew members would have minded. If I had been a 'barking' Guide Dog they would have let me in! "Grr" it made my blood boil.

After surviving my belittling night in Claire's car, I jumped out and quickly forgave Mum who was feeling very guilty, when she waved a peace-offering sausage that she had saved from her breakfast.

We retraced our steps around the harbour and I

strutted my stuff down the millionaire's strip of land called Sandbanks, which hosts the most expensive beach huts in Britain, and felt much more important again. The Sandbanks chain ferry took me across to the Isle of Purbeck, which isn't an island at all, and onto the beautiful soft sand of Studland beach, which does condone naturism! Luckily, it was a chilly day, so not a bare bottom in sight. Here I started the 630 miles of the South West coast path to Minehead.

The white chalky footpaths and short grass made the walking easy going for me, but the ascents and descents were very steep and without four paw drive Mum and TEB found it hard going. I would race on ahead and then wait at the top of the hills for them to catch up. The sun was getting much hotter and fresh water to drink was becoming harder to find. Every day Mum carried water for me but it quickly ran out, resulting in me drinking from the filthiest puddles which sometimes upset my tummy. We were sleeping in the tent more often now, as the weather was better and a small piece of flat grass to camp the night was usually easy to find, but by the time we got to Swanage it was getting late and we hadn't passed any such area. We had already been refused from a couple of possible stop-overs and it was nearly dark, so the tent was erected discretely behind some bushes in the corner of a public park. We had a peaceful night, and I slept well, but in the morning, as I was sitting beside Mum watching her fold away the poles, a 'jobsworth' park warden came along and gruffly said, "Did you camp here the night?" (It was pretty obvious that we had) but Mum just said "No!" Speechless and disgruntled, he shuffled off muttering. I smiled wryly to myself.

The South West Coast Path took us past Dorset's famous 'lost' village. Unbelievably, during the Second World War, villagers of Tyneham were given just twenty eight days to pack up and leave their homes. They hoped one day to return, but sadly this never happened and now it is part of the army ranges. Luckily they weren't using it for firing practice as we walked quickly through and over the chalky white Purbeck hills. Way below me I saw Old Harry Rock and an archway called Durdle Door sticking boldly up out of the sea, refusing to be eroded by constant battering from the waves. Then, after sleeping in a dead horse's stable for the night, (he wasn't still there) we managed to 'break camp' and march along the military road past Lulworth; early, before the Army closed it to the public to practice their morning military manoeuvres.

It had been a hot day and I was desperate for a refreshing drink as we walked right past numerous pubs and cafes along Weymouth sea front. Beyond the pretty painted fishing boats, with my tongue now almost dragging on the ground, at last I spotted a Hasher called Gravel Rash, waiting for us outside a retro teashop in the rejuvenated harbourside. So, beneath the ornate, metal table and chairs, whilst the others drank hot tea, I downed a whole bowl of beautiful clean cold water, it tasted amazing.

That evening, back at her house, she cooked an enormous leg of lamb and invited some other members of Hardy's Hash round for dinner, so while they were eating and chatting in the dining room, I was allowed the whole bone to myself and spent the entire evening in the garden gnawing away to my heart's content. Gravel Rash walked with us the next day onto the rocky land-spit of Portland and out to Portland Bill lighthouse, past the intimidating barbed wire fences of the Young Offenders' prison, balanced perilously on the end. It was rough under paw and apart from the odd mouthful of rabbit poo, I didn't like it. As far as I was concerned it was another pointless waste of energy, as we ended the day back exactly where we started that morning.

To avoid the eight miles of pebbles on Chesil beach, which apparently are smaller at one end than the other and would have been good to witness but painful on my paws, we diverted around a big lagoon of water called The Fleet, through the Swannery at Abbotsbury, and on to Seatown in the search of gold.

Jurassic Coast to Newport

Through a field of wobbly new born lambs, ahead of me was the highest cliff on the south coast, Golden Cap. It was a breezy day and quite hard going even for my four legs to climb the six hundred feet to the top. I fought my way through the overgrown gorse bushes which scratched across my face as I charged on ahead to the summit, leaving Mum and TEB scrambling up on all fours. Then I raced down the other side to Charmouth, gravity assisted and with the wind behind me I was there in no time. While waiting for them to catch up, I went off for a sniff around in search of Mum's dead budgie, which apparently Grandpa had buried there when she was little, though without success. I was soon distracted by the sound of plastic rustling and the aroma of chocolate biscuits appearing from Mum's pocket.

I spent most of the time walking with my head down, looking for fossils along the shore to Lyme Regis. Although not quite a whole diplodocus, Mum did find a few bullet shaped Belemnites and some lumps of gold (well, 'fool's gold', but it was still exciting) I was having great fun and wanted to stay longer just rummaging and chasing pebbles on the beach, but TEB insisted we moved on.

It was lunchtime by the time we reached Lyme Regis and drizzling with rain. Mum popped into a shop and bought two pasties, then we sat in a bus shelter to keep out of the rain. Suddenly, around the corner appeared Nanny and Grandpa from Bath. I was so pleased to see them. I hadn't seen anyone I'd known for so long I went crazy, jumping up and down, squeaking silly noises and wagging my tail so hard it nearly fell off. Unbeknown to us they had been following our progress through Claire and Geraldine, the area Fund Raising Managers, who had told them we were due to be in the area on that day - it was just luck that we were on schedule. Poor Grandpa was still waiting for his knee operation and couldn't walk very far, so could only hobble as they accompanied us slowly past the Cobb. I was reluctant to say goodbye and kept looking back as we slowly climbed the steps to the Undercliff without them.

From Lyme Regis, we were back on home territory. I had walked the Undercliff to Seaton before. It is a seven mile landslip of amazing Jurassic jungle. Slippery, narrow, rocky paths weave in and out of the mud and large leaved bushes, twisted vines hang from bended trees, waiting to be swung from and mossy green bogs that seem eager to swallow you up. I love it there. Off my lead I ran freely exploring every nook and cranny, checking out smells old and new, which soon took my mind off leaving Nanny and Grandpa behind.

The South West coast path is one of the best signed coastal paths in the whole of Britain but the steep rise and falls of the Devon hills in the warm spring sunshine made tough going. The narrow paths and steps down to each little beach jarred my back leg, so I resorted to hopping on just three, which was less painful.

Branscombe brought the famous sandy cliffs of Devon and also a new excitement to the area. Just a couple of weeks before our arrival, a ship called the MSC Napoli had floundered and sunk in the bay, spilling its container load. Looters from far and wide invaded the shores of

Branscombe in the hope of retrieving something of value washed up onto the beach, but by the time we got there, salvage boats were trying to secure the ship and clearing the area of debris, so unfortunately, I came away empty pawed!

Friends from Teign Valley Hash House Harriers joined us at Budleigh Salterton and brought a fantastic picnic to share, which included my favourite cold sausages, then walked with us along the cliff tops to Exmouth, where local Guide Dogs and puppy walkers came out to support us. We stayed the night at Melon Picker's house in Exeter (who, as you will find out later, became a huge part in my life) and the following morning we managed to get a lift by car to Dawlish Warren, which is just across the mouth of the River Exe from Exmouth, to continue our walk. As we were now on local territory, Teign Valley Hashers had organised for someone to accompany us each day. Arbie and Doris through Dawlish, then Wigwam and Mig Man joined us in Torquay, where we stopped briefly by the Harbour for a photo shoot with the local Guide Dog committee. The area was packed with tourists and a great opportunity for rattling the collecting cans. I wanted to stay longer and collect more money, but typically the Hashers dragged us off to the pub for lunch. That evening Brixham's inshore Lifeboat had been organised to carry us across the harbour. This was a lovely thought but stupidly, somebody also thought it a good idea to let off fireworks! OMG, Mum almost had to sit on me to stop me jumping out of the boat or even worse - digging my claws into the rubber dingy walls. Safely on the other side, a big welcoming party was waiting for us in the yacht club and all my Hash friends were there to feed me tit bits from their plates. Hannah and Scott had managed to make it too which was nice, as I had missed them terribly. Sadly, it was all too soon to say our goodbyes to everyone and be on our way again. We stayed the night with Broken Man and Fallen Woman in their cosy little character cottage overlooking Brixham harbour, twinkling in the moonlight. The next day Flowery joined us as we climbed the steep hill onto Berry Head. Mini cyclamen carpeted the banks either side of the footpath and the gorse bushes were vibrant against the clear sky. It had been lovely seeing all of our family and friends back in Devon but once Flowery left us at Sharkham Point, we were on our own again.

The sun was high in the sky as we took the ferry across from Kingswear to the pretty fishing town of Dartmouth. Hundreds of expensive, brightly coloured yachts bobbed about in the estuary overlooked by the grand Naval College, where Queen Elizabeth II had met Prince Philip, way before I was born. Lots of wealthy people visit Dartmouth so it was a great place for fund raising.

In the South Hams the coastal path undulates over more gently rolling cliff tops. The grass was short and the footpaths easily defined, so I could run ahead and chase rabbits. Mum would occasionally shout and warn me if I got too near the eroding edges of the crumbling cliffs. It was annoying but I knew it was in my best interest. I stopped briefly to take a look at the derelict Hall Sands, sat eerily at the bottom of the cliff. Most of the village was swept away by the rough sea in 1917, but still the remains of a few houses cling on to the land for dear life every time a wave crashes against the shore.

We rounded Start Point lighthouse standing proudly up on its rocky peninsula, looking down over the beautiful sandy beaches below. We scrambled down the cliff just in time to cross on the passenger ferry to the quaint little fishing town of Salcombe. It usually rains whenever I go to Salcombe but today the sun was out and its warmth beat down on my back as I gazed over the side of the boat and watched sunbeams sparkle and dance on the surface of the rippling water below me. High above the sea, the footpath from Salcombe to Bantham snaked ahead and was progressively getting more rugged. The jagged rocks above me looked like the backs of sleeping dinosaurs, so I tiptoed past trying not to wake them, and around each corner was a mesmerizing new rocky cove, each one even more spectacular than the last. By now the primroses were in full bloom and the Blackthorn hedges festooned the narrow paths as we approached Bigbury-on-Sea. Ahead of me through the blossom, I caught my first glimpse of Burgh Island, where an amphibious tractor carries people at high tide out to the old white washed Pilchard Inn. I have ridden and walked across this causeway several times before, but not today, as I had a bed waiting for me in Challaborough, where we stayed the night with South Hams Hashers Ging Gang and Goolie in their luxury bungalow overlooking the sea. Silly Goolie kept forgetting my name. Every time he went down to the cellar to fetch another bottle of wine, he would come back up and call me something different. I forgave him the following morning when bacon was served with my breakfast.

We were lucky enough to catch a low tide as we waded across the river Erm, under close surveillance from the panicking beach lifeguard on his quadbike. Then, after a good shake and roll in the sand to dry off (that was just me), we made our way along dry sandy tracks, through fields of grazing cattle around Gara Point into the compact holiday cottage village of Noss Mayo. Standing on the edge of the little stone quay we managed to attract the attention of the one-man rowing boat ferry for our complimentary five-minute ride across to Newton Ferrers, where charming little houses worth millions of pounds, fight for an elite river side frontage.

In the distance, through the heat haze I could make out the tall grey buildings of Plymouth. I knew we were there when I saw a big plaque set in the ground that read,

"Welcome to Plymouth, please wipe your feet". A lady called Rosemary put us up for the night, once we had eventually found her house. I had met her previously a few months before starting our walk, when I was collecting money standing in the freezing cold outside the shopping precinct in Plymouth. She had promised to raise lots of money for us doing cake stalls and raffles. She had even organised a charity barbeque the evening we arrived. Her husband was busy down in the garden cooking and charging their family and friends for burgers. But of course, I got mine for free.

Another beautiful day, another ferry. This time to another country – well almost. Cornwall is like another country, with its own language and road signs. We arrived on Mt Edgecombe and continued the rocky coastal path into Looe, a busy fishing village with its colour washed houses and brightly painted boats and yachts, bobbing up and down in the harbour. A young lad called James brought his Mum's Retriever Guide Dog, Jacob, to meet us outside the RNLI shop where he is a voluntary helper.

From Looe we wove our way through the narrow streets of Polperro. Rotund holiday makers sat outside quaint cafes eating Cornish cream teas and ice creams, so I stared at them hopefully, sucking my tummy in and trying to look emaciated as they were busy spreading jam and cream on their scones, - or should it be cream then jam? I'm not sure, but they were far too engrossed expanding their own waistlines to be concerned about the state of mine. I managed to drag my weak body past their tables and was soon back on the sunny cliff tops chasing a cabbage white butterfly, completely forgetting that I had been almost starving to near death.

The footpath began to get hilly again. Mile after mile the narrow track rose and fell. The bracken had not yet grown tall, so I could clearly see the dusty path in the distance, like a never ending thin snake in the grass, slithering along the coastline ahead of me. It was hot, thirsty work so I stopped at every opportunity in the bottom of each gully and eagerly lapped the clear water from little streams searching to find their way to the sea. After yet another ferry crossing across the river Fowey, the coastal path took us through the working China clay depots of Par, where all the trees, bushes and grass were covered in a layer of white china clay dust making it look like frost in mid-winter.

The three mast sailing ship Hispanola, moored in the harbour of the historic museum village of Charlestown, made me think of sunnier times. Unfortunately the sea's erosion had caused the collapse of a big chunk of cliff and the footpath was blocked off. A polite sign suggested we take a five-mile detour inland and back, but after a discussion which included me for once, it was decided that we would be impolite, ignore it, and try to make our way along the eroding cliff. With 'gentle persuasion' I was squeezed under the barriers and edged my way gingerly along the ever narrowing path. I daren't look down and held my breath. Mum grabbed onto the hedge for safety with one hand and took my lead in her other and pulled me quickly across the cracked narrow gap. "Phew!" That was close. I was relieved to climb the barrier the other side, where I could safely breathe again.

We had been walking due west since Plymouth, but now the long path to St Mawes headed south, hugging the grassy undulating cliff tops that were dotted with primroses and little dog violets. I tried not to stand on them but it was impossible as there were so many. We had to wait a while for the ferry to Falmouth; enough time to curl up on the soft grass for forty winks in the sunshine. Then around Rosemullion Head to catch our last ferry for a while, across Helford creek, before reaching Lizard Point the most southerly tip of mainland Britain.

Despite still trying to reach Land's End, we were now

heading north around Mounts Bay, where I got my first view of the derelict remains of old chimneys and engine houses left behind from Cornwall's tin mining days. These now litter the cliff tops on this very rugged part of the coast and started to make my feet sore. From Cudden Point I could see St Michaels Mount, a little island complete with its very own castle perched upon the top, linked to the mainland by a causeway and only accessible on foot at low tide. We were invited to stop for refreshments outside a kind local man's house, and luckily, by the time we reached the Mount, it was still low tide and we were able to walk across the slippery concrete causeway; but guess what? 'NO DOGS' "Oh for furs sake!" Who decides that dogs aren't interested in castles on islands? Is it the National Trust? Mmm? Someone should look into this discrimination. Maybe, after I've finished this book, I will.

Oh boy! It was getting hot now as we set off on the final stretch to Land's End. At any opportunity I had I would lie in the shade and rest. The sea looked so clear and refreshing below me. The little coves of beautiful soft sand were tantalizing and calling to me to roll on them and play, but there was no way down to reach them, it was so frustrating.

I paid my respects (as doggies do) whilst Mum read out loud from a plaque remembering the whole crew of the Penlee Lifeboat, who tragically lost their lives in the disaster of 1981. I was interested, but my mind was elsewhere, as I searched desperately around for any dead mice. Knowing that the next town was called Mousehole, I was adamant there would be one lying around somewhere that I could add to my ever increasing list.

"Yay, at last!" If I screwed my eyes up, I could just make out the white buildings of Land's End in the distance. I had no idea what was there, but I had heard talk of it for so long that I was almost running to greet it. It is truly a landmark for Britain and for me. I had walked halfway round the country; well not exactly in mileage but from top north east corner to bottom south west corner. As you can imagine, I was a little disappointed when I got there. No brass bands or well-wishers out to meet me, just hundreds of holiday makers all enjoying their own company and totally oblivious of mine. I tried walking up to people to get them to read my jacket and Mum tried rattling her can, but everyone was far too engrossed in spending their money on ice creams and amusements to even notice us. We had a quick photograph taken by the sign that read 'Land's End' and Mum signed the special book that is kept in the pub, to record that we had walked there from John O'Groats. Then, as unnoticed as when we had walked in, we sneaked quietly away along the

coastal path, this time heading in a north easterly direction.

When we had stopped at Penzance the night before, we had met a couple that lived just past Land's End and they had offered to put us up for the night in their house when we reached it. Their house was 'homely' and had two Collie dogs which I got on well with, so as Mum and TEB set off to walk the next morning, I was happy to watch them leave without me and stayed the day at the house just resting and relaxing with their old dogs. I really needed rest and recuperation. My pads had become sore and my shoulders really ached with the constant pounding on the rough flint rocks. As I lay in the garden licking my painful paws, for the first time since we began, a wave of doubt crossed my mind as to whether or not I would complete the walk. However, as I had no idea where we were going, I quickly brushed the doubt aside and consoled myself with the thought that as I had no idea how far we were walking, then it would probably soon be over. Mum and TEB were brought back again that night to sleep and I joined them walking the following day. Early next morning I was first at the gate and raring to go again.

Almost every day on the dry footpaths around Devon and Cornwall, I saw a dead mouse or shrew just lying there and I still couldn't fathom out what had made it die? Surely a buzzard or hawk would have carried it off or a fox would have eaten it? I was still trying to puzzle this over in my mind as I crossed the lovely sandy beach at Sennan Cove, but then the return of relentless dry, winding footpaths brought me back to reality as the sharp stones dug painfully into the pads on my feet again. I was trying not to limp but Mum (who I think has eyes in the back of her head) noticed, and the next thing I knew I was pinned to the ground and she popped one tiny shoe onto each paw. I frantically shook each leg and danced manically, trying to release them but they wouldn't detach and I was getting left further and further behind.

Eventually I had to give in and just walk as best as I could with these ridiculous clumsy items firmly attached to my feet. By the time I passed the ruined chimneys and wheel houses of Levant and Geevor tin mines perched perilously on the edges of the steep rugged cliffs, I was used to them and only the noise of crunching stones beneath our shoes broke the blissful silence. Enjoying the solitude as we approached Godrevy Point, I could hear crying. I thought it was children on the beach below but when I looked over the edge, I saw another enormous colony of seals just lying on the sand basking in the sun, waiting for the next tide to come in and wash them back into the sea. I barked at a lone gull which swooped overhead laughing at me in my shoes, as it played in the wind.

The cliffs were getting higher and the paths were getting steeper. A few wispy clouds were cooling the midday sun but I was desperately thirsty and in need of a rest. Atlantic FM radio had invited us to go into their studio for a live interview when we reached St Agnes, and thankfully someone gave me a drink as I arrived. Unfortunately I was so tired I curled up and went to sleep under a man's desk and missed the interview - but I'm sure Mum did a good job on my behalf. The hills flattened out and the soft grass and sandy beaches made it easier walking to Newquay, where I hoovered my way through the chip and burger covered pavements. We carried on towards Trevose Head lighthouse and Padstow's newly constructed Lifeboat station. Ahead I could see lots of big tents, cars and people with cameras, silver screens and huge big lights. Surely no one had gone to all that trouble to film me? Sadly no, I discovered that they were making a TV advert for the new Renault Clio car. After shaking our buckets amongst the film crew, they allowed us to sleep in their marquee that night and I even got bacon for breakfast in the morning from their portable café. From Padstow we caught the ferry over to Rock, where the RNLI were waiting to give us our official half-way celebration. Claire was there to greet us along with all the crew members, and their inshore Lifeboat was out of the water up on the harbour wall. Inside the boat was a little table with a white cotton table cloth laid up with china cups and saucers and plates of scones with jam and cream (or cream and jam.) We didn't need to be asked twice as we climbed aboard and posed for our photos before tucking into the delicious Cornish cream tea – scrummy.

Still licking the cream from my whiskers, we climbed steeply out of Rock. Bluebells and red campion grew thick on either side of the dry coastal path towards the quaint little fishing village of Port Isaac. I recognised it as Port Wen from the TV, as it is where they filmed the popular series Doc Martin.

Further along the cliff tops we met Will Smith - not the famous singer but an elderly gentleman from St Ives who enjoyed walking. He had heard about our adventure and had set out to find us. He walked with us for most of that day and popped up again several more times along the South West Coast Path. He explained how he had found it difficult getting over all the wooden stiles. On one occasion he had tried to use the dog flap, but it had swung down between his neck and his rucksack, completely trapping him. He said, "Good job no one had come along behind me otherwise I would have been buggered!" I didn't understand quite what he meant but it made Mum and TEB laugh.

Oh my goodness, Tintagel! – There were hundreds of wooden steps and bridges climbing across and up to the castle. They had to be joking. Surely they weren't going to make me walk there? But yes, they did. Mum asked the man in the ticket kiosk if he would kindly look after our rucksacks and panniers until we returned, but unfortunately, 'jobsworth' that he was, said he wasn't allowed. - But we left them anyway, (nobody was likely to steal them; they were far too heavy!) and off we set. I could hardly feel my poor little legs as we climbed the last few steps up to the castle, then, after what seemed like only a few minutes rest, it was time to walk all the way back again and unluckily no one had stolen the bags.

My legs were on automatic pilot as I somehow managed to drag myself down the hill to the quaint little fishing village of Boscastle, quietly nestled in the sunshine at the bottom of the valley, with its almost dried up river trickling under the little stone bridge. It was hard to believe that in the storm of 2004, this had been a raging torrent, washing a car downstream and completely blocking the bridge, thus flooding the whole town! Hot and desperate for a rest, I almost collapsed exhausted on the cobbled pavement outside the shops, when a kind man came out and asked if I would like an ice cream. Mum just had to watch as the man fed me the refreshing cold vanilla treat from a cone, but it certainly did the trick, and I was soon recovered and ready to go again. After a long day's hot walking we pitched the tent earlier than usual and I was almost too tired to eat my tea. I ate slowly so that I didn't bring it back up again then crawled in on top of Mum's cosy sleeping bag, curled up as tightly as possible and within seconds I was asleep, not moving so much as a whisker again until morning.

As we left Cornwall behind and made our way back across the border into Devon, we climbed the black rugged cliffs towards Hartland Point. I couldn't help thinking that the stranded rock stacks looked like old people bending over in the sea. It was another beautiful day, the cloudless sky and the calm sea looked the same; I couldn't see where one ended and the other began. It brought back happy memories of going there when I was a young pup on a Hash camping walking weekend with Ollie and his Collie dog Bill. We were so high now on the cliff top coastal path I could see right over the tree tops to

Clovelly. We passed through the Visitor's Centre at the top of the hill and were allowed free entry into the heritage village where narrow streets led steeply down between the tall houses to the quay below. The cobbled road had lots of ridges that ran across like shallow steps, and they were awkward to walk on and hurt my back leg as I bent it. It seemed another one of those pointless exercises to me and I grumbled under my breath, as once we reached the bottom, we turned around and walked back up again! Apparently, the residents used donkeys to help drag their shopping up and down the hill on sledges. Well, I could have done with one of their donkeys to drag me up the hill. I did not want to walk back up and tried every delaying tactic I knew, but despite all the sniffing and weeing there was no alternative but to retrace my steps to the top.

The footpath to Westward Ho! was so beautiful. Bluebells carpeted the floor beneath the trees for as far as I could see. I tried sniffing out rabbits but the smell of the bluebells was intense and camouflaged any scents they may have left. The weather was really warming up now and I stopped whenever I could to snatch a quick drink from any nearby stream. By the time I reached Appledore, I was so hot that I tried the trick that had worked so well in Boscastle. I walked boldly up to the ice-cream stall and stood there wagging my tail, hoping that someone would feel sorry for me but this time it didn't work and I had to make do with water from Mum. It effectively quenched my thirst and I was ready to board the little boat which took us across the River Taw to Braunton Burrows and North Devon's beautiful long sandy beaches. It took forever to walk along trying to dodge kite strings, runaway pooches and snotty nosed children. From Watermouth Bay the coastal path was described as 'Undulating'. I would describe it as 'Barking hard going', and the steep path with loose gravel under paw ran slightly inland through thick woodland. As I was about to give up the will to live, suddenly amidst the greenery, a pub appeared in the middle of nowhere like a mirage and two men were sitting outside on a bench chatting and enjoying a peaceful drink. Without a second thought I climbed up onto the younger man's lap and moved my nose towards his beer. He declined my advances but allowed me to sit on his knee while he finished his refreshments and I was grateful for the rest. We pitched the tent that night in a nearby grassy clearing, only to find by morning we were all crawling with minute ticks, "Yuk!" The route to Lynmouth was spent with Mum picking them off one by one, and luckily none of them managed to attach themselves to her or me.

The Exmoor woodland eventually cleared as we started climbing once more but the ground was rocky and rough with clumps of spikey grass. I daren't look down as it was a steep drop to the sea below, so Mum held tightly onto my lead. Up in front, I could see animals nimbly jumping from rock to rock completely unfazed by the fact that there was a perilous drop below them. They looked dark in colour and definitely weren't sheep. Mum said that they were mountain goats, which then followed me inquisitively as I stumbled through the Valley of the Rocks into Lynton. We stopped briefly to watch the quaint funicular railway. Two little trains counterbalance each other and work on gravity by having a tank that fills and empties with water to make them go up and down the steep hill (Just like me) I wanted to take a ride down - but we had to walk.

As one of the charities we were collecting for was the RNLI, during my walk I saw, and even went on, some of the most up-to-date Lifeboats available, with their modern technology engineering. At the bottom of the hill in Lynmouth, I saw a very old wooden Lifeboat that men had used to row out to sea to rescue people. Many years ago, 1899 I believe (before even Grandpa was born), there was such a bad storm that the men were unable to launch their Lifeboat from Lynmouth, so they dragged, pushed and cajoled it 13 miles up Congresbury hill and down the other side to Porlock Weir and heroically launched it from there. Well, I followed in their footsteps and copied their route to Porlock Weir, but it was all I could managed just to drag myself up that barking hill. So I have great admiration for those brave men. It was early evening and I was on my last legs by the time we got there. The pubs and streets were full of noisy people totally absorbed in their own self-indulgence, not interested in a knackered scruffy little dog like me, who had just re-enacted a piece of local history. There was nowhere to stay and the only grass was a pathetic bit of stony land next to the car park, where every visiting dog had got straight out of their car and used as a toilet! I enjoyed all the different smells but I must admit it was not terribly hygienic for humans.

After another long, tiring day walking through the heather and gorse of Exmoor National Park, we eventually reached Minehead, the official end of the South West Coast Path. We had been given permission to stay in a chalet at the huge Butlin's holiday camp. We were all tired, but TEB had been horrible to Mum all day and was getting nastier. Whatever she did or said seemed to be wrong in his opinion. I crawled underneath one of the beds so that I couldn't hear him shouting at her. She retreated to the bathroom crying, but he only yelled louder until someone in the neighbouring chalet banged on the wall! He immediately stopped shouting, picked up one of the collecting boxes and disappeared out for the evening, leaving me to console Mum yet again.

As usual, he apologised for his aggressive behaviour the next day, and the walk continued. The coast here was not very pretty as the sea was a long way out, so apart from the odd strong whiff that caught my attention there wasn't much else to do but follow Mum's footsteps. Many of the seaside towns had flat concrete promenades so we moved along at quite a pace. Everything was going fine; Mum and TEB were talking again and the miles were ticking away. Then we reached the banks of the wide river Parrett!

It would have been a lot of extra mileage to walk inland towards Bridgewater and find a bridge, but the estuary was far too wide, deep and fast flowing for us to wade across. Mum and I sat on the grass to rest whilst TEB went in search of someone with a boat who would be willing to take us over. He returned ages later saying he had found an old man that would row us across to the other side. Well, he really was an old man and was recovering from a recent heart operation, so he said Mum and TEB would have to row us across and he would row himself back. We all piled into his tiny little wooden boat complete with all our baggage, untied the ropes and off we went. The current was strong but slowly they rowed us across. The old man sat in the back and I sat right up in the front directing them across. At the other side, thick grey mud made it impossible to get right to the shore, so the old man dug his oar into the mud to secure us and out we got. I immediately sunk up to my armpits and Mum was nearly up to her knees in the horrible gloopy mud as we gingerly waded our way up to the grass. I turned around to watch the old man row himself back, with my heart in my mouth as the current took him further away from his moorings and out towards the sea, but thankfully, he slowly inched his way up the far side, eventually making it back. I breathed a huge sigh of relief and thanked God for keeping him safe after he had been so kind to us. I managed to remove as much of the mud as I could by paddling in a nearby ditch and wriggling in the grass. The open land was flat with a labyrinth of deep water filled drainage ditches to cross, which we navigated our way around, eventually finding civilisation and pavements again. TEB was beginning to feel unwell and was desperate for a toilet. He struggled on but was feeling faint and disorientated by the time we reached Highbridge just below Weston-Super-Mare, and felt that he could go no further. Mum phoned Uncle Andrew who drove over from Bath and took us back to their house for TEB to recover. He reluctantly visited a doctor, and then after a tub of tablets and a week's rest, we resumed our walk from exactly the same crossroads that Uncle Andrew had picked us up from.

The beaches from Burnham on Sea to Weston-Super-Mare are almost as wide as they are long, with sand or mud for as far as I could see, but we had a lot of miles to catch up so playing was out of the question. A pretty Golden Labrador Guide Dog puppy called Bumble, came along to meet us with her owner. Bumble was very young and had so much to learn, so I whispered in her ear that she was a very special puppy and had a hugely responsible job ahead of her and I kissed her lightly on the nose and wished her luck in her training. Later that day in Clevedon I met four more puppies in training but they were much older and knew exactly what was expected of them - but I'm sure secretively they wished they could swap places with me.

Avonmouth docks was our next obstacle, providing miles of high metal fences and huge grey metal buildings to negotiate our way around. I have never seen such a big car park! There must have been thousands of newly manufactured cars all parked in colour co-ordinating blocks, row after row after row. We eventually made our way out of the car maze and found ourselves amongst some dingy terraced houses, completely out of place amid this metal industrial estate. If someone above had a gigantic magnet, this whole area would disappear leaving only these little houses marooned like an island. Above my head I could hear a peculiar loud droning noise and as I strained my neck to look up I was surprised to see cars whizzing along the M5 motorway, crossing the muddy river Avon. I really couldn't cope with another crossing in a little rowing boat, so there was no alternative but to walk along the side of the motorway. Not many dogs (or people) know this, but there is an official path that runs over this bridge. We found a footpath sign and followed it up a steep flight of steps to the motorway above. I was so high the houses looked like dolls houses and the cars in the carparks below just looked like toys. It was very noisy crossing the bridge and I was glad when we descended the long flight of steps down the other side. (Every time we've crossed the bridge since then in the van, Mum says "We've walked over this bridge, haven't we Havoc?" I smile to myself and remember it clearly.)

Continuing our route up the edge of the Severn estuary, I could see the first Severn Bridge crossing over into Wales. It was mostly hard pavements under paw and I was physically and mentally exhausted, but I knew we were heading for a campsite. It had been a long day and thought it mustn't be far now as my tummy was beginning to rumble. We walked right underneath the bridge, passing the gigantic concrete buttresses that held it up, and started looking for the campsite that was clearly marked on Grandpa's map. Unfortunately, the map was dated 1964 and the campsite no longer existed! My heart sank as my legs turned to jelly. What on earth were we going to do amidst all this concrete where there was nowhere to pitch a tent? I managed to drag my body another mile or so until we reached a residential mobile home site, where Mum asked if they would allow us to put our tent up on their grass for one night. The man wasn't too keen but sympathy got the better of him and he reluctantly agreed to let us stay. After passing under the second Severn Bridge we made our way through fields of buttercups and cows, past Berkley's ugly power station to Slimbridge Wetland centre with all its pretty ducks. We then travelled up the Gloucester and Sharpness Canal and into the centre of Gloucester's renovated dockland area, where Mum's cousin Neil was waiting to meet us. I stayed at his house for two nights while Mum and TEB walked the next day without me, so I could have an extra rest. It was warm and sunny so I slept for hours in the garden. Neil came out occasionally just to check that I was still breathing and hadn't escaped, but most of the day I had to myself - it was Bliss. I was firing again on all cylinders the following day and back walking to celebrate crossing the border into Wales.

Newport to Gretna Green

I had been looking forward to reaching Newport for my second transporter swing-bridge crossing. The last one took me across the river Tees to Middlesbrough. Disappointingly, this one wasn't working and we had to walk a little bit further to find an alternative bridge to cross the River Usk.

Cardiff looked particularly gloomy when we arrived as the weather was overcast. I have visited the capital of Wales a few times before but the sun had always been shining. We didn't go into the town centre today but just kept to the coast and worked our way around more never-ending hard pavements, from Cardiff Bay towards Penarth. We were following footpath signs, trying to negotiate our way between a huge metal fence and the sea, when we found ourselves lost in the middle of a huge coal depot, faced by a ditch full of shiny black water. I started to panic as I could hear big lorries rumbling around me. I looked down and thought my feet had disappeared, as they were so black that they blended in with the ground. Thinking I was going to get run over, we managed to scrabble up a steep slope to get our bearings, when I heard an angry voice shouting "You're not supposed to be in here!" Suddenly, the front end of a lorry was driving towards us with a man leaning out of the window, yelling. With profound apologies given, Mum explained all about our charity walk and that we were only trying to follow the footpath signs. His face mellowed and he invited us to climb into the cab with him. We all squeezed aboard, complete with big rucksacks, and he drove us out of the coal yard and deposited us safely back on the road to Barry.

The coast around Barry and Llantwit Major was not very special and I longed for clean soft sand or lush grass to play on. It took until nearly Porthcawl before I could come off my lead and run freely again along the long sandy beach. The tall, white lighthouse beckoned to us from around the bay and pointed us in the direction of Port Talbot. The enormous steel works were silhouetted against the sky and belched out smoke, which drifted across the road and up into the valleys. To avoid getting lost again amongst all the factories, we took an inland road which ran parallel to the coast and through the tiny village of Tai Bach. The Roman Catholic Church had a large grassy area at the side, so Mum asked the vicar if we could pitch our tent. He agreed, and said that there was a party in the hall that night and the kitchen would be open for us to get water. When the party people arrived, they invited us to join their celebrations, which included the food. Well, I was straight in and in my element just wandering around from table to table, while people fed me from their plates with sausages, sandwiches, bits of pie and crisps. It was amazing! Later in the evening there was a cabaret show for us to watch, after which they passed around our charity buckets for a collection. It was quite late by the time we crawled back into our tent but a very successful evening was had by all.

Compared to the South West of England, the coast path around Wales so far was relatively flat, although the concrete pavement around Swansea Bay seem to go on forever. I could clearly see the Mumbles Lifeboat Station in the distance but I didn't seem to be getting any closer. With sore feet and gasping for a drink, we eventually arrived at the Yacht Club, where we were welcomed by the Mumbles Lifeboat crew and a well-inebriated Leaky Willie, (a Hasher called Williams – from Wales, great name) who was a good friend of theirs. It wasn't long before Mum and TEB joined in and I was entertaining them all with my handstands. If Mum puts my shoes on just my back legs, it feels so strange I walk with them waving in the air. Everyone was in fits of laughter, asking me to do it again and again. Thinking I would be sleeping at the Lifeboat station that night, it was worth doing anything for a warm bed to lie on. It turned out even better, as after I got all four feet back on the ground, Leaky Willie took us to a guest house, where he had arranged for us to stay for the night.

Back on track the following morning, I was walking along minding my own business, when I picked up a pleasant smell of baking wafting through the air. My pace instinctively quickened in the direction of Port Eynon Lifeboat Station. I could see people sat at tables eating, so I put on my well-rehearsed, pathetic starving dog look, sucked my tummy in and headed towards them. The station was having a fund-raising Open Day and the crew were cooking fresh Welsh Cakes. This is a small scone-like pancake, sprinkled with sugar and they were delicious. I managed to scrounge at least three whole ones, just in bits, from people's plates. A great way to start the morning's walking.

The next couple of days the wind picked up and gales literally blew us around the Gower peninsula, where the beaches were deserted and stray sand blew into my eyes making me squint. The grass around Worm's Head had been eaten to 'within half-an-inch of its life' by the thousands of resident rabbits, but it was easy walking and I bounced happily along, eventually reaching Three Cliffs campsite, where many tents had already blown over and collapsed. Our little 'two-man and one-dog' tent that had been kindly donated by Terra Nova was brilliant. Yes, it leaned a little and shook a lot, but the wind just blew right over the top. I put my paws over my ears to block out the sound, curled up as tight as I could to keep warm and closed my eyes, knowing I was safe, snuggled up in our little portable home.

At a speed of approximately 4 miles per hour we sped along the north coast of the Gower and picked up the new tarmac Millennium Coastal Path, which started just outside Llanelli, but compared to other coastal paths I'd walked on, it was ugly and made my feet sore. I longed for the higgledy piggledy dry stony paths lined with gorse bushes, wild flowers and grazing sheep. Any sheep here would have been mown down by the speeding cyclists! At last we arrived at Pendine beach in thick sea mist, where a plaque on the wall informed me that between 1924 and 1927 five World Land Speed Records had taken place there. Ignoring the notice 'NO DOGS' on the beach, we set off at top speed along the sand, dodging the holiday makers who were trying to see enough to build their sand castles. I was just glad Malcolm Campbell wasn't trying to break any land speed records today.

Two little plaques set in the ground at Amroth told me in both English and Welsh that this was the start of the 180 mile Pembrokeshire coast path. There were plenty of holiday makers about so we walked slowly to take the opportunity to do some fund raising. TEB had phoned ahead earlier in the day and spoken to the crew of Tenby's Lifeboat, but they said that they were unable to accommodate us in their brand new station. I was gutted, as it had been such a long day. My legs felt so heavy and trudged unwillingly around the seaside town, which was now beginning to shut down for the night, as we encouraged the last few remaining tourists to put money in our cans and looked for somewhere else to stay. We came across a hall that was meeting place for The

Salvation Army. Remembering that all denominations of churches had helped us out around the country so far and knowing that the 'Sally Army' help the homeless, Mum enquired within, but I could not believe my floppy ears when they rejected us - that was twice in one day!

I poked my head out of the tent. It was another beautiful day, warm but not too hot, the grass was lush and the early summer flowers were beginning to show. The cliffs were safe for me to be off my lead for most of the time and I could run ahead to play or chase bunnies whist Mum slowly caught me up. Rummaging in the grass, I found the most pungent bit of fox poo to roll in and thought I smelt divine. Mum, on the other hand had other ideas and dragged me off to the nearest cow water trough, dunked me in and then used human shampoo to try to eradicate the smell. Luckily fox hangs around for ages so despite 'aloe veras' best efforts I still thought I smelt acceptable.

Mum put me back on my lead as the nearing cliffs were high and dropped away steeply around St Govan's Head. We were entering military owned land again and another sign told me not to pick up any military debris in case it exploded – as if I would! Following a narrow animal track close to the edge, I noticed a flight of stone steps which led down to a tiny church nestled between the rocks. Hundreds of years ago, so the rumour goes, St Govan hid between these rocks from pirates. He must have been there an awfully long time to be able to build a church. Just beyond, I passed a narrow cleft in the land with a very sheer drop to the sea. Another story tells of a huntsman who leapt across the gap on his horse, but, when turning around to see what they had safely cleared, he apparently died of shock! So, for Mum's sake I decided I had better not attempt to jump it.

Pembrokeshire National park has 186 long miles to walk around, and the little town of Angle sits all on its own, miles from anywhere, jutting out to sea opposite Milford Haven. The locals are quite rightly, very proud of their Lifeboat Station, which of course we visited before making our way around Pembroke docks. There was a strange scent in the air. I'd smelt it before, but it seemed out of place amongst the green hedges and wild flowers. It reminded me of back home when Mum took the car to the garage to be repaired. - It was oil! The smell lingered in the breeze as we wound our way along the narrow paths towards Pembroke. The foxgloves swayed gently way above my head and the busy bumble bees flew from one glove to another gathering nectar. My favourite flower of them all was the dog rose with its white petals delicately tinged on the edges, wide open to reveal their enticing centres begging for the bees to come and pollenate them. I caught a glimpse through a hole in the hedges of the enormous Texaco Oil refinery across the water, with its numerous towering, shiny metal chimneys resembling something from outer space. It looked and smelt very sinister as I walked underneath one of the jetties. Thick pipes carrying oil ran above my head and I couldn't believe that such a beautiful place could be hiding such a blot on the landscape.

We finally reached Pembroke and stayed with a lovely family for the night. They had two dogs; Lucy a retired Golden Retriever Guide Dog who just sat and stared at me and Bart an almost-white Labrador that was a working Guide dog for Eifion. They joined us on our walk the next day and I quietly watched Bart in his harness working with such responsibility. I know I couldn't do it, as there would be too many distractions for me. He wasn't allowed to sniff lamp posts or pick up food in the street or even cock his leg on the corner of garden walls, but he seemed happy working and looked so proud. I couldn't believe he was the same dog that I had been fooling with in the garden the day before.

Foxgloves, Bobby's buttons and ox-eyed daisies guided us along the lush grassy footpaths of the Milford Haven estuary and past the ugly pipework of the new LPG depot (which, I believe stands for liquid petroleum gas, whatever that is). The coastline eventually resumed its rocky characteristics and beautiful wild flowers as we made our way slowly around St Anne's head.

The tiny island of Skokholm was clearly visible to my left and I could see the bird sanctuary island of Skomer straight in front as we turned the corner at Wooltack point and headed into the chilly wind. As we arrived at Martin's Haven a little boat was preparing to leave the quay, packed with bird watchers off to visit the puffins that come to nest on the island and rear their young. I would have loved to slip onboard the boat to see the cute little black and white birds that live in burrows, but surprise surprise,

'NO DOGS ALLOWED'

"Grr". So, I sat disappointedly and watched the little boat leave without me, until it had completely disappeared out of sight.

The dark cliffs ahead and fields of mud stained sheep reminded me of the south Devon coastline, the grass was high and I had to jump up occasionally to check the sea was still there. Small spotted butterflies fluttered across the path in front of me unable to decide where they wanted to land as we descended our last hill. The sun had beaten down on me all day and I was hot, tired and thirsty as we arrived in Little Haven. Mum cooked sausages for tea and we shared them sitting on the sea wall watching fire fill the sky as the sun set into the sea.

Yet another beautiful day and soft grassy cliff tops made walking pleasurable as we left the sheltered estuary of Solva, with its little fishing boats and tiny yachts. We were making our way towards St Davids, the smallest city in Great Britain. There were no huge department stores, tube trains or heavy traffic belching out stinking fumes and I almost trod on some wild orchids as I raced down to the little stream for a paddle. A red kite soared gracefully overhead and I could clearly see his forked tail against the cloudless sky. This was not a bit like any other city I had visited before. I was also slightly confused as it wasn't Sunday but I was visiting the huge cathedral, seemingly out of place in the centre of this little town, but there were plenty of visitors about so made it a perfect opportunity to rattle our collecting boxes before setting off around St David's Head.

The dry stony coastal paths seem to go on forever into the distance and disappear into the cloudless sky making the mileage impossible to judge. Like many footpaths around Britain's coast they were only single file, and we had no particular pecking order in which we walked, but today was a good day so I was out in front. The afternoon sunshine warmed my back, there were no sheep, no dangerous steep cliff edges and I was off my lead as free as a? - a dog. I was as free as every dog should be, and loving it. At that moment, I forgot the times when my feet hurt, or my legs ached or when I was cold and soaked to the skin or hungry. This was the life of a travelling dog and I was lucky enough to be the one experiencing it.

In the distance, perched on its own little island, I could see Strumble Head lighthouse. Here I met a lady called Elly, who explained how the mysterious little piles of stones, called cairns are made. She said if everyone that passes places a stone on the top the cairn it gets bigger and bigger. I picked one up in my mouth but couldn't quite reach top, so Mum did it for me to mark our journey. Elly also showed us a very rare flower called spiked speedwell. She said it was blue, and I'd never seen one before and I've not seen one since. Along the Pembrokeshire coastal path, the gorse bushes were in full bloom, smelling of coconut and reminded me of the suntan lotion that Mum uses. As I squeezed between their spikey branches I tried to avoid standing on the large black beetles weaving between the stones. I was fascinated as they skilfully manoeuvred their bodies like little articulated lorries, trying to cross the path in front of me. Horrible jet-black flies hovered in the air dangling their hairy legs in my face annoying me (well I hope it was their legs) enticing me to snap at the air and bite them, but when I did, "Yuk" they tasted awful!

We had been promised a night's stay at Fishguard Lifeboat Station just a few more miles around the corner. It was getting late in the afternoon, I was dog tired and my pace was getting slower, so I was relieved when we finally stopped to look over the wall onto the Lifeboat Station nestled in the busy port below. To my dismay though, there was a locked gate and tall fencing, preventing us from accessing the secure port via the flight of overgrown stone steps at which I was at the top. The official pedestrian access to the port was about another half a mile further on, (and then we would have had to walk another half a mile back to the station) I collapsed to the ground, my little legs had given up for the day and I could walk no more. Fortunately, after a few frantic phone calls from Mum, one of the crew came running up with a key and released us. I almost fell down that flight of steep steps and was soon gobbling down my tea in the warmth of their mess room. That night, I sat looking out of the window mesmerised by the illuminated Stenna ferry arriving from Ireland, not realizing then, I would be lucky enough to be traveling on one of those ferries in nine years' time.

As we left Fishguard Bay the path got considerably steeper, the bracken was high and the foxgloves towered above me. I couldn't actually see the sea but I could hear it crashing against the rocks below so I knew it was never far away. The cliff edge dropped away steeper now so I walked close to Mum, carefully watching every step I took, till we reached the home of Jess the collie, perched on the cliff top where we stayed the night. Now Jess's dad was a lepidopterist and I've not stayed at a lepidopterist's house before but it reminded me of Grandpa's, with memorabilia and books everywhere. He had a fascination for moths, and catches them in his home-made moth catcher which he puts outside in the evenings. Then in the morning he takes close-up photos of them before releasing them again outside. Unfortunately, lots had escaped in the house and big moths were perched everywhere on windows and walls and I had to really restrain myself from sticking my tongue out and eating any.

Apparently, from a geologist's point of view, the rugged coast and high cliffs around Dinas Head are spectacular with its perfect rock formations. As I am not a geologist, the arrival of Poppit Sands was all I was interested in. I ran straight past the Lifeboat Station and headed across the beach, forward-rolling into a full-on back scratch wriggle. Bliss. To celebrate reaching the end of the Pembrokeshire Coast Path, we stopped for refreshments at the nearby Webley Hotel. A local man told us that apparently for a while it was called The Poppit Inn. For some reason the good ladies of the church didn't like the name, so it was changed back to The Webley!

There was no obvious way across the river Teifi and the banks were thick mud which would have gobbled me up in an instant, so we kept to the road and headed inland towards the town of Cardigan. We had been promised a night's stay further up the coast in Aberystwyth by Guide Dog supporters who owned a guest house. It was very late and already dark as we made our way around the final grassy headland by torchlight and into the town. We had walked so many miles that day that my legs ached, I was thirsty, hungry and exhausted and I desperately wanted to stop and pitch the tent for the night, but the couple were expecting us so we had to keep going. When at last we arrived, they gave me a much needed bowl of water, then immediately showed us to our room, which, if I fought my way through the net curtains, overlooked the sea. Mum gave me my tea which I gobbled down, followed by another bowl of water. I then curled up by the side of her bed and went straight to sleep. The next day was Sunday so it had been decided that we would spend the morning looking around the town and continue our walk in the afternoon. After a bit of a lay-in Mum and TEB got up, gave me my breakfast, then went down stairs for theirs, but I needed to wee! They had left me in the room and there was nowhere for me to 'go'. I waited for a few minutes but they didn't return. I paced the floor, went to the door, considered the mat but then thought, "Where would it be least obvious if I weed?" So, I jumped up on the bed and relieved myself! I knew it was wrong but I couldn't hold it in any longer. I slouched in the corner when they returned and hoped they wouldn't notice, but as Mum was packing her rucksack she suddenly shouted, "Havoc's weed on the bed!"

Luckily, she didn't tell me off, as she knew she should have taken me out before they went down for breakfast. Usually I have the bladder of a camel but I had drunk so much the night before I couldn't wait. I hoped they wouldn't tell the lady and I felt so embarrassed. Mum stripped the bed and put the duvet in the sunny window to dry, then stuffed all the sheets into her rucksack. We slipped quickly out of the front door and headed towards the launderette. Mum put the sheets in the washing machine. Then once they were washed, one of the sheets went into the drier but the other sheet had a rubber backing and she thought it might melt, so we walked around Aberystwyth waving a huge white sheet, trying to dry it. Mum slung it over a picnic bench in the park and luckily it was a windy, sunny day so by lunchtime it had dried. We returned to the guest house and Mum re-made the bed. We picked up our bags, said a quick goodbye and made a hasty retreat out of town. I don't know if the lady ever knew - but she will now when she reads my book.

Still feeling ashamed of myself, I trudged reluctantly up the steep hill next to the funicular railway, wishing I could hitch a ride. I gazed thoughtfully out into the sparkling ocean and could clearly make out four or five dolphins breaching the water. I added them to my mental list and pulled on my lead so Mum would pause and observe them as well. TEB didn't want to stop and continued puffing his way to the top while we stopped for a few moments to watch these elegant creatures gracefully playing in the water as if they were sending us on our way.

The weather had cooled considerably as Dave the Lifeboat man gave us a lift across the river Dovey in his own little motorboat. Inland, I could just recognise Snowdonia, the highest mountain range in Wales, looking mysterious and uninviting against the cloudy grey sky. I have climbed Snowdon before so was glad I didn't have to climb it again today.

From Harlech castle we walked inland slightly to get around the Traeth Bach estuary and arrived outside the gates of an Italian style village called Portmerian. As expected, a big sign read, 'NO DOGS'. Mum started to explain to the lady on duty that we were walking the coast of Britain and had to pass through, and without further ado she welcomed us in. Naturally I was the only dog in the village walking amongst the brightly painted hotels, cafes, shops and holiday cottages, so became quite a talking point for the visitors, who then felt obliged to drop money into our collecting boxes. My good luck continued as we walked along the beach to Criccieth Castle because Mum didn't even have to ask; the lady on the gate just said, "Come on in."

The Lleyn Peninsula had numerous beautiful sandy

beaches for me to play on. Porth Oer was particularly entertaining as the sand strangely whistled or squeaked beneath our feet. (Apparently it's something to do with the shape of the sand grains rubbing against each other, but they were far too small for me to examine closely) Following the Lleyn's 'waymarked' coastal path was almost impossible. The number of times we went the wrong way and had to backtrack, was tiring and frustrating, so we stuck to the shore whenever we could. You would think it would be relatively easy following a coastal footpath but The Lleyn Peninsula had other plans for its walking visitors. Big clear signposts when the path was obvious and you didn't need them, but then no signpost when you needed one the most, leading us into all sorts of places where we shouldn't have been; across busy main roads, into people's gardens and around numerous fields into farmyards with no obvious way out. I think the local Welsh council could do with a visit to the Southwest Coast Path to see how it should be done properly.

When Mum was confident that we were on the right track, so long as no sheep were mowing the grass, I was allowed off my lead to enjoy the freedom. Early one afternoon I was running on ahead when something made me stop in my tracks. I was about to climb over a stone wall stile when I noticed something on the top that looked wrong. It had black arrow markings and I instinctively knew it could be dangerous. TEB couldn't see it and was shouting at me to go on, but I didn't want to move. Mum climbed the wall by my side and recognised that it was an adder snake. She pulled me back quickly and we walked safely away giving it plenty of space. It frightened us both and certainly made me more aware of where I put my feet.

Later that day, I was walking along the footpath next to the Welsh mountain railway line into Caenarfon. My nerves were still on edge and I jumped in the air each time I saw a bent stick. Suddenly a train came chugging up behind me, frightening me out of my fur. I barked angrily and ran after it, Mum called me back but I was already in full flight and ignored her. I sped off into the distance but the train got faster and faster and I got left further and further behind, so with no more gears I eventually had to give in. The trouble was that during the chase I strained my bad leg and was hobbling on my other three by the time I returned to Mum. I thought she would feel sorry for me and give me lots of sympathy, maybe even carry me, but no! I even sensed from her tone of voice that she might have been a tad cross with me and said it was my own fault, so remorsefully I hung my head and had to limp the last few miles into Caenarfon. I understand Prince Charles was invested as The Prince of Wales at Caenarfon Castle but unfortunately he was out, so I couldn't stay the night. Luckily, two Hashers that we had met previously in Norwich, had recently moved there and they were in, so let us stay with them in their tall Victorian house, where I had a good night's sleep and thankfully was fit to walk again by morning.

If I squinted my eyes, though the drizzle, I could see the south coast of the Isle of Anglesey across the water. It was far too wide and deep to wade across and still a long walk up to the Britannia Bridge, so TEB did one of his disappearing acts again and came back smiling. He had managed to find a kind man in the Caenarfon boat club who was returning to his house on Anglesey and offered us a lift across the Menai Straights in his rubber boat. It was raining harder and a bit scary to say the least, so Mum held me tight as we bounced across the waves. The salty water splashed into my face as I watched Caenarfon slowly get smaller and eventually blend into the grey misty sky.

By the time we landed on Anglesey the rain was lashing down. I was miserable and walked with my head down to keep the rain out of my eyes till we took shelter in a farm barn. When I looked up there was a semi-circle of antique tractors around me, with headlamps that looked like eyes peering down. I thought they looked friendly and it cheered me up, but I kept my eye firmly on them whilst Mum ate her lunch just in case one of them should attempt to move closer.

It didn't stop raining but we had to press on. Luckily Anglesey's coastal path was clearly signposted making things slightly easier, so with poor visibility we slowly made our way clockwise around the island. Everything was sodden. We camped out a few nights but the tent didn't dry and was packed up each morning still wet, which made it heavier for them to carry. I wore my waxed raincoat so couldn't carry my panniers and we hardly saw another person on the coastal path, making fund-raising difficult. TEB would go off on his own most evenings and collect from the local pubs, but Mum and I were too shattered so would try and get some extra rest. We visited most of the Lifeboat Stations on the island and the crews were pleased to see us, offering their big drying rooms for our kit, so luckily, we were able to dry things out between the showers.

From one island to another we ventured onto Holy Island. The weather improved slightly and from the top of the mountain I could see both the North Stack and South Stack lighthouses. From the other side of the mountain, I sat looking down onto the town of Holyhead and enviously watched the Irish ferries leaving for Dublin. I cheered up slightly as we left Holy Island because we made our way north along a massive sandy beach, which stretched as far as I could see, and despite the drizzle Mum took off my coat so I could wriggle on my back. This catharsis only lasted a few seconds before three jet aeroplanes from RAF Valley came screaming over my head, and I immediately sprang to my feet, almost pulling a muscle in my back, and ran to Mum tucking myself in behind her legs. The deafening screams continued along the entirety of the beach. It felt like they were using us as target practice as we were the only ones in sight and they swooped down so low. This occasion was one of the only times in my life that I was glad to get off the beach.

The northern coast of Anglesey came and went through thick cloud and torrential rain. We took respite in Moelfre Lifeboat Museum and I sniffed round an old Lifeboat called Birds Eye, which made me feel a little home sick as it reminded me of two things back home, a Hasher with the same name and of course fish fingers. "Mmm" maybe Mum will cook some tonight. Towering above me, standing at the helm of his ship, stood a statue of Dick Evans, one of the most decorated Lifeboat men in Britain. I felt a bit sorry for him as the wind and rain were lashing in his face and he was getting nowhere. Goodness knows how long he'd been fighting the storm! I walked past trying not to distract him, still thinking of the possibility of fish fingers for my tea.

Red Wharf Bay wasn't quite what I had expected. Mum had told me earlier that she remembered from her childhood, the beach being a vast expanse of beautiful sand. Unfortunately, when I arrived the tide was in and I had to carefully pick my way through broken glass bottles and discarded plastic around the edge of a stony, grassy covered mud plain. Must have been a different Red Wharf Bay on Anglesey that she remembered.

Penmon lighthouse stands at the most easterly tip of the island. It had stopped raining for once and I could see out towards Puffin Island. I couldn't see any puffins though and neither did I get to see any doves in the old stone bee hive shaped dovecot, but I did get to see Ron and Pam. I had been looking forward to meeting them and they let us stay in their cosy bungalow for the night. Ron and Pam were good friends of Nanny and Grandpa.

Mum said that they used to have lovely camping holidays together on Exmoor when she was very young. I was glad I got to meet them, but I will always remember Anglesey for its rain; I think it rained every day.

We said goodbye to Anglesey and crossed the Menai Bridge, doing our best to avoid the busy main roads which tried everything to block our route to Bangor. Once we reached the city, we headed for the cathedral, which again I thought strange as it wasn't Sunday. It was a massive, old building and echoed inside. Mum was looking for something but eventually had to ask, "Where are the old dog tongs?" The verger looked down at me and smiled, then took us to a small room where he showed us some rather painful looking wooden tongs. A notice beneath them read 'Dog Tongs – used by the sextant for removing unruly dogs from the church.' This pair had been restored in 1892, so goodness knows how old they originally were. Apparently, John Merrill had mentioned them in his book, so Mum wanted to see them. I was glad she wasn't about to use them on me, I know I can be unruly at times but these seemed a little barbaric.

The road from Bangor to Conwy was scary, as we walked the pavement alongside the main road between the sea and railway line to my left. We were insignificant to the juggernaut lorries that hurtled past, squeezing us up against the sea wall and spraying me with dirty oily water from the road. The sky was full of dark clouds above Conwy castle, but at least it wasn't raining when a little old lady dressed in Welsh national costume and tall, black felt hat edged with white lace, posed for a photo with us outside the smallest house in Great Britain.

As if I wasn't walking far enough on Britain's mainland, I thought doing the islands as well was going above and beyond. So, when it came to walking around Great Ormes Head off the top of Llandudno, meaning extra mileage on predominantly pavement around a rocky outcrop of land, I considered it completely unnecessary so sulked and dragged my feet the whole way.

St Trillo's church, is the smallest in Great Britain at Rhos-on-Sea and was just my size, made from little stones and pebbles cemented together, with white washed walls inside and a cobbled stone floor. It had an arched end in front of the marble topped altar complete with 5 tiny wooden chairs and was full of flowers making it look so pretty.

The seaside towns of Rhyl and Prestatyn have both seen better days and looked sad and neglected in the drizzling rain. It was a long monotonous walk around the Dee Estuary on my lead on mostly hard pavements which jarred my now very painful joints. How I yearned for the open cliff tops of Yorkshire, the short soft grass of South Wales, the never ending sandy beaches of Northumberland or even the steep hills of Dorset. So, to avoid walking all the way up the river and into Chester on more pavements, we managed to find a little metal bridge which took us across at Queensferry onto the Wirral. There are no roads that follow the coast to the town of Neston, where TEB's aunt lived, so we trudged knee deep (my knees are quite low) in sticky mud around fields of potatoes to reach her house in time for tea. I had not enjoyed today's walk at all so really appreciated their lovely warm house and a comfortable bed that night.

Before leaving the Wirral peninsula, I paid my respects in the only way I know how, to a little statue of a Guide Dog in harness at New Brighton, where in 1931 Guide Dogs for the Blind was founded. I then crossed the River Mersey into Liverpool, by ferry of course.

We made an early start and despite the misty morning, from the ferry I could see the Liver birds standing boldly on top of the Liver building. I stopped outside the famous Cavern Pub where many music artists rose to fame, while the statue of a young John Lennon leaned on the wall and watched as I humbly drank in the street from my bowl.

Dirty pavements took us around the industrial dockland area out of Liverpool and up the coast to Crosby. I had the fright of my life as I witnessed a man stuck in the quicksand drowning as the tide came in. He didn't try to run or turn around and shout or wave, just stood there as the waves splashed round his feet and then rose higher and higher up his body. I couldn't understand why Mum just stood looking at him and didn't run for help. Then I noticed more men along the beach, further out to sea with the water up to their waists and necks. Why wasn't anyone trying to save them? So, I started barking to raise the alarm, but Mum just laughed at me saying, "They're not real, silly." I soon realised there were about a hundred of these men, all made from cast iron, stretching for over a mile along the beach. I learnt later that they had been made by Anthony Gormley, the same artist that designed the Angel of the North. Apparently, the Lifeboat gets called out regularly on false alarms to rescue these 'drowning' men from the sea.

I was starting to feel like a proper holiday maker now as I could see Blackpool Tower in the distance. TEB was being horrible to Mum again and an argument started out of nothing just because she needed a wee and he had to wait for her in the pouring rain. I got the brunt of it as he was holding my lead. Quite unnecessary I thought but that's humans for you. There weren't many people strolling along the beach, but still the horse-and-carriages trotted merrily past and the electric trams smoothly glided along, sheltering tourists from the rain. We didn't bother stopping to collect money and made our way into a side street where the double fronted New Guilderoy Hotel and its owners Simon and Rhona, Black Pudding Hashers, cheerfully met us. We were given a cosy little room that overlooked the kitchens and I quickly bedded down for the night. Next morning things looked brighter all around, the sun was shining, Mum and TEB were talking again and Rhona gave me the biggest plate of breakfast scraps you could imagine; Bacon, eggs, sausage, fried potato, beans and of course black pudding, I had to decline the mushrooms and tomato due to my flatulence but scoffed down the lot. A perfect way to start the day in Blackpool.

As we hadn't managed any charity collecting the day before, we caught a tram back down to Lytham St Anne's and walked the Golden Mile for the second time, but today was sunny. It was August now and holiday makers from everywhere were digging deep into their pockets and throwing coins into our buckets. I loved the happy atmosphere with people laughing on the fairground rides, children playing on the beach, donkeys giving rides and the smell of hot doughnuts and fish and chips filled the air. Glancing up at the huge metal tower I smiled to myself as I bounced happily along the prom in its shadow.

After losing a bit of time looking at vintage vehicles in Fleetwood, we caught a late ferry across the Wyre estuary and arrived in the tiny village of Knott End on Sea early Sunday evening. A car pulled up alongside us and TEB asked the way to the church (in the hope that they might let us sleep in their hall for the night.) The man gave us directions and as he pulled away shouted, "The service starts in ten minutes". We had to run, but made it just in time and slipped quietly in at the back of the church. Coincidently we found out that the children were having a tea party afterwards, to which we were cordially invited. Sandwiches, sausages, cakes, biscuits, jelly and ice cream. I was in my element, allowing the children to take turns in feeding me their leftovers. After the children had left the party and the room was tidied, we were invited to sleep the night on the hall floor and the remaining food was left for us to nibble on during the night.

From Lancaster, we trudged a thick, muddy, tidal route

around Sunderland Point then continued past the front of a pretty little holiday park with rows of flower adorned caravans, spoilt only by their obtrusive panoramic view of Heysham power station. We squeezed along the narrow footpath that skirted the perimeter metal fences and headed along the sandier coast towards Morecombe, where I tasted local prawns and posed for a photo with a statue of a man called Eric Morecombe.

Morecombe bay is renowned for its fast incoming tides and sinking sands. Apparently people have died trying to cross from one side to another, and only a few years ago, 23 Chinese cockle pickers perished because the tide surrounded them and they got stuck in the sand and drowned. Yep, you guessed it – I was going to cross! Luckily, Mum had contacted a man known as 'The Queen's Guide' called Cedric, who reckoned he was the only person that knew a safe route across and he offered to show us the way. Cedric was due to lead a large sponsored walk across the bay the following day and was preparing the route by sticking laurel branches into the mud as he crossed, which the group would then follow. He met us at Arnside, told us to just follow his tractor tyre imprints and off he drove across the bay. He drove his tractor quite fast across the muddy sand but I could clearly see the laurel branch markers. Even when we crossed the river Kent, which flows across the middle of the bay I kept walking, well I was almost swimming, as it came up to my armpits. All that cold water made me desperate for a wee, so when the next laurel branch appeared in the sand I cocked my leg with relief. A lady called Marion, who we stayed with the previous night, did the perilous crossing with us. Our indirect 'U' shaped crossing seemed to take hours but we all eventually made it safely to the other side. At Grange-over-Sands, Marion treated us to a celebration drink and piece of cake. We sat outside of the café in the sun and waited for her lift to collect her before we triumphantly set off again on our journey.

After my life threatening adventure across Morecombe Bay, more by luck than judgement, we successfully managed to negotiate our way through Barrow-In-Furness Dockyard and found the bridge to Walney Island, just for the promise of fish and chips for tea. "Oh I do love a bit of crispy batter and tender white fish." In the morning, we set off north again across the little causeway that is only accessible at low tides, along the A590 towards Milom. The coast from Haverigg to Ravenglass was amazing; beautiful soft, clean sand for as far as I could see and Mum took my panniers, jacket and lead off so I could have the freedom of the beach. We were the only ones around for miles so I could roll, on my back, paddle in the sea and chase pebbles to my heart's content. If I stopped to sniff Mum would just keep walking. I had my safe distance that I would allow her to get away, then I would run like the wind to catch her up. I knew she would never lose me but I couldn't cope with being on my own for too long.

We reached Ravenglass by late afternoon and Mum asked at the station what time the next train was due in. I thought this strange, as I knew we wouldn't be needing one. I followed her over to the nearby pub, where we plonked the bags down and sat on the wall outside and just waited. Eventually, a train rumbled into the station and onto the platform jumped a smiling Leaky Willie. He had travelled all the way from his home in Swansea, complete with a full size suitcase and rolled up umbrella. He was on his way to the Far East (that is another country, not Norfolk) and thought he would join us on our walk for a day, then catch his aeroplane from Glasgow. I thought he was quite mad but as he paid for us to stay the night in a hotel room again (only a Hasher would do that), I was happy for him to join us, at least it was extra company and someone else to make a fuss of me. He was not really equipped for the walk. I don't think he realised quite what our adventure entailed: Not beautiful man-made footpaths or tarmac pavements all the way around Britain's coast. Our first obstacle was a thick black muddy ditch, so he took off his brand new trainers and waded ankle deep across. Our second obstacle was the river Ehen. Clearly shown on our map was a footbridge for us to cross, adjacent to the railway bridge, so we put our best paws forward and headed in that direction. When we arrived, there was a sign that said, 'footpath closed' and two men were working on the bridge. Mum told them about our walk but they were adamant that we couldn't cross. TEB took his shoes off and waded across the river but it got deeper and deeper, then he had to lift his rucksack above his head as the water reached his waist. While the railway workmen were curiously watching him in the water, Leaky Willie slipped past behind them on the railway line. (I believe if he had been caught there would be a fine of £200.) That left just Mum and me to cross the river. We couldn't follow Leaky and Mum didn't want to wade up to her waist and I certainly didn't fancy a swim. She pleaded with the men to change their minds and again explained about our walk and I put on my most pathetic expression. Although not happy about it, eventually they gave in, but insisted they must escort us across the footbridge, telling us not to step on the wet tarmac between the paving slabs. It was easy-peasy; two skips and a jump and we were over. (Why wouldn't they let us do that in the first place? such 'jobsworths.' I will never understand humans)

Our third obstacle to negotiate that day was only a nuclear decontamination station! Sellafield is positioned right on the coast and there was no way they would let us through. Reluctantly we had to follow the arrows and detour around its high metal fences and warning signs that made sure we couldn't get too close. I felt a weird and tingly feeling in my fur and I'm sure my wee glowed in the dark that night!

Deviation accomplished and safely back on the shore, the soft sand turned to shingle and was more painful on my feet. It was getting near tea time and my tummy started to rumble as we passed cute little wooden holiday homes. Some were perfectly painted, neat and tidy, whilst others were ramshackle and well loved, but the smell of cooking was wafting towards my nose from beyond their wooden verandas. I wanted to stop and join the holiday makers for a meal but Leaky's train was due soon and we had to get him to the next station. We arrived at Braystones with just seconds to spare, as a train rumbled into the station behind us. Leaky boarded the train with his now tatty suitcase and filthy rolled up umbrella and trainers, then with a quick wag of my tail the train slid away up the track in the direction of Whitehaven, where I was heading on paw.

The coast from Whitehaven northwards was not very pretty, full of chemical factories and hard pavements. My pads were beginning to wear out and lose their knobbly pattern, so Mum insisted I wore my shoes again. They rubbed a bit on top of my toes but she had been collecting sheep's wool and padded them out making it more comfortable. Although I didn't like wearing them it did take the hard impact off of my paws, giving them a chance to recover slightly.

From Maryport the sand reappeared, but it wasn't soft and golden and nobody played on it, so we kept to the pavements till we reached Silloth Lifeboat Station, where I politely posed for a photo shoot with the crew. From here, across the Solway Firth, Scotland didn't look far away. All that lay between us was squidgy wet lands, wildlife reserves, the river Eden, the river Esk, a main railway line and a massive motorway construction site. We popped into Carlisle to deposit charity money at the bank and Mum bought another map and replenished the food supply. I sat outside of the shops with my head cocked to one side, ears pricked up and shiny bright eyes to make me look cute so that shoppers would drop money in my bucket. It worked a treat every time.

The construction site was enormous, there were signs telling us we couldn't pass but we had no option. Amidst thick clouds of swirling, choking dust, we inched our way along the newly built stony embankments, while enormous lorries rumbled past completely unaware of our presence as we were so small. I was petrified and tried to walk as fast as I could with absolutely no time for sniffing. We clambered fences and crossed temporary bridges over rivers and railway lines, passed workman's huts and portaloos (which Mum conveniently used) I just peed on the outside. At last we made it back to the main road. For once I was relieved to feel solid pavement under my feet, the oncoming lush grass verges and bright flowerbeds of begonias welcomed us at last into Scotland.

Gretna Green to Outer Hebrides

Against the clear sky, I could see the white cross on the flag of St Andrew fluttering gently in the breeze on top of the first house in Scotland. At Gretna Green, we stopped for a well-earned rest and looked around the visitor centre with the other tourists to see where traditionally the blacksmith marries people that run away to marry without their parent's permission. I just thanked God that we hadn't walked all this way for Mum and TEB to do that! Luckily, I just posed by the sign for a photo.

The days were long and the weather was dry so we slept in the tent more often. I couldn't do much to help erect it, but I was always the first one in to test the beds. The large front canopy was designed for keeping bikes under, but as we didn't have bikes it was a useful space in which to keep the bags and for Mum to cook tea on the little stove. This gave me more room to spread out inside the sleeping area.

After a good night's sleep, I was usually ready and raring to go next morning. There was only one occasion I remember in the early days of my walk when I did not want to start the day. I just stood outside the church we had been staying in and let Mum and TEB walk right down the road without me. I thought Mum wouldn't leave me but she did! She just kept walking, looking back then laughing at me to see who gave in first. I have a mental distance gap allowance between us set where I know I can still feel safe, but she was beginning to stretch that gap too far. I couldn't stand it any longer, so I was the one that eventually had to give in and run like mad down the road to catch up. I never played that trick again.

Thick grassy banks lined the estuary up to Dumfries. It was a beautiful warm summer and I was enjoying the freedom off my lead. Fishermen waded waist deep in the water with poles stretched out either side, with their nets hanging down to catch fish. Along the shore of the Solway Firth, at low tide I saw hundreds of fishing nets stretched between poles as far out as I could see, just waiting for the tide to come in and fill them all with thousands of wriggling shiny fish.

We reached a busy little estuary village called Rockcliffe, where picturesque stone and white washed cottages overlooked Urr Water. Plenty of yachty holiday makers were sat outside of the pubs in the sunshine enjoying lunch, still wearing their lifejackets, so Mum rattled her collecting can as I ran up to greet people, allowing them to read my jacket. For our lunchtime break I flopped down in the shade and stared out across the shimmering water. Little sailing boats fluttered past and fishing boats bobbed rhythmically up and down on the waves. As I lay there wondering how we were going to get across to the other side of the bay without having to walk all the way round, a family of four that was about to leave the quay in their old motor boat invited us aboard. The boat was very small but we all squeezed aboard and slowly chugged across to the other side. The boat grounded on the bottom before we got to the beach, so I jumped in the water and paddled the last few feet ashore. The mother invited us to join them for a drink in their garden, so Mum accepted. We followed the family up the beach and pushed our way through a hole in the hedge. The other side opened onto their huge sloping front lawn, at the top of which was one of the biggest houses I have ever seen. This lovely family were the owners of Auchencairn House, so while everyone chatted and drank lemonade on the patio, I lay on the neatly mown grass and soaked up the sun. My tummy started to rumble and I was just beginning to think it was about time we left when the mother asked if we wanted to stay the night. "Please say yes, please say yes" I was thinking.

Luckily, my telepathy worked and Mum accepted, so we were shown to the 'Yellow room'. It was massive with an 'en suite' bathroom for Mum to wallow in deep hot water and luxurious carpets for me to curl up on and sleep. Their two Retrievers shared their food with me (I'm not sure if they were consulted) and the family shared their roast dinner with Mum and TEB.

After the most comfortable night's sleep I've had in weeks, I sauntered down the enormous winding staircase and into the marble floored hallway. Pillars towered above my head and huge paintings of people I didn't know stared down at me as I explored the downstairs, popping my head around a couple of doors to peep into the other gigantic rooms. One room had a long table in the centre laid out with candelabras, silver knives and forks and glass goblets to drink from. I backed away and thought better of going in in case I knocked something over.

We left Auchencairn House across the front lawn again and I glanced back over my shoulder, still not quite believing where I'd stayed the night. We made our way in the sunshine through the grassy flat fields that hugged the coast, in the direction of the little fishing town of Kirkcudbright.

We camped the night on the shore of Fleet Bay where I sat trying to judge the distance to the far bank across the water, as there had been talk earlier in the afternoon about walking across. I was right! The next morning at low tide, despite Mum's reluctance and the thick mist, off we trekked across the sand towards the other side. I kept a careful look out in case the tide rushed in, but thankfully it wasn't too far and we were soon safely over.

It was now heading for mid- August with ragwort in full bloom. The terrain was mainly flat farmland around Wigtown Bay to Burrow Head, the sun had cooled considerably and walking 15 – 20 miles a day was a doddle. I enjoyed passing the time of day with the locals, said "Good morning", to a couple of donkeys and sympathised with some poor little black piglets who had just been recently separated from their mum, but I avoided making eye contact with the huge brown bull that the farmer had put in his field to ensure our right to roam was almost impossible.

I was merrily trotting, minding my own business along a dusty, narrow lane between the open fields, when a 'chink, chink, chink' metallic sound made me stop in my tracks, Mum was lagging behind so I ran ahead to investigate. I could see a dog next to the fence obviously distressed, frantically jumping up and down. As I drew closer, I could clearly see it was a fox not a dog and he was caught in a trap with a wire noose around his neck. However, the more he panicked and tried to pull away the tighter the noose became. I could see the terror in his eyes but didn't know what I could do to help him. Mum came running up to assist but the fox was the other side of the fence. If she had put her hand through the wire the fox would have bitten her to be sure, as he was so frightened. The only thing Mum could do was to unwind the wire from the fence end, which she did. The noose went loose and off the fox ran across the ploughed field, dragging the wire behind him. My only hope was that when he stopped panicking he would be able to put his paw under the slack noose and pull his head out. Well we did our best to help; it was up to him now.

The main A747 hugs the coast from Monreith, next to which I noticed a small bronze statue of an otter and a plaque which remembered the life of Gavin Maxwell, the man that wrote the story 'Ring of Bright Water' (one of Mum's favourites). This main road, took us pretty much all the way to the Mull of Galloway. The weather soon deteriorated into a thick mist, but above a sea of fragrant heather I could make out the shape of the lighthouse, jutting out at the bottom of the Mull, on a finger of land to warn ships from crashing into the rocks.

We slept that night still in a tent but indoors. It seemed very strange, but the people of Port Logan had used the community Marquee a few days earlier and were drying it on its frame inside the village hall and had given us permission to sleep inside. So, amidst the tables and chairs plus all our junk I found a warm spot in front of the portable gas fire, curled up small and dreamt of running on sandy beaches and chasing bunnies. My legs still did all the actions and I squeaked every time I almost caught one (but woke up before I actually did). The only time I've ever caught a real rabbit was years ago, when we were laying a Hash trail in south Devon. The poor thing wasn't very well and couldn't run away, so I sat on it feeling very pleased with myself, but then I didn't know what to do. Mum told me off and said it had myxomatosis, so I reluctantly let it go and I've never managed to catch one since. (But I will keep on trying)

We walked to Portpatrick across the rugged cliff tops amongst the blooming heather and although I cannot appreciate the different shades of colour the busy buzzing bees and strong scents told me everything I needed to know. I stood and gazed for a moment across the shimmering water. In the distance I could just make out the coast of Ireland only 28 miles away and wished I could be sailing there on one of the big ferries I'd seen leaving Fishguard. "One day, maybe one day".

At the northern tip of the Mull of Galloway, standing high on the grassy cliff top, was Corsewall lighthouse, now a hotel tidily painted and looking inviting in the evening sun. I cockily strutted past some grazing cattle down the long gravel drive behind Mum, who proceeded to ring the bell beside the hotel door, then explained to the manager about our charity walk and asked if he would allow us to put our tent up in their grounds. (I think in the hope that he might offer us a room for the night, which has happened on many occasion before) To Mum's surprise and all of our disappointment he said "No"!

Reluctantly, we re-traced our weary steps back up the drive past the cattle which I swear now had smug grins on their faces and on along the road. At the next farm we came to, Mum asked the same question to the old lady who was standing outside in the yard. She hesitantly replied "I'll just have to ask my husband". She was gone absolutely ages, so I thought the answer was going to be no again and we would have to keep walking, but her jolly looking husband followed her out and said that we could sleep the night in one of his gypsy caravans. In the yard were two beautifully painted wooden caravans with curved canvas roofs. The farmer told us that he had made three of them and had been planning to start a horse-drawn holiday business, but unfortunately the girl that was to lead the tours had let him down, so he decided to scrap the idea and sell the waggons. He had already got rid of one but still had these two to sell. They were very basic inside. Just a double bed, a bowl for washing and an area to put a little cooker, but so cute and cosy. I thought it would be a perfect idea to continue our journey in a horse drawn caravan. What a great talking point that would be. Although Mum loved my idea, she said we must continue on foot. (Or paw in my case)

From the busy town of Stranraer, we walked the relentlessly hard pavement parallel to the main A77. Just a low wall separated us from the Irish Sea, which crashed noisily onto the rocks beneath me. As the main road left us and wound its way inland through Glen App, a gap in the mountains, we kept firmly to the cliff edge and slowly made our way through the grazing sheep around the coast. From here I got my first glimpse of Ailsa Craig, a big round rock the shape of a Christmas pudding that sticks out of the sea and can be viewed for miles along the coast.

I don't know what caused it this time! But Mum and TEB were having the biggest row ever. He was yelling and she was crying. TEB had hold of my lead and was dragging me along, as he knew Mum would not leave without me. I hated the arguing but there was nowhere for me to hide. I hung my head and tried to dig my claws into the ground but he yanked me along still shouting.

Mum followed reluctantly behind, tears pouring down her face. After hours of silence between them we walked up the downhill of 'The Electric Brae', an optical illusion with the land either side of the road, making it look like it is sloping the opposite way. Therefore Mum's coke tin unbelievably rolled slowly up the downwards slope! Yes, it did my head in too, but at least got them communicating again, if only in grunts.

The following morning the arguing had subsided (slightly), Mum was adamant she wasn't going home and was determined to finish the walk. It had been her idea originally so she was going to complete it, with or without him. You could cut the air with a knife, so I made sure I didn't put a paw out of place as we walked around the edge of the famous Royal Troon Golf links and made sure I didn't have a poo in the middle of the pristine grass.

From Ayr, the coast seemed like one sandy golf course after the other and throughout the day I'd found a collection of golf balls which I'd presented to Mum and chased rabbits by the hundred. We arrived in the town of Irvine early evening but apart from the golf course there was no grassy area to put the tent on. I was on my last legs again as we trudged towards Irvine's Fire Station, so Mum popped in and asked if they would allow us to sleep there for the night. Blue Watch were on duty and welcomed us in, and actually gave us a room with proper beds in, but, just as I was enjoying the last few mouthfuls of my tea, deafening alarm bells started ringing and men were running everywhere. They abandoned their chips and just left! Within minutes, we were completely on our own in a fire station surrounded by uneaten meals. I wanted to finish the food but Mum said they would warm it up again when they returned so I had better not. I just could not get to sleep that night. All I kept thinking of was those chips waiting to be eaten but alas by morning they had gone.

Sandy beaches took us to Ardrossan, where a big black and white boat with its mouth wide open was waiting to gobble us aboard. Caledonian Mac Brayne had generously offered us free crossings on their ferries to all the islands we planned to visit on our journey. My first Cal Mac trip took me to the Isle of Arran. I didn't feel sick just a bit wobbly in my legs. I stayed up on deck with Mum and enjoyed watching the sparkly water splash against the sides of the boat. The flag of St Andrew fluttered above me from the back of the boat (which I now know is called the stern) as I watched the port of Ardrossan disappear, and from the front (which is called the bow) I could see the rugged hills of Arran getting closer. It didn't take long before we arrived at Brodick, the capital of the island, and walked up the hill to the small bed and breakfast where a Guide Dog supporter was putting us up for a couple of nights. It was so homely and comfortable; tea and coffee in the bed room for Mum and TEB and homemade Scottish tablet (a hard sugary crystallised fudge) for me – well, I presumed it was for me and ate most of it before Mum had the chance.

We didn't walk around the whole island; just the main A841 from Brodick, which hugs the coast as far as Sannox then crosses the island at the top to Lochranza. However, during our stay we did visit Lamlash Lifeboat Station to sign the visitor's book, and took a day off 'to rest' they said, but walked me 874 metres up Goat Fell Mountain! The climb was hard going for my tired little legs, and the ground was uneven and rocky, tripping me from time to time, but the clear fresh air was invigorating and the view from the top was worth the effort. I could see right back across to the Scottish mainland and still see Ailsa Craig to the south, sticking up proudly like a pimple out of the sea. On Arran, I saw my first ever red squirrel, although to me it looked the same colour as a grey squirrel (Mum told me it was red) but I suppose it was a bit smaller and had tufts on its ears. It was running sideways along the wall that led down to the house of Lady Jean Fforde, the oldest serving president of the RNLI, who was really grateful for what we were doing and kindly posed with us for a photograph.

From Lochranza, I boarded my second Cal Mac ferry, this time to Claonaig on Kintyre, which is almost an island but not quite. The weather was hot again and I found my thick fur a burden, so I took every opportunity to paddle in the sea or if I found a burn (The Scottish word for a small stream) I would jump in to cool down. The water is a funny colour on Kintyre and it looked like I was swimming in cold tea, I could barely see my legs paddling beneath me.

The warm evenings and boggy countryside brought out midges by the million. Our road hugged the coast and didn't give many opportunities to pitch camp, luckily we passed a lady pottering in her garden who invited us to put up our tent there. Unluckily, as soon as I stopped walking the midges honed in on me and start biting, I hated them, they made me scratch like mad. The kind lady was very interested in our walk and sympathetically offered Mum a bath, as she had an outside bathroom attached to the house, but afterwards Mum said that the water came out of the tap a rusty brown colour and she felt almost as dirty as when she got in. (But at least she smelt sweeter)

Campbeltown has a Severn Class Lifeboat, which the crew were very proud of and just about to take out for a test drive as we arrived, so offered us a ride. I relish travelling in boats now and eagerly clambered on board. Wow! We went so fast my whiskers were wet in an instant. I loved the thrill of looking over the edge at the sparkling water splashing against the sides of the boat and the thump, thump as we broke through each approaching wave. They let Mum have a turn at steering the boat, she does have her power boat certificate from when she used to work at the school, but she had never steered a boat this size. Luckily, it didn't faze her and she skilfully turned the boat one way then the other, drawing patterns in the water with the wake. I tried keeping my eyes fixed on Davaar Island lighthouse but all too soon I was feeling queasy. I lay on the wet deck and felt my tummy lurch up and down in concurrence with the boat, until at last it was time to return to the quayside. I stumbled ashore feeling quite sick, until Mum prepared my tea, then as if by magic, I instantly recovered and gobbled it down.

It was a much colder start to the morning as we ventured down to the Mull of Kintyre. We left all our bags at the Lifeboat Station so walking was easy but the weather began to deteriorate, the hedges were high, the lanes were narrow and just like the words in the song, 'The mist was rolling in'. Today, I was glad of my thick, furry coat as the water droplets clung to each hair. Spider's webs in the gorse caught the mist and hung like mystical fairy hammocks. Mum kept looking at the map but I wasn't convinced we were actually walking in the right direction. The rough track seemed to go on forever, higher and higher we were climbing, then suddenly, out of the thick mist, the white buildings of the lighthouse emerged. Visibility got even worse until I couldn't see a paw in front of my face let alone a lighthouse, so unenthusiastically we retraced our steps to Southend then managed to catch a bus back to Campbeltown. After collecting our rucksacks and panniers, we found the A83 which led us across to Bellochantuy Bay, then followed the Kintyre Way which was marked by painted posts and hugged the west coast northwards to Tarbert, where a mile strip of land keeps Kintyre firmly attached to the mainland.

The further north we walked, the more the weather improved and we spent the night on a lovely campsite at Tayinloan, right next to the beach in the Machair (fertile low lying grassland). I nestled down in a comfy spot amongst the spikey grass and lay on the sand in the warmth of the remaining evening sun. I gazed out to sea over Gigha Island and wondered if I was ever going home again, or was I to continue walking every day for the rest of my life? Anyway, where was home? I can't even remember. In my short life so far, I've had four homes and now I'm sleeping in a different place each night; but I still have Mum by my side and I'm safe, and that's what really makes a home. Every day was a surprise. I never knew where I was going, who I was going to meet or what I was going to see, and maybe that was what made it exciting? Or unsettling? I eventually drifted off into a restless sleep, dreaming of being chased by the sheep with big curly horns that I'd seen earlier in the day. I twitched and squeaked until Mum woke me and settled me for the night, back in the safety of the tent on the bottom of her sleeping bag - home.

From Kennacraig we caught another Cal Mac ferry on a long but smooth crossing to Islay, arriving at a quaint little town called Port Ellen, with its pure white painted terraced cottages with their pitched grey roofs, which encircled dormant yachts and little fishing boats tied up to pontoons bobbing around in the shallow bay. It was late afternoon by the time we arrived and it wasn't worth starting to walk, so we pitched camp early on sandy grass in the grounds of a local hostel. I didn't get much sleep though, as our groundsheet was above a mouse hole and I could hear him running about all night underneath me! I waited to pounce as they broke camp next morning, but he ran away too quickly for me to chase him. I ate my usual tinned meat breakfast in the sunshine (although I would have preferred fresh mouse and I could have added him to my ever increasing 'dead mouse a day' statistic) and we set off around the beach of Laggan Bay. At the far end of the beach, we met a lady called Becky who was wandering aimlessly about on the shore, as if looking for something. We stopped for our lunch break and I watched her from a distance. She was collecting discarded items and placing them into one pile. Mum's inquisitiveness got the better of her, so approached Becky and asked what she was doing. They got chatting and she explained that she was a student artist and was collecting rubbish found on the beach to make into a sculpture of something else. She was fascinated by our walk and offered us a night's stay in her house in exchange for help with creating her sculpture. I picked up sticks whilst the others dragged over bigger items. Rusty corrugated iron made an excellent ribcage and body, a redundant electric cable spool made a neck frill and a big lump of tree stump made a head with an open mouth. Becky finally added a couple of golf balls for eyes and 'hey presto', our dinosaur was created, it looked mighty scary too! With pictures of evidence for her course-work taken, we all wandered back to her house, where she prepared tea and we settled in for the night.

From Becky's house, we walked the sandy west shore of Loch Indaal, then made our way north east, across the island towards Port Askaig. To make us feel like we were still on the coast we explored the footpaths around the edge of the beautiful Loch Ballygrant. The rosebay willow herb flowers were past their best and the old man's beard was looking as weary as mine, but the trees on the islands in the middle of the loch, the hills in the distance and the fluffy white clouds in the clear sky reflected a perfect mirror image in the still water. I was so hot and the loch looked irresistible, I just had to go in and disturb the picture in the water. Round and round I swam like an indigenous otter. It was only the bribe of a lunch time sandwich crust from Mum that eventually enticed me out. As I sat and watched the water, slowly the beautiful picture returned.

We made Port Askaig by evening and headed straight

for the Lifeboat Station, in the hope that they might let us stay the night. The guys on duty were so grateful for our fund raising efforts that one man invited us to stay in his comfy house. To my relief Mum agreed and we were guided to his home. While they chatted around the supper table, I sneaked into another room and found something to occupy myself with. It was in a small sawdust filled wire cage on the floor, with fluffy bedding in one corner that moved occasionally. I spent all evening religiously staring at it, hoping something mouse-like might appear, so that I could add another 'dead mouse a day' to my statistics. I had watched that blooming cage for four and a half hours by the time I went to bed and not so much as a nose had poked out. Feeling rather dejected I slumped upstairs with Mum. The bugger then kept me awake all night, running around in his squeaking wheel. Apparently, it was a golden hamster, but mouse enough for me to add to my list if I'd got hold of him.

Next morning, bright and early we were on the ferry to Colonsay, the Paps of Jura majestically watching us from above as we sailed betwixt them and the huge white whisky distillery of Islay.

The ferry docked in Scalsaig where we were met by a lady called Lesley, who had organised our free passages on Cal Mac ferries. We posed for a quick photo, then waved her off on the return ferry. I was surprised how small the island was, with just a few stone and traditional little white cottages then cove after cove of sandy beaches sheltered by heather covered rocks and of course sheep; always lots of roaming sheep on Scottish islands. We ventured along the only road heading south and stopped long enough to enjoy a bay which overlooked the even smaller island of Oronsay. I wriggled in the sand and paddled in the water, while Mum and TEB rested and watched me play. We didn't walk very far that day – (well there wasn't far to walk) as we had to leave again from Scalsaig, the only port Cal Mac use. So, after just one night camped in a local's garden, we were heading towards Oban on yet another black and white ferry. I hated the hustle and bustle of a mainland town after the tranquillity of the islands. It was a shabby looking, noisy, old seaside town and everything moved far too quickly. Mum was almost dragging me across the streets so that I didn't get run over. Luckily, we were only using Oban as a stepping stone, I couldn't wait till next morning when I could catch my next ferry to the Isle of Mull.

Well, what a contrast Craignure was from Oban. Despite a few cars queued up waiting to get on our returning ferry, a couple of shops and a tourist information office there was not a lot else there. The main road follows the coast north, so with panniers strapped firmly on my back, off I happily trotted. I didn't see much of the Sound of Mull as private woods and houses obliterated my view, but every now and then there was a clearing in the trees and a triangular road sign with 'OTTER CROSSING' would appear, so I would stop and gaze across the water desperate to see one of these strange furry, web footed, amphibious creatures.

As respite from walking the main road, we deviated along an inland route through Glen Aros and around the shore of Loch Frisa, apparently noted for observing Golden Eagles. The track was stony but relatively safe to come off my lead again and explore at my own pace. I regularly got engrossed with trying to decipher smells and would get left behind, so intermittently I needed to glance up just to check Mum had not gone beyond my 'safe distance'. If she had, I would panic then run like mad to catch up, sending the gravel flying. We stopped for a lunch break by a wooden bird hide to try and spot an Eagle, but all the wildlife had obviously heard my noisy arrival and were hiding away in the dense woods.

By mid-afternoon, the cloud was thickening and rain

threatening, my paws hurt and I needed cheering up as I trudged reluctantly on my lead downhill into Tobermory. Mum pointed out the brightly coloured buildings in the town, and as we arrived at sea level I recognised the crescent of painted houses and shops surrounding the little fishing harbour. It was Ballamory, from the children's programme I'd seen on the telly. The sun then slowly emerged from behind the clouds as I trotted happily along the water front, singing the theme tune in my head and into the Lifeboat Station ready for tea.

There were many tourists in town that evening, so Mum suggested we went for a walk and maybe take the collecting cans to the pub to see if we could raise some money. It was dark when we left the Lifeboat Station and I could hear a strange high pitch chattering sound coming from below the sea wall. "That's otters!" Mum whispered. We rushed to the top of the steps and slowly peered over the edge. In the darkness I could just make out the shape of two, wet, cat size creatures with a shiny fish on the steps below. I made a low grumble from my throat and Mum gently held my mouth closed so I couldn't bark and together we watched the otters with their fish before they slipped silently back into the water. It was a very special moment and I'm so glad that I didn't frighten them away. We had a good collection in the pub too which was a bonus.

After a satisfying night's sleep in Tobermory Lifeboat Station, my next ferry took us across to Kilchoan on the Ardnamurchan peninsula (what a great name), the most westerly point on Britain's mainland. A few small roads take you across the peninsula but none actually skirt the coast, so we yomped our own way as best we could around Ardnamurchan Point, through the spikey grass hummocks heading towards the lighthouse. The area is very remote, just a few single story white crofts dotted amongst the fields (these are low rental cottages given to people in exchange for farming the land) and the most amazing soft white sandy beaches I've ever walked on, which we had all to ourselves. It was another gorgeous day with not a cloud in the sky, so we stopped for a rest at Sanna Bay. As I tried to relax on the warm sand I had a strange feeling that someone was watching me, but whenever I looked up all I saw was rocks and sand. I pretended not to be bothered and lowered my head on my paws, deliberately keeping one eye on the lookout. As Mum threw me her last piece of sandwich crust I caught a glimpse of something black run between the rocks and I instinctively jumped to my feet. It looked like a long rat and I wanted to add it to my 'dead mouse a day' list. Then I saw another and another. Mum said they could be mink. I needed to chase them but she warned that they might be vicious and held my lead tight so I couldn't follow. I relented and reluctantly sat down beside her like a coiled spring as we watched them frolicking between the rocks.

Through this uninhabited terrain we followed any animal track that we could find if it was going vaguely north. Sometimes we were heading away from the sea and I was worried that we were walking the wrong way, but Mum was doing the map reading and I trusted her expertise. Amongst the bracken the heather was in full bloom and towered way above my head, the tracks were quite boggy in places and squelched between my pads; a funny, cold feeling that I haven't felt for a long time. I kept close to Mum's legs. It would be too easy to lose sight of her amongst the tall vegetation and as we started to gain height around Rudha Aird Druimnich Point a thick mist began to fall.

We pitched camp and ate the supplies we were carrying as there were no shops to buy anything. Mum warmed up sachet meals for them and I always kept a couple of days' worth of dry food in my panniers, so no tinned meat tonight but it kept me alive till morning.

Tioram Castle looked eerily impressive on its little island as it appeared out of the morning mist. I hoped to see knights in armour guarding the drawbridge as I trotted by but alas it was a ruin and nobody living there, although I'm sure it was haunted, as I felt my fur stand on end and a shudder go down my spine as I passed.

The ground was wet and boggy for most of the way and the paths were difficult to negotiate. The rocks that jutted out to sea were covered in the type of seaweed that otters love to play in. I tried to watch where I was putting my feet and keep one eye fixed on the shore line, as I'm sure they were there, but despite intense searching I didn't see one. Eventually we came across a sign that read, 'Aird Molach' which means scrubby heights. A demanding 5k, muscle-building trail around Moidart which should take 2.5 hours in good weather. Well, today was miserable weather and my leg muscles already hurt, so I hoped we would take the shorter, less challenging route that the sign suggested as an alternative. I looked up at Mum with a pathetic look in my eyes, hoping that she would take the hint but no use, off we set into this, I quote, "Ancient forest, stepping back in time through tranquil wood to enjoy peace and serenity". My paw! - It was tough going and I'm not too proud to admit it. The steep path started off OK, recently renewed and gravelled, but gradually became unkempt, muddier and rocky. Suddenly miles from anywhere, we came across a man with only one arm driving a mini digger along the side of a bank at a perilously steep angle, digging out trees and making the new path. He stopped to let us past, bid us "Good Day", and continued with his digging. Mum was concerned that his digger might tip over and no-one would be able to rescue him, hopefully that never happened. The path narrowed and got increasingly more difficult as we continued. The moss covered rocks were slippery and the undulating gradient intensified. My legs weakened each time I lifted a paw out of the mud and by the time we reached Kinlochmoidart Castle I was completely exhausted and I couldn't use my back left leg as it ached so much. I hobbled up to the huge wooden door and stood there covered in mud looking dishevelled. Luckily the lady that owned the castle was expecting us and welcomed us in. (She was a friend of Spud's - the girl that walked her own poor dog around the coast of Britain). Inside the castle, which looked more like a French Chateau (as you will discover later, I have a wide experience of them also) was dark and had many of its original features: a lattice metal gated lift took us up to the second floor and a bell from each room rang in the hall way for the butler. The old fusty smell tickled the back of my nose and made me sneeze as I waited for Rif Raf to appear! The lady didn't look anything like Magenta but I sure felt like Brad as I followed her down the narrow corridor to our room. I kept one eye open just in case Rocky appeared but thankfully, nothing Transsexual happened in the night! Despite still feeling tired, I made sure I was up early and the first one out of the door and down the path in the morning.

It was a grey day but the coast was stunning as there are so many little islands just off the west coast of Scotland. As I walked, I kept a look out to sea hoping to get a glimpse of another otter, feeling sure these were perfect conditions to see one amongst the floating seaweed until my concentration was somewhat distracted by the sound of splashing. I squinted across the shimmering water to see my first Salmon farm; huge cages of fish hanging between floating pontoons in the middle of Loch Ailort. The light reflecting on their shiny bodies as they jumped out of the water was almost hypnotic.

Crofts, midges and tumbling rivers led us to the port of Mallaig where we caught the now familiar black and white Cal Mac ferry across to Armadale on the Isle of Skye.

September had just begun but the weather was still warm, the grass was high and the rowan trees were laden with berries along the main road that pretty much hugged the coast up as far as Loch Na Dal. As the traffic was infrequent walking was easy, so I trotted happily along by Mum's side, ears flapping up and down with each step (mine, not hers). I glanced briefly back across the Sound of Sleat and saw two little bumps in the water, so I pulled back on my lead so Mum would stop and look also. "An otter" she confirmed. It was quite a way out but I had definitely spotted an otter swimming alongside us.

We camped the night next to Loch Na Dal and TEB lit a fire to keep away the midges that were beginning to become a nuisance. The following morning, we surrendered the A851 and made slow progress along our own route, picking our way across bogs, sphagnum moss and uprooted tree stumps, through the old oak woods of Kinloch back out towards the coast. With black mud splattered from my toes to my armpits we eventually found a drier narrow gravel track and despite being miles from anywhere surprisingly met a lady on a bicycle. She stopped and chatted for a while, explaining she was touring Scotland in a campervan with her two dogs. "What a fabulous idea, why can't we do that?" I thought. She cycled on ahead to put the kettle on, inviting us to call in to her van when we passed. As we arrived her dogs were barking incessantly, so she shut them in the tiny bathroom enabling us to enter. There wasn't enough room inside the van for my panniers and the big rucksacks, so they were left out on the path, but were quite safe as there was nobody else around for miles. I curled up under the table listening to them talking and soon an hour or so had passed. I gave my whole body a good stretch before jumping out of the van and landing beside the rucksacks which I barely recognised, as they were now completely black and covered with midges that had been attracted to our sweat! They were everywhere; all around my face, in my ears and in my fur. I couldn't breathe without them going up my nose and I started to panic. The only way I could lose them was to run, so off I set down the track with Mum chasing after me, still trying to pull her rucksack onto her back. Eventually I shook them off and could slow down enough for Mum to catch up with me and re-attach my panniers.

We left Skye briefly from Kylerhea back to Gleneig on the mainland via a little private ferry which pivots on its base. The sea current is so strong through the narrow gap of Kyle Rhea that the ferry must moor along the lee side of the stone jetty. The top then rotates slightly so that the cars can drive from the side of the jetty onto the deck of the boat, which then straightens itself to cross, rotating again the other side for the cars to drive off. Clever eh? – Well I thought so.

We slept the night in Gleneig church hall after joining them for yet another unusual Sunday service with no music. The next day we left our bags in the hall and headed south. "No!" I kept stopping, limping, sniffing, weeing, pooing, finding every excuse not to walk, and trying to signal to Mum that we were walking in the wrong direction, but she insisted she was right. I understood why, when we reached a beautiful little area called Sandaig. There was no beach as such, just rocks that jutted out to sea with heather and spikey grass between the gaps. A small 'cold tea' coloured stream separated us from a neglected, derelict white washed stone cottage. Mum crossed the stream via a rope 'postman's walk' bridge. (I recognised it from when we used to work with the naughty boys back home in Devon, as they made one once tied between two trees. It had a lower rope to walk along and a higher rope to hold on to.) However, it was quicker for me to jump down the bank and just wade across the water as it wasn't too deep. At Sandaig were two plaques, one marking the

Canoeing on the river Wye with Ian

Christmas Fancy Dress

My bike trailer and Mum at Rye Harbour

My ridiculous coat and panniers I wore on my coast walk

My visit to London

Oranges in Spain

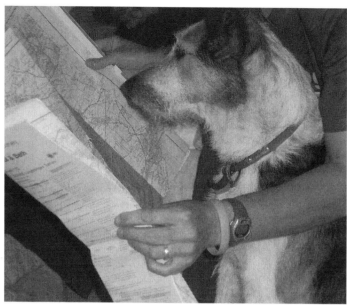

Planning the route

Ride in a Lifeboat

site of the ashes of Gavin Maxwell, who wrote the book 'Ring of Bright Water', and the other to mark the resting place of Edal his otter, whom the book was written about. (Although in the film I watched on TV with Mum, the otter was called Mij which was confusing.) It was a lovely story, but had a very sad ending and I had to soak up Mum's tears when Mij dies.

It was such a peaceful, surreal place. I just lay on the rocks in the warmth of the sun, gazing out to sea watching a yacht playing on the crests of the waves, until Mum interrupted my siesta and reminded me of the long return walk to Gleneig.

After a second night in the church hall, we stayed on the mainland and walked north this time towards Loch Alsh, where we managed to cadge a lift in a Salmon farm boat. The men picked us up from the shore and took us out to the floating farm, where I could peer right down into the fish pens to see the different sizes of the developing salmon. One man threw a handful of fishy flavoured food pellets into the water to entice the fish to come splashing to the surface. It was all Mum could do to stop me jumping in after them, and when a few fell on the pontoon I gobbled them up quick. After the man stopped laughing he took us the rest of the way across the loch in his fishy smelling boat to the opposite shore, where we only had a short walk to the dismal town of Kyle of Lochalsh. This sad, neglected town is currently ignored by passing travellers who drive straight through in oblivion, rushing onto the Isle of Skye over the arced concrete Skye Bridge; elegant in its construction but totally out of place amidst this naturally beautiful landscape. However, I was glad of it to walk over to save yet another ferry back on to Skye.

The main road hugged the north coast up this peculiar shaped island to the town of Portree. With the Isles of Scalpay and Raasay on my right, the views were stunning, even to a dog. Today was a good day. The sun reflected on the water making shiny dancing stars on the surface, the little white washed crofts dazzled amidst the lush vegetation and I was feeling great. My legs were strong, nothing ached and the mountains in the distance beckoned me on, as I passed the impressive Dunvegan Castle standing majestically on the banks of Loch Dunvegan.

Scottish weather can change so quickly from one day to the next and from lovely sunshine the following day was overcast and drizzly as I passed Loch Fada and Leathan, but it so was difficult to distinguish between the water and sky I almost missed them. I heard a rumour that there was an Old Man of Storr residing in the mountains here but I didn't see him as he is very shy and was hiding away in the low cloud. From the small town of Staffin we were recommended to cut through the stunning Quirang Pass. Higher and higher we climbed the winding tarmac road, through the misty stone needles. Breathless I stopped, digging my claws into the road for security and looked back over my shoulder as the hairpin bends meandered their way down the pass beneath me, dropping to sea level. Feeling dizzy headed and needing oxygen, I eventually reached the top. It was too cool to stop for long, so off we set and with gravity's help made a much quicker descent, through the sparsely scattered cottages to the port of Uig, where I acclimatised to my altitude sickness and camped the night.

Outer Hebrides to John O'Groats

Yet another ferry ride took me on a slightly longer passage across 'The Minch' to the Outer Hebrides and into the port of Tarbert. Dogs are generally expected to travel in the 'pet area' on Cal Mac ferries or up on deck, but today as it was raining, Mum sneaked me into the restaurant and shoved me under her table, which was the one nearest the doorway. At first, I was quiet and nobody knew I was there but suddenly I saw a poodle with a silly haircut messing about outside in the gangway, so I gave a quick disapproving bark and hence we were asked to leave (much to TEB's annoyance) "He he." Reduced to the 'pet area' again, Mum got chatting to a man about our walk and he offered his caravan for us to sleep the night in. He told us that when we arrived on Harris, we should go to the gift shop in Tarbert where his wife would give us the key to the van. This was great news until we got there, because she took one look at me and said apologetically, that her daughter was allergic to dog hair and I was not allowed in the caravan! Seeing the disappointed look on Mum's face she quickly added that there was a 'cow bus' I could safely sleep in. This seemed a weird statement at the time but made perfect sense as we walked around the corner and up the sandy track to find the caravan. Parked on the side of the hill, slightly on an angle next to the well loved holiday van, was a gutted minibus painted black and white like a Friesian cow. I wasn't sure, but after tea Mum checked the security of the door, made me a bed from her coat and settled me down for the night in the belly of the cow! I had a cold, dark, lonely, restless night that seemed to go on forever and it reminded me of when I was a puppy and TEB had made me sleep outside the pub in a

shed. I shuddered at the thought and buried my head into the armpit of Mum's coat. At last, the darkness faded and I could see the first glimpse of morning light squeezing itself under the bus door. I welcomed Mum eagerly and nearly knocked her flying as she arrived with my breakfast and let me out for a desperately needed wee.

Harris looked desolate as we headed north, sticking to the A859 in the drizzle and lingering mist. It was almost a lunar landscape; rocky with very little vegetation or life. Way off in the distance, I could hear an odd sheep bleating and occasionally a car would speed past then disappear into the barren, bleak horizon. The rain intensified, my tummy rumbled reminding me it was lunchtime and we were due a rest. As we approached the brow of the next hill, out of the mist appeared two military-looking vehicles with caterpillar tracks, abandoned by the side of the road. The rear vehicle was a personnel carrier – without the personnel, so we clambered aboard dripping water all over the floor and sat on the little wooden seats (yes and me) to shelter for our lunch break.

The driving rain continued as we cut across grassland trying to avoid walking all the way round a hairpin bend, only to find ourselves deep in a bog and eventually walking further than we had originally needed just to avoid drowning. Disheartened and soaked to the skin, we slowly squelched our way up a seemingly endless hill, where at the top we found an oasis in the form of The Scaledale Youth Activity Centre. Mum convinced the bored, uninterested duty member of staff into letting us stay the night and he showed us where we could sleep. He then just vanished, so I think we had the place to ourselves. There was a warm-air drying room, so Mum spread their now non-waterproof clothing and rucksacks out to dry. It had been a long, hard day and I was exhausted, so I wriggled myself dry on the pile-less carpet, curled up as tight as I could and was asleep in seconds (after my tea of course)

The next day was cold but at least it had stopped raining as we crossed the borderless border from Harris to Lewis and to my relief there were no guns or gates or men in sentry boxes, just a sign that welcomed us. I liked Lewis, as it was not quite as desolate as Harris but tranquil and remote; almost as if it had been left behind forty years in a time capsule. There was a rich, sooty smell that filled the air as we approached the villages. It was peat burning in the fireplaces of the cottages. I had passed little piles of it drying by the roadside where it is dug from channels out of the ground, and now I could see its smoke rising from the chimneys. It was a lovely homely smell that I will never forget.

We arrived at Stornaway, crossed the lawns of the

impressive Lewis Castle, and made our way across the river and through the busy town past the tempting wet fish and smoked kipper shops to the working fishing harbour, where we stayed the night in the Lifeboat Station. The crew were extremely friendly and one of them even offered his dad's driving services to show us around some of the island that we hadn't walked. True to his word, the following morning I was lifted into the backseats of a car and chauffeur driven around in luxury. I saw the Butt of Lewis right at the very top (strange place for a butt to be) with its magnificent lighthouse standing on the cliff edge, I was mesmerised by the dark sea, which turned white as each wave crashed against the rocks, but the piercing squawk of gulls hurt my ears as they soared overhead. As we were driven down the North West coast I visited a Blackhouse museum and village. These cosy little white cottages were built hundreds of years ago, with double thick stone cavity walls filled with soil for insulation. They are topped with a thatched reed roof and covered in netting, weighed down by large pebbles to stop it blowing away. Inside, tiny little beds were built into wooden boxes, (a bit like a kennel.) The people must have been very small in those days and their beds looked so inviting covered in knitted wool blankets, protected from the cold by long floral curtains. If I hadn't been on my lead I would have willingly curled up inside with the comforting smell of burning peat wafting through the air.

The stones at Calanais have been standing boldly looking out over the stunning white sandy beaches on the west coast of Lewis for thousands of years and against the clear sky, amidst the buttercups and Bobbies Buttons, they certainly looked impressive, standing way taller than both me and Mum put together. I left my calling card and we were returned to Stornaway to catch the last ferry of the day back to the mainland town of Ullapool, sheltered safely just inside the mouth of Loch Broom.

The annual Loopallu music festival was on that weekend and the town was rocking with visitors, filling all the Guest Houses, campsites and anywhere else you might try and erect a tent. Eventually we found the coastguard, who allowed us to sleep on the floor of his office. I didn't get to see any of the bands playing but the thud, thud of the base music resounded through the floor and echoed around my head 'till the early hours of the morning.

Still muzzy eyed, we set off on our trek across formidable terrain. A notice told me it was eleven miles to Achiltibuie and that I was entering 'a remote sparsely-populated area over potentially dangerous mountain country'; a good clue if ever I saw one to turn back! 'Bridge crossing unsafe and temporarily out of use,' was another strong hint. I tried my hardest to convince Mum to stop but she just laughed at the signs, picked me up under her arm and carried me across the 'unsafe' bridge with my paws frantically making swimming movements lest we should fall into the deep gully below. The path was no more than an animal track that completely disappeared in places, with wooden stakes occasionally marking the way if they weren't broken or missing. Higher and higher we climbed, with Mum in front and me close to her heels, in fear of getting lost amongst the long grass or hidden bogs. We rested often to catch our breath and relished looking back to see how far we had ascended. The hidden rocks made walking tough and we all stumbled from time to time. Sphagnum moss and hidden pools soaked our feet but there was no place I'd ever seen before quite as natural and beautifully unspoilt as this.

Mum had spotted a Youth Hostel on the map at Achnacarinan, so that's where we were heading, hoping for a bed for the night. We reached the tiny wooden building by sundown and watched fire fill the sky as the sun slowly went down over the sea. My heart sank as we walked up the garden path, as the hostel looked totally deserted and locked up for the winter. The grass in front of the hostel was flat so Mum suggested we pitched camp there and started unpacking the tent. I barked in agreement but TEB had other intentions. He poked and prodded the old sash window, pushed it up and within minutes we were inside! The building hadn't been used for quite a while, and all the chairs were stacked up on the tables while the beds were folded up with the mattresses piled at one end of the upstairs room in the roof. I sniffed around in the hope that I might find a stale crumb but only found a stiff dead mouse in the corner under a table. It didn't look very appetising but at least it was another I could add to my statistics list. I followed close behind Mum's heels as usual as she went into the kitchen to start cooking tea. "Oh look, someone has left some cheese, corned beef and bread!" she exclaimed. I thought that was odd, as nobody had been staying there for weeks, but the food was fresh and I wished I'd found it first. "I'll eat it, give it to me," I thought, looking pleadingly up at her but she ignored me and left it on the side to continue cooking their meal. It had been a long day's arduous walking and we were all tired, so straight after tea was finished we climbed the wooden stair-case to the attic room, dragged out a couple of mattresses and went to bed. I curled up on the bottom of Mum's sleeping bag and drifted off eventually, feeling a bit miffed that she hadn't given me the corned beef and my tummy was still rumbling. I had only been asleep for a while when Mum whispered, "There's someone downstairs!" I listened hard and sure enough, there was somebody walking about downstairs. I almost jumped out of my skin when a man shouted up the stairs "Is anybody there? Come down, whoever you are."

I was so frightened, I couldn't walk properly. My little legs were shaking so much as I followed Mum and TEB downstairs. Waiting in the dark hallway was a very angry, slightly shifty looking man with a dim torch that he shone in my face. He asked what we were doing and was panicking that we had used the electric. Mum kept quiet but TEB explained about our charity walk and that the hostel had been closed when we arrived late and tired. The man asked how we got in and TEB lied, (he was good at that!) He said that the door had been unlocked and with a push it opened. The man didn't believe him but TEB insisted he was telling the truth. (He was so good at lying he could even convince himself he was telling the truth sometimes!) The man calmed slightly when TEB offered him some money for the use of electric, but continued to use his torch and reluctantly let us stay the night, insisting that we left first thing in the morning. I hardly slept a wink because my heart was pounding so fast and I kept one eye open just in case he came upstairs to where we were sleeping. We got up early the next morning but the angry man had already left. I gobbled down my breakfast and was ready waiting by the door eager to be the first one up the path. Thinking about it later as I walked down the road, I don't reckon that man was supposed to be in the hostel either. Why didn't he want the lights to be put on and why was he eating cold food from a plastic container? No wonder he was quick to take our money; he probably just put it straight in his pocket.

The day improved. The Summer Isles on my left, made up of a multitude of tiny islands, littered the water just off the coast but the clouds were low and it was difficult to see where the mainland ended and the islands began, mingling together making it appear magical. I imagined a big, scaly dragon living amongst them, which comes out at night and gobbles up nasty men from Youth Hostels.

Following the road around the coast of the Coigach peninsula till there was no road, then squelching the remaining miles through boggy spikey grass, I came across what I thought could only have been a yeti! Do yetis live in Scotland? Anyway, it was much taller than me and covered in long untidy hair, at first I thought it had no eyes, until I realised it was peering at me with beady black ones through a thick mangled mane. I've never seen a creature so woolly. It had four legs like me, but I knew it wasn't a dog as it was far too big and had two enormous pointed horns stuck out of the top of its head, making it look intimidating. I kept my distance as it watched me slink past, hoping that there were no more around the corner. The grass became progressively drier and springy, which encouraged me to bounce across it towards Stoer lighthouse, perched on the end of the cliffs. I cautiously looked over the edge to see the huge stone pillar of the Old Man of Stoer standing alone, protruding off the coast with waves crashing around his ankles, looking bravely out to sea. I'm not sure if he was related to the Old Man of Storr on the Isle of Skye, but he was far less shy and much easier to find and at least this old man wasn't shrouded in fog.

The narrow road to Kylesku Bridge, was how I imagine being on a switch back rollercoaster would be. Up and down we went, bending to the left then quickly swerving back to the right but it was great fun. I would run the downhill bits, then pull Mum up the steep uphill bits. The sea below me was clear enough to see the bottom, the grass verges were thick and lush, the heather had a beautiful smell and the air in my nostrils was so clean and fresh it tingled. I stopped briefly to look over a wall, intrigued by the sparkling baby salmon jumping out of the water in their fish farm play pens. These young fry live here until they are big enough to eat, and are then shipped all over the world as a delicacy. You never know, maybe one day I will sample some. Hidden amongst the shady trees in the bottom of one of the dips in the road was a fish farm company with a few square concrete buildings. It was getting late in the afternoon, so Mum approached a man who was just getting in his car to go home and he agreed to let us sleep the night in his office on the floor. It wasn't quite the Ritz but it was warm and dry, albeit a little smelly. I had run out of my dry dog food and we hadn't passed a shop all day, so I ate Marmite on cream crackers for tea, Mum kept apologising but actually it made a nice change. As we left in the morning, outside the door in front of the step was a dead rat – how lovely. Another one to add to my ever-growing mental list of dead mice. (After all a rat is just a big mouse, but I still wondered how it died and why did it expire just there?)

My observation of dead mice counting became an obsession. It seemed that every stone path throughout Great Britain presented a dead mouse a day, and I explored every blade of grass, little stone and nook and cranny to see if one was lurking. If I hadn't seen one by the evening, I would sit by the door of the tent for Mum to let me out. Thinking that I needed a wee she always obliged, but I only wanted to have a last check for a dead mouse. Sometimes they were stiff and crispy, although other times they were quite fresh. I didn't want to eat them, just add another to my ever growing mental list. (Years later, I still get a twinge of excitement whenever I see a dead mouse on my path as it reminds me of my incredible journey.)

If I was counting yetis as well, I could add another two to my mental lists. I was walking along sniffing through the long, wet grass for whatever dogs sniff in long wet grass for, when I came face to face with another huge, hairy, four legged, twin horned creature, breathing hot air down on me from his wet dribbling nose that was bigger than my head. I turned on my paws to run back to the safety of Mum, but this yeti was accompanied by a cloned miniature which had approached me from behind, penning me in. Well, I nearly peed myself! I crouched as low as I could then skidding in the mud, shot between the little one's legs before he had chance to head butt me. Mum laughed, clipping my lead back on, saying they were only highland cattle. I'm not sure whether to believe her or not, as cattle back in Devon are usually black and white friesians, and confronting this hairy mammal was a close shave (excuse the pun) that I never want to experience again.

Eventually, my legs ceased shaking and I could enjoy the scenery once more. The single-track gravel road was dotted with sheep poo that I tried to pick up and eat as I walked along. Mum would yank my lead to try and stop me but I was always quicker than her and managed to snatch a quick snack. The summer bracken was beginning to die back and the road rose higher so I could see far out to sea. The west coast of Scotland has numerous uninhabited little rocky islands just off its coast that we couldn't walk on or around. Some are quite flat and some are like mountains, but most are dark and mysterious, poking menacingly out of the clear water. Not many trees survive the harsh weather in the barren highlands, although I noticed that a few pine forests have managed to nestle around the sheltered edges of Locha Chairn Bhain, as we made our way towards the concrete Kylesku Bridge. Similar to the Skye Bridge it was elegant in construction but totally out of place in this area of outstanding natural beauty.

At the Kylesku Hotel, we stopped for a break by the water. I played with a little black and white hairy mongrel, whilst Mum and TEB chatted to people about our walk in the hope that they would donate their loose change. A kind young man who lived a few miles further on down the road offered us a roof over our heads for the night in his house. He said that he wouldn't be home when we got there, but explained to Mum where to find his hidden front door key and said that we could help ourselves to any of his food. I don't think he meant I could eat all of it and we did have our own food as we had passed a shop, but it was a trusting, generous offer to people he had never met before. He came home later that evening and we all sat outside, I snuggled into Mum to keep warm and together we watched an amazing sunset over the sea.

It was a slow climb up the steep main road on the other side from the bridge so we paused for a quick bag rest and drink. As I sat on the damp grass contemplating, I could hear a roaring sound, like a lion. Mum climbed the bank and I followed close behind (yes behind, for safety). From the top, we could see right across the valley. Amongst the tufts of tall grass was a big herd of does, blissfully grazing, with one big stag protecting his harem. On the opposite hill was another stag challenging him, bellowing out his protests which echoed through the valley. I was glad that they were below us and a little way off, as I feared a confrontation could be about to materialise.

Our evening walk downhill to Kinlochbervie was scary, as huge refrigerated container lorries rattled past, forcing us to walk in the ditch to avoid getting squashed. They sped into the fishing harbour to swap their empty containers for ones full of frozen freshly caught fish, and then once loaded, would rumble back up the hill again to deliver their prized fishy loads around the country. Their headlamps shone straight in my eyes and temporarily blinded me, causing my tired legs to frequently stumble, so I was relieved when we eventually arrived in the village. There were cars parked everywhere, on every spare inch of grass, leaving us nowhere to pitch our tent. We soon discovered that there was a wedding in the village and everywhere was full. I felt like Mary and Joseph again arriving in Bethlehem, but luck was with us that night as the Morrison family kindly said that they had room in their stable (well, attic of their garage actually.) I couldn't climb the steep wooden ladder so Mum had to haul me up into the loft space – very undignified, but once up there it was quite cosy as I snuggled down between spare sleeping bags and camouflage netting for an acceptably comfortable night. As a bonus, we were sent off in the morning with bacon and egg sandwiches to help us on our way along the road to Sheigra, the last hamlet before Sandwood Bay, the most northerly beautiful beach on the west coast of Scotland.

From Sheigra, the footpath sign directed us through a little wooden gate and along a stony track, four and a half miles to the beach. I was off my lead as there wasn't a sheep in sight and trotted pannier-free happily along in front, with the occasional muddy puddle being no problem, which I leapt with the greatest of ease. The sand dunes were filled with frolicking rabbits running and diving for cover the moment they saw me but I only had eyes for the beach. The last few hundred yards I ran at full speed, then, from a forward roll landed on my back and wriggled in ecstasy in the soft pale sand, massaging every inch of my aching spine. By the time Mum caught up I was already paddling in the sea, with the gentle waves and salty water soothing my sore legs and paws. Although I was walking the coast daily it had been a long time since I actually dipped my feet in the sea and played on a beach. Mum and TEB stopped for their lunch break but I wasn't even distracted by the thought of a left over crust. I was far too busy sniffing and rummaging through the flotsam and jetsam washed in by the tide. We walked the entire length of this vast beach in the shallow water as it lapped onto the sand, before heading back through the sand dunes in the direction of the aptly named Cape Wrath.

The Parph peninsula is the most north westerly point of Britain and apart from the lighthouse at the tip, is a totally uninhabited wilderness of grass and bogs and probably why the military use it for bombing practices. Mum had phoned ahead to check that the Army weren't firing the day we wanted to cross, so at least I could relax knowing I wouldn't be blown up - just eaten by the carnivorous plants that thrive amidst the sphagnum mosses! Luckily, they only eat insects, not dogs.

After a long day's demanding hike we found a flattish area of grass near an area called Keisgaig, where we pitched camp for the night. I was far too tired to chase the local rabbits, so while Mum cooked tea I curled up tight in the soft long grass and dozed in the evening sun that, despite being nearly the end of September, still had a bit of warmth. We had a long day ahead of us so once the sun had gone to bed so did we.

An ideal day for walking this formidable terrain, with just a few wispy high clouds, made visibility perfect and within an hour of leaving camp I could clearly see the top of Cape Wrath lighthouse, though it just took forever to get there. The landscape looked flat but ditches and bogs hindered our route, and it seemed the more I walked, the lighthouse didn't get any closer. At last, stone walls finally came into view and funnelled us in towards the white washed buildings. My legs were aching and I was desperate to rest but out from nowhere shot a gang of springer spaniels that hadn't seen anyone for days and wanted me to play. I tolerated them for a while whilst they sniffed me from head to toe, but a quick curl of my upper lip and they retreated as fast as they had appeared. I was appreciative of their full water bowl and as there was no café open, the friendly lighthouse keeper made Mum and TEB a mug of steaming tea, and then proceeded to give us a guided tour of the lighthouse and museum. I tilted my head and raised my eyebrows from time to time to make it look like I was interested, but I just couldn't keep my eyes open and within minutes, I was snoring loudly under the table.

A quick dog nap and I was raring to go again, walking easily down the tarmac military drive for the seven miles to the Kyle of Durness. A white minibus of waving tourists passed us on their upwards journey to see the lighthouse, it was a shame that they hadn't arrived when we were there, as we could have collected money from them. The little ferry boat that had brought them across the Kyle was still moored up at the quayside when we arrived, so without hesitation we quickly jumped aboard for our lift across the water. Unfortunately, the boat jerked forward causing Mum to fall backwards, still with her pack on and she banged the bottom of her spine on one of the wooden seats. She didn't yelp, but I could tell by the look in her eyes that she was in a lot of pain. The boat ride across to Durness was quick and smooth but Mum had difficulty getting out of the boat on the other side. TEB marched on ahead as usual. He never showed sympathy to anyone, so I walked slowly by Mum's side, I could see she was struggling, as every step she took jolted her back making it painful to walk. We stuck to the main A838 road which hugged the coast, making walking slightly easier for Mum. I deserted her briefly for a quick back wriggle on the irresistible white sand of Sangobeg beach but returned to my care duties around Loch Eriboll, which took us nearly all day, while the dark mountains loomed above us. We found a picturesque camping spot sheltered in the bottom of a valley on the grassy banks of the river Hope, just above Loch Hope. A fire was lit to keep away the midges and after a paddle in the babbling river to cool my burning pads I settled down to watch another stunning sunset over the bay.

Mum woke with a very stiff back the next morning and found the day's walking around Whiten Head agony. There was no path, so we had to make our own route as near to the coast as possible. The ground was uneven and intermittent clumps of grass between hidden deep bogs made for an uneven gait. With TEB way on ahead of us, I was trying to jump from tussock to tussock, but more often than not fell into the obscured black bog, and poor Mum was wincing in pain with every unpredictable step.

Amongst the quagmire, TEB was waiting for us to catch up by a little stone built bothy and as we were all in need of a rest we went inside for a look. The sympathetically painted fireplace with sooty black pots and pans surrounded by old wooden chairs, looked so cosy that I wished it was bed time so we could stay the night, unfortunately we still had a long way to go and the pace was slow. The view from the tip of Whiten Head was dramatic. The steep cliffs fell away to the sea and below me giant stacks of rock protruded out of the water, enormous waves pounded at their base and swirls of white wash made menacing patterns on the surface, as swooping gulls screeched over my head. The crispy heather on the cliff tops was dying back and the spikey grass was dryer and shorter from where the hardy sheep had been grazing, making walking a bit easier. At Strathen we converged with a small tarmac road which quickened our pace considerably. Mum politely passed the time of day with an elderly man who was gardening outside his cottage, who then proceeded to have a 'right go at her' for wearing shorts. Apparently, his recently departed wife had been a shorts wearer and had picked up a tick walking in the countryside, subsequently dying of Lyme's disease. Mum empathised with the man as she bid goodbye (though she still wears shorts every day in the summer) but it made me paranoid. I hate ticks and always make sure I have a good check of myself from time to time, just to be certain I have no pesky parasites grabbing a free meal.

Back on the A838, the main road crossed the Kyle of Tongue, where out to my left I could see Rabbit Island. I'm not sure if it is named for its shape or its inhabitants but I wanted to go there, positive I would be guaranteed to catch a fresh lunch, but boring Mum insisted we trek on. The rocks and seaweed around the edges of Kyle of Tongue looked a perfect place for otters to reside. Again I watched every moving thing that was wading or dipping. I caught a glimpse of the occasional heron but there wasn't an otter in sight.

Mum's back was easing up so we followed a small track to Scullomie, then trampled our own path through more bogs around the cliff tops to Torrisdale Bay, where the beach was immense. I bounced and played my way along the flat white sands which banked either side of a small estuary, funnelling us to the hillside village of Bettyhill. We were promised a night's stay here by Monsoon Drain from Edinburgh Hash with his sister in law who owns and runs the post office. A quiet, reserved lady whom I think may have been coerced into accommodating us duly provided an evening meal then showed us to our room. Their home, behind the post office/village shop was quaint but homely and by morning Susan, I think her name was, had relaxed and was bustling around in the kitchen brewing tea and cooking breakfast. A cheery farewell wave from her husband Pete, who seemed slightly keener having us stay, probably because Mum had just bought oatcakes and cheese from his shop, and we were then on our way again following the jagged coast towards Strathy Point. Although the cliffs are high above the sea, the landscape from a distance looks relatively flat so I could see the lighthouse from quite a long way off, standing bravely on the last bit of rock that jutted out from the land, glowing pure white against the dark ocean behind. Glancing back over my shoulder to check on Mum, I could see the evanescent jagged coastline of northern Scotland, silhouetted by the vast mountains I had recently walked around. I thrived in its pureness, freedom and natural phenomena. I had never felt so fit and now looked forward to each day's new challenge.

That evening after tea, while just resting in the tent, I

overheard Mum talking on her mobile phone to Nanny and Grandpa. They said that they were coming up by train from Bath to welcome us back at John O'Groats in a week's time. "How exciting!" But then a horrible lump came into my throat, as that meant that I had nearly completed my mammoth, circular journey. I would have only one more week of walking and sleeping in a tent and seeing beautiful places that most dogs only dream about. The vast, empty sandy beaches, the sparkling, fresh water streams, the lush grassy fields, the Scottish lochs, the unfamiliar wildlife and all that open moorland, which I would probably never visit again. I squeezed my eyes tightly shut and made a wish, that one day I would return to at least some of these beautiful places. I gradually drifted off into a restless sleep.

From Strathy Point, our route was a mixture of gravel tracks, boggy moorland and the main A836. This was bordered with Caithness stone slabs which looked like tomb stones lining the road and fenced in a field of cows, completely oblivious that they were grazing on land next to Dounreay, a Nuclear Power Station. I only knew this because their cow pats glowed. I didn't like the feeling in my fur, so tried to hurry Mum along by pulling on my lead in the hope that we wouldn't hang about too long.

Not far enough along the road for my liking, we stopped by a clearing amid some trees in the grounds of a little old cottage. It was getting late and there had been nowhere obvious that we could pitch the tent so TEB knocked on the door, explained about our walk and asked if they would allow us to camp on their grass. The young couple enthusiastically agreed and being interested to find out more about our walk, they invited us to join them for dinner. "We are eating out," they said, "bring your food and we will share ours". I sat in the small grass clearing and watched the unfailing military procedure of Mum and TEB putting up the tent, trying to puzzle out what the young couple meant by 'eating out'.

Not understanding quite what they meant either, Mum took along her packets of dried stew, and found the young lady busily preparing more food in her kitchen. The mystery unfolded when the guy called us outside. He had lit a fire and over it was a rack attached to a pole that could be swivelled over the flames to cook food and raised or lowered to adjust the heat – clever eh? I appointed myself head chef and didn't take my eyes off that rack for one minute. Jacket potatoes, burgers and stew; what a feast. I had remnants from everybody's plate and even licked the stew pot clean. Tummy satisfied, I curled up on the grass absorbing the heat from the glowing embers whilst the others chatted till late and the moon was high in the sky, providing enough light to guide us safely back to our tent.

It was now 7th October and we were only a couple of days off completing our journey. Nanny and Grandpa weren't due to arrive at John O'Groats until 13th October, so to 'waste' a few days we caught yet another ferry out to the Orkney Islands; a purely vocational trip, not intended to be part of our charitable route. I was glad I wasn't walking as it was a miserable, drizzly day when we left the harbour side at Scrabster. The crossing took about an hour and I felt a bit queasy and light headed as we approached the islands. A stone column emerged out of the thick mist, which at first I thought was a statue of Bart Simpson, till Mum correctly informed me it was The Old Man of Hoy. The ferry moored at Stromness and we found a hostel that would accommodate me as well, I think they were officially closed for winter as we seemingly had the place to ourselves. That afternoon we went for a stroll around the narrow streets of this grey, pebble dash and stone built town and found 'Mrs Humphries' house, which had been a temporary hospital between 1845 and 1846 for scurvy ridden whale men that had been trapped in the ice for months. I didn't know what scurvy was but Mum made a face so I sensed it was horrible. The following day TEB hired a car so we could explore as much of the island as possible during the three days that we were there. We visited Scara Brae, a 5,000 year old village, which had been buried under the sand until it was uncovered by a massive storm in 1850. The remnants of this stone village topped with short grass is now a tourist attraction. Luckily, not too many visitors were there at the same time as me, so I could explore the little houses and closely examine the stone beds, fireplaces and cupboards without getting under people's feet or them over mine. Next to the village was a beautiful, curved sandy bay which I found far more appealing, so I wandered off on my own for a play, until in a panic Mum found me.

Over the next couple of days, we also visited The Brough of Birsay and the Broch of Gurness but I was far more interested in the Lidl of Kirkwall where Mum came out with a carrier bag of goodies to eat.

All too soon it was time to catch the ferry back to Scrabster to continue the final stage of our walk along the top of Scotland. Nothing surprised me or seemed strange now, as in the pouring rain the tent was unpacked for the penultimate time and we were the only ones camping the night on a Thurso campsite that was shut and all closed up for winter.

After continuous rain all night, a wet tent was packed away and more Caithness stone slabs led us along the main road to the last white sandy beach of my walk. Luckily, I didn't realise this at the time, otherwise I don't think I would have ever left it. The sand and the sea were so clean; no flotsam or jetsam for me to investigate and not even a pebble for Mum to throw into the sea for me to chase, so I patiently paddled and wriggled whilst Mum and TEB ate their lunch.

We popped in briefly to the Dunnet Wildlife Visitors

Centre, which had recordings on the walls of sightings of Orcas swimming off Dunnet Head. Wow! I couldn't wait to begin counting killer wales and start another OCD mental list. As we squelched across our last boggy, marshy headland I kept my eyes firmly fixed on the sea to my left. Every wave, splash, ripple or diving bird I thought was an Orca. I was getting left behind and Mum had to continually call me to catch up, but it was difficult to concentrate on the sea and look where I was going. I was tripping and falling in ditches but never once took my eyes off the surface of the water. We reached Dunnet Head, mainland Britain's most northerly point, but still saw no Orcas and I was beginning to get a stiff neck from constantly looking over my shoulder. Dunnet Lighthouse is perched 127 metres above sea level on top of cliffs. Mum lifted me onto the wall for an even better view which made me feel dizzy looking down, but I desperately wanted to see a whale. I didn't want to leave, until reluctantly I had to turn my back on the lighthouse and walk away, desperately disappointed that I hadn't seen a killer whale. Maybe one day Mum will take me on an aeroplane to Canada to see one; I know you can see some there. That afternoon we visited Dunnet church, so while Mum and TEB climbed some rickety steps to look at the old church bell in the roof, I whispered a little prayer to the big man above and asked if one day he could arrange for me to see a whale.

A little further along the road was the Castle of May, the Queen Mother's favourite holiday home; not quite like the chalets and caravans I had passed on my walk but homely never the less. Unfortunately, she was out, so I didn't get invited to stay the night, which was a shame as I'm quite 'au fait' with castles now.

We spent our last night in the comfort of our own familiar abode. After eleven months of routinely erecting the tent, unrolling mats and sleeping bags, lighting the meths stove, cooking and eating tea, it was strangely quiet, and I felt excitement but apprehension in the air. TEB wrote in his daily diary while Mum and I snuggled up in bed. I couldn't wait to see Nanny and Grandpa tomorrow but it meant that that was it – the walk would be over. Then what would we do? I've known nothing other than walking for nearly a year; how strange it would feel to go home – wherever that is? I tried to remember home but could only recall arguing and shouting and I didn't want to return to that! I shuddered at the thought and pulled myself in closer to Mum, eventually drifting off to sleep.

John O'Groats to Home

I was up early with the sun but snoozed on the grass while Mum and TEB packed away the tent for the very last time. They loaded on their rucksacks and Mum strapped my panniers onto my back and we walked in silence along the road from Kirkstyle to Huma. Then the last mile was along the cliff top, skirting the edge of farmers' fields, to John O'Groats. Visibility was good and I could see the buildings in the distance and quickened my pace, pulling Mum along behind me. As they drew closer I could see a man with a big white beard. It was Grandpa, my Grandpa, walking around the side of the hotel! Mum let go of my lead and I ran towards him barking. Then Nanny appeared and Grandpa started clapping as Mum and TEB followed close behind me. We had made it. We had walked 5,000 around the coastline of Great Britain. Mum signed us back in in the special records book kept in the still 'less than friendly' hotel and we made our way to the famous sign post, where Grandpa had arranged for the official photographer to come out specially (as it was winter) and take our photo, with '13th OCTOBER AROUND BRITAIN 5,000 MILES' written in black lettering on its white arms. On one of the signpost's other arms it read 'LANDS END 874 MILES' but that is 'as the crow flies', straight through the middle of Britain. I went 'as the dog walks', over 1,000 miles more than that to get there, walking clockwise around the coast and that was not even half of my journey.

Photographs taken, hugs given and conversation in full flow we bundled our bags into the back of Grandpa's rented car (which he had had to lie about his age to hire.) I climbed onto Mum's lap in the back seat and off we were driven for about a mile, to where Grandpa had booked us all in to a hotel for the night. I had my usual tinned meat tea then went on up to the bedroom, while the grown-ups had their meal and a lot to catch up on. Nanny and Grandpa stayed with us the next day and we showed them Whaligo Steps, Dunnet Head and the little church at Dunnet where I had said my whale prayer. They returned their hire car and we all got on the train at Thurso station. They were returning home to Bath and I presumed we were continuing on to Devon.

I presumed wrongly!

Mum, TEB and I only travelled as far as Aberdeen, then off we got, waving to the others as their train pulled on out of the station. Where on earth were we going now?

Huge grey buildings towered above my head as cars, buses and lorries belched out fumes level with my nose. We dodged between traffic, trying to cross busy main roads and passed people shopping who were far too interested in their own affairs to notice us. Nobody wanted to know who we were or what we had just achieved, and no one stopped to read my jacket or donate money. Mum was in a hurry, so I wasn't allowed time to sniff lampposts or street corners to check who'd been there before me. On and on we marched from one side of Aberdeen to the other. I couldn't understand why or what was the hurry?

Up a shaded avenue we stopped by the gates of a big house I vaguely recognised. I was checking out the gate post but Mum twitched the lead so I walked hesitantly up the path. As the door creaked opened I heard a familiar Scottish voice; it was Olymprick! We were welcomed inside and as they chatted I began to piece together the intriguing jigsaw.

Now Halloween was only a couple of weeks away and Olymprick owns a fancy-dress shop. Knowing my Mum is 'The Queen of Dressing Up' he offered her and TEB a fortnight's work in his shop at its busiest time of year. He said he would donate a considerable amount of money towards our charity walk. – Well, how could they refuse?

We were shown to the top flat of a small block of three, sparsely furnished but warm and dry. I trotted happily in, knowing that it was often frequented by visiting Hashers. (Olymprick's brother lived in the middle flat and an old lady with her cat lived on the ground floor.) But here I stayed for two boring weeks. I was only taken out occasionally to relieve myself around the neighbouring concrete tenement blocks. I hated it! "Come on Mum what are you doing to me?" I was used to the freedom and fresh air of the sea and countryside, not being penned in

in a miserable flat with only empty beer cans as company.

I nearly went stir crazy as the time passed so slowly. I couldn't even see out of the windows, because they were so high. I slept a lot and looked forward to lunch times and the end of each day when Mum would come home and let me out. I knew she was desperately sorry for leaving me. (Although, I think she quite enjoyed working in the fancy dress shop) Halloween eventually came, and for once I wasn't the one dressing up.

Two boring weeks later, at last I was sitting on a train heading for Devon. TEB had spoken to the guard about our charity walk and asked if we could collect donations from the other passengers. It was agreed and announced over the train's loudspeakers that we would be walking through the carriages collecting money in our cans and asked people to give generously. Well, as you can imagine, I was in my element. I was important again; a celebrity. The ladies wanted to stop me for a cuddle or a smooch or quick pat on the head as I walked past. Most passengers were very interested and wanted to find out as much as they could in a short time about our trip. They dug deep in their pockets and donated generously, although some people just politely said, "no" which was fine, while a few miseries buried themselves in their newspapers and pretended that we never existed. I hope they never need a Guide Dog or a Lifeboat to rescue them.

After a very long day's travelling, the train slowly pulled into Newton Abbot Station at about 6.30 Monday evening. Mum gathered up our bags and we disembarked the train. We were greeted by a sea of people. The platform was absolutely packed with all our Hashing friends, Guide Dogs, puppies and owners, a man dressed as a big cartoon Lifeboat man, Hannah, Scott and of course there were my Nanny and Grandpa again; all come to welcome us home. As it was a Monday Hash night we joined in the trail, not much running, mostly walking and talking, but then into the pub for celebrations. Grandpa drove us home and dropped us off outside the house, and as I walked in the door I knew then, it was time to hang up my lead.

Havoc Bathard

Home for a while.

L ife resumed to some sort of normality once we got back to Devon. A few photo shoots and newspaper interviews were '*fait accompli*' (wow - look at me speaking French) Well, we had raised £50,000 for charity. We moved back into TEB's old cottage, as the tenants that were renting it had found themselves a house to buy. It was mid- November and Christmas 2007 was fast approaching. Mum had no money for presents so had to find a job. She went to a few interviews in schools for naughty children but either she didn't like them or they didn't like her. She ended up with a job in a local green grocer's shop, where the hours were variable, so I wasn't left at home on my own for any length of time.

It wasn't long before the friction started and arguing began again between Mum and TEB. He said it wouldn't happen if she didn't go back to work at the school, but I knew that was a lie. I hated it and would run upstairs, crawl under the bed and try and cover my ears. Mum would cry and we would try and get away, but he would block our path, and continued to rant and rave as we cowered on the stairs. I won't go into too much detail, but Mum was getting very down, and losing her sparkle, so eventually she went to the doctors who gave her some pills, they worked a bit but she was not her usual self.

Although Mum enjoyed working at the green grocer's

and the girls that worked there were nice to her, the money was poor and she hated leaving me at home, especially when TEB was alone with me. She started to think about what else she could do; something that was still in the outdoors and we could both do together. That was when she had the idea of becoming a dog walker. The business started slowly at first but soon became quite busy with dogs from the three local villages. She bought a little white van and had it sign-written with the name "2feet 4paws" and my picture on both sides. This was a massive way to advertise and I soon had lots of new friends that we picked up daily and took for nice walks in the surrounding countryside. I always rode 'shotgun' in the passenger seat and looked proudly out of the front window. The other dogs would try and beat me to it, but I never let them win as I was in charge and it was a very important seat. On Fridays, we collected other dogs and always went to the sea side, which of course was my favourite walk, having spent so many months walking along all of Britain's beaches. We also offered a pet sitting service, which meant that we would stay for a few days in the dog's own homes and look after them while their owners were on holiday. I was a bit reluctant at first but soon put the other dogs in their place and let them know that I was still top dog, whoever's house we were in. Some houses we returned to many times and they became quite familiar. My long walk had made me very nomadic so I settled easily into new surroundings and quickly made them feel like home.

By now, the relationship between TEB and Mum was unbearable, the arguing was becoming more and more frequent, he was becoming more and more scary and burly policemen visited more and more often. I felt useless because there was nothing I could do to help. I would get shouted at as well and shoved out of the way, all I could do was comfort her. Sometimes we did manage to get away, and would drive up onto the moor and just cuddle in the van. She would sob uncontrollably into my fur, but after sitting for hours, and nowhere else to go, we had to return. The following day he would apologise, saying that it would never happen again, but I knew they were empty promises and he would undoubtedly lose his temper again.

Then one day, Mum did pluck up enough courage to leave TEB, and while he was out of the cottage, she took all our stuff and we returned to our old house where Hannah still lived. But I can tell you, he wasn't happy about it. (Scott had already moved out and lived with his girlfriend Emma)

Now I don't know what solicitors are, but I knew they were in town, and Mum couldn't take me with her when she went to see one. Anyway, the long and the short of it is, after a few visits, TEB did eventually leave us alone, and slowly life began to calm down.

Two new little people came into my life soon after. In the October, Scott and Emma had a baby girl called Lottie, and then eleven months later, just as I was beginning to get used to it, they had another baby girl called Lyla. At first, I wasn't too keen on these noisy intruders, as their crying confused me and once they started moving about it was even worse, and I felt threatened in my own home. One day Lottie came far too close for comfort. I couldn't help myself and quick as a flash I gave her a warning snap and caught her on the lip. Oh my goodness, did I get a telling off! – I was so embarrassed that I ran upstairs and hid under the bed. Every time they visited after that, as soon as they came in the door, just to be on the safe side, I would take myself upstairs and stay under the bed till they had gone home. Eventually, I realised that they weren't coming to hurt or frighten me, but were actually to my benefit as they were moving food depositors. So, I then followed them everywhere, waiting for a stray crust or biscuit to be dropped. As they got older we built up a trust and understanding. Sometimes they would stay overnight and I would curl up on the floor near their beds to protect them. We would go on lovely walks together, and I would take treats gently from their hands, then once they were old enough to sit still I would snuggle in for a cuddle.

I took my work duties seriously - Mum would deal with the humans and I would sort the dogs out, teaching the young ones how to behave and fit into the pack and trying to chivvy the old ones into keeping up and not get left behind - I stood no messing about. (Never thinking I would be one of the slow old ones one day) We stayed in some grand homes, with outside hot water taps to wash off dirty dogs, indoor running machines for dog walks when their owners were too lazy to take them out. Chaise longues for dogs to lie on and even fake grass to pee on. As soon as I entered a new pet sit house I would let the dogs know who was in charge; "Your house but my rules". A few of the dogs we looked after regularly, especially Skye and Max the Collies and Alfie and Barnie the Westies, became my very good friends once they had learnt their place in the pecking order. There were a few others who spring to mind though, that tried my patience right up to the end.

There was just one dreadful home that we stayed in that absolutely stunk, it was horrible! The two dogs ate tripe that Mum had to de-frost in the microwave and the smell made even my tummy turn. The Jack Russell was constantly cocking his leg around the house, the two cats were forever being sick, had diarrhoea and kept missing their litter tray. The smelly carpets had no pile left in them at all, so I slept on the bottom of Mum's bed at night. We kept the window open to let in clean air but the seagulls on the roof woke me up at 5am in the morning and the cooker was so old that Mum fused the house when she used it. Needless to say, we never pet sat there again.

Apparently, the solicitors in town sent TEB a letter and thankfully, he never turned up at our Hash evenings again, so Monday nights became a sanctuary for us to enjoy our free time. Occasionally we would take a pet sit dog along with us, chasing through the long grass and woods, crossing rivers and getting so muddy that their owners would have gone bananas, but the dogs loved it and always slept well that night.

Mum and I had two years of fun and independence together. I had nobody to rival for Mum's attention and it was great. I slept on her bed every night, shared her food and ALWAYS had the front passenger seat in the van. A couple of 'waste of time' male acquaintances came and went, but I stood by Mum, and together the two of us made an excellent team - Who needs a man around.

In the January Mum celebrated her 50th birthday in style, starting with a red dress run, where everyone – me and poor old Grandpa included, had to wear a red dress and run through the town. It finished with a barn dance in a local pub for all our Hash friends and family. She traded in her van for a Land Rover Defender and I thought life couldn't get any better.

Well, apart from Holly: I forgot to mention Holly! For a few months, Hannah had a little tabby kitten called Delilah who yelled a lot. One day she went to the vets to be 'spayed' but she never came back. Hannah and Mum cried and cried. I don't know what happened to her at the vets but I don't ever want to be spayed. The house seemed so empty without Delilah.

The following Christmas Mum and Hannah went to look for another cat and what did they come home with? Yes Holly. Holly was a tabby and white slightly older kitten and we had a love/hate relationship - she loved to tease me and I hated it. She would hide behind a chair or the curtains then rush out and bop me on the nose, encouraging me to chase her, but then I would get told off, which made her parade around looking so pleased with herself. To get my own back when she wasn't looking I would jump on her and pin her to the ground, but then I got told off for doing that also. Life just isn't fair. But she was company and we had many hours entertaining each other when everyone else in the house was out.

A few days after Mum's 50th birthday party, she brought a man home called Ian, or Melon Picker. I knew him from Hashing. Ironically I had stayed at his house on our walk but he had never been to our home before. I liked him. He had obviously had dogs himself as he knew exactly where to tickle me. He brought me treats and visited our house more and more often and we regularly went out in his car to exciting new places for lovely long walks. I was a bit worried at first about him trying to take my mum from me, so I decided to put him to the test on our first date to see how much he really liked dogs. It was a fairly warm day and Ian had hired an open canoe for us to paddle down the local canal for a couple of hours. Of course, I am quite familiar with canoeing on the canal and waited for just the right moment to catapult myself out of the boat and into the murky cold water for a swim about. When I had cooled down enough I swam back towards the canoe with a pathetic look of anticipation on my face. Then, gentleman that he is, Ian hauled my dripping wet body over the side and into the boat, absolutely soaking his jeans. I followed that by shaking myself, so as to get his top half equally as wet. Mum fell about laughing and when Ian joined in I knew then that he had passed my test. He got his own back a few months later by taking us to The Forest of Dean and we spent a whole day in a canoe paddling down the river Wye. Another time, he hired a canoe on the Bridgewater canal and we ended up getting chased by an angry swan.

Ian certainly had his benefits though; he took us on

holiday, helped with dog walking and pet sitting, taxied us about in his car (despite me trying to shed as much fur as possible on the seats) and genuinely made Mum happy, although I admit I was a little put out when I was banned from sleeping on her bed anymore!

We had weekends away in hotels with Ian and camping week holidays in the tent, he came up to Bath and met Nanny, Grandpa and the family and treated Hannah and Scott like his own offspring. We stayed at Ian's house sometimes, which I loved, as he had a garden with grass that I could sit out in and watch the world go by. It was quite a long way for Mum and Ian to drive up and down to see each other, so after about a year, our house was put up for sale. Hannah and Holly moved out first into a little house that she bought with her boyfriend, and although I hate to admit it I missed Holly as we had become good friends. Then Mum and I packed our belongings into boxes (which unsettled me again) and moved temporarily into Ian's house for a few weeks until we found the perfect house that suited us all. Five months later Mum, Ian and I moved into our new home. It was great, as I could wander around at my leisure, sleeping in a different room every night if I wanted. It had a lovely big garden for me to patrol, over-grown bushes to hide in and a lovely lawn to sunbathe on, and it was big enough even to allow other dogs to stay occasionally if we looked after them overnight.

Alas, we weren't the only occupiers of our new house! I began to itch and scratch so Mum treated me with my usual 'little visitor' treatment, but the itching continued, followed by constant scratching. It was driving me crazy! She bought me an expensive flea collar that the vet recommended but still the problem persisted. Next I was bathed in flea shampoo and even I could see the little buggers floating on the water, but I was still scratching! Eventually the penny dropped and Mum realised it must be the house. The previous owners had had cats who obviously left me their little friends behind as a present! Several cans of household flea spray later meant the problem was solved and I could sleep peacefully again.

Ian still drove to work from our new house every day, but most of the time Mum and I had the place to ourselves and it was perfect. Then, after 3 months, Ian finished working full-time and took a part time job with a local Charity shop doing handyman repairs, which meant he was home much more and able to spend lots of time with me. I always joined Mum dog walking on the first walk of the day but then I could rest back at home knowing Ian was around for company. We spent a lot of time in the garden together digging, planting and sunbathing and sometimes he would take me for a walk down to the river for a play and swim. I loved this time we had together because it brought us much closer and I began to trust him more and more.

We continued to go Hashing twice a week, although I was beginning to find it increasingly difficult to keep up. My hips and legs ached and I found the noisy group gatherings distressing. I was 12 ½ years old now and old age was definitely catching up with me! I had already had a couple of little 'wobbles'. Once when we were walking along the river, I lost control of my legs and fell over, my eyes were flicking and my head was ticking. I was very frightened, so Mum held me tight. It only lasted a few minutes, then I was OK again jogging along as usual. Another time, a few months later, I woke up and one of my eyes had disappeared up into the top of my head. I looked very odd and it felt strange but again this didn't last long and by lunchtime had returned to normal. I've had shaky legs for a number of years but more recently they occasionally lose their natural rhythm for walking. I stumbled badly more recently at Auntie Sally's house which made me panic and pant. Mum thought they might have been mini-fits but I was determined not to give in; there was still a lot of life in the old dog.

Grandpa too had been taken ill a couple of times and was finding it increasingly difficult to look after and walk me if Mum and Ian went 'abroad' (wherever that is). So, I was introduced to Anne the dog boarder, where I had one night's trial sleep over. Mum warned Anne that I was not good at sharing food or the space around food, or the anticipation of food, or even the thought of having to share food! I tried, I really did try to be good. I liked Anne and her dry witted husband John. They were real doggy people. Their house was our house and although I hated being left there, I soon settled down knowing that Mum would come back for me soon. "He was as good as he could be!" Anne told Mum, which meant I wasn't very good at all. The other dogs got on my nerves and tried pushing me about but I was having none of it. I had a go at two of the little ones and made sure the bigger ones knew exactly who I was and what I was not putting up with. When John tried to put me in the back of his van with the others I really let rip! I was marched straight out of the back and made to go in the front and sit on Anne's knee. ("He he", that little plan worked a treat) I stayed at Anne's a few times in the end and actually tolerated it better each time I went. I gave up my safety den under her table and sneaked up onto the sofa between Katie the elderly greyhound, and Darcy the retarded Golden Retriever for cuddles. They had a lovely garden full of mud, doggie smelling bushes and big trees which shaded my resting spots. John had a man cave at the end of the garden, where I could join him when we wanted peace and quiet from Anne and the other dogs.

Like me, Ian enjoys the little luxuries in life and he bought a VW transporter camper van to use instead of the tent. It had a little built-in kitchen, a pull out bed for him and Mum and the roof popped up so that they could stand up, and was where Lottie and Lyla slept if they stayed the night. So now we could holiday in comfort. We went to the Peak District, the Lake District, Yorkshire, Wales, Wiltshire, Cornwall and Dorset. At first, I wasn't sure that I liked it. I couldn't see the point of having a lovely house then driving hundreds of miles to sleep in the car! So I would protest and sit outside at the far end of my long lead, as far away from the van as possible. But again, the more I did it the more I got used to it. We would arrive at our destination and Mum would tie my long lead to the van so that I could enjoy the afternoon patrolling my new territory, keeping a look out for intruders and bunnies.

One weekend at the end of May 2014, we camped on the outskirts of Tavistock with Scott and his family on a lovely site adjacent to an old railway line that was now used as a cycle path. Scott, Emma and Vinnie their one eyed French Bulldog (he lost his eye in an attack by a Jack Russell - poor bugger) slept in their tent, while their girls slept in the pop-up roof section of our van. The Saturday was beautiful and we all cycled into Tavistock. Now I'm older I have a drag-along kiddie trailer which Mum tows behind her bike, but Vinnie could not keep up at all and was puffing and panting, getting himself all hot and bothered. I felt sorry for him so I got out and walked, letting him ride in the trailer.

We got back to the campsite late afternoon after lunch in the pub. Vinnie and the girls got a lift back in a car and I rode in my trailer. Mum had a message on her phone from Auntie Sally (her sister) to say that Grandpa had been taken seriously ill and was in hospital. We didn't stay the rest of the weekend camping and drove straight to the big hospital in Bath. I wasn't allowed in to see Grandpa but I knew things weren't good from the length of time I was left in the VW and by the look on Mum's face when she eventually returned. We drove back to Devon but Mum was very quiet and constantly on the phone to Auntie

Sally. The following Friday, Mum and I returned again to Bath and stayed with Nanny for a few days. A phone call came in the middle of the night from the hospital to say Grandpa had 'passed away'. I wasn't too sure what that meant but I never saw him again! Everyone was so sad and I got the message to be quiet and comforting to anyone who smoothed me. I was allowed to sit in the front row at Grandpa's funeral, which was a long service held at his church with another shorter one at the crematorium. Mum counted over a hundred people at the service who came to say goodbye, along with his Morris men team who carried his coffin. They danced outside afterwards, respectfully leaving one place missing. Afterwards, at Grandpa's 'festival' (as little Zoe called it) I played in the stream, but part of my heart was missing and things were never quite the same when we went up to Bath. We took Grandpa's 'Dust' to Exmoor and with the help of Nanny and the rest of the family, scattered it over the grass in a remote spot alongside the river, where they used to camp when they were younger.

Their house now was lifeless and quiet. I would sit at the end of their garden amongst the vegetables just waiting and watching. Nanny wasn't herself and was getting more and more forgetful. She had a vacant look I knew something wasn't right. She wasn't coping without Grandpa and took a tablet overdose. (Mum thought I had done that once when I was a pup and was rushed to the vet to have my stomach pumped, God was I sick – again, and again, and again! No tablets. "No Mum, I hadn't swallowed them!") Nanny went through the same procedure (but not at the vets) and was kept in hospital for a few days. I never saw her in her old house again and visited her now at 'Greystones'. Outside was a sign that read 'Residential Home for the Elderly'. "And that's telling me!" she would say. She seemed very happy there and returned more to her jolly old self.

Every weekend, for the next four months was now taken up travelling up and down the motorway to Bath and back, emptying and re-decorating Nanny and Grandpa's house to eventually sell it. Gradually bit by bit, piece by piece, the memorabilia that they had collected over the last 59 years was removed. It was a horrible feeling and I hated going in their house without them being there. It echoed their absence. Instead of cakes and dinners, it smelt of paint and cleaners. The carpets were thrown away and the wooden floorboards felt cold and unwelcoming, so I stayed outside whenever I could and even found a hole in the hedge to escape! Twice Mum found me wandering around the neighbourhood looking for Grandpa. So very, very sad.

On a happier note, the following May Mum and Ian got married, and apart from having to dress up as an Oompa Loompa, it was a magical day. It took four months for Mum to make her amazing dress out of purple chocolate wrappers and Ian was dressed as Willy Wonka. The 100 guests all wore fancy dress and the ceremony took place in a beautiful local orchard beneath the apple blossom. I was to give Mum away (that meant give her to Ian) but, as we walked through the apple trees with fairies as bridesmaids following Teapot playing the bagpipes, I caught sight of Father Christmas, then a tiger, cowboys and pirates! Immediately, I dug my heels in and refused to go any further, luckily Auntie Sally, who was dressed as a box of Roses chocolates came to my rescue. She took off my silly Oompa Loompa outfit and I went to sit on the bank with my friends Skye and Max and watched the wedding from a distance. It was a pagan ceremony with the binding of hands with coloured ribbons and jumping over broomsticks, so not quite the norm, but then that's my mum! Grandpa's Morris side, Bathampton Morris Men, travelled down specially and danced in his honour and then everyone joined in and danced in the sunshine. After which we all paraded through the narrow streets of the village, lined with picturesque thatched cottages. I went back to Skye and Max's house for the night while the humans ate hog roast (Mum did save me some) and barn-danced late into the night.

After all that excitement, the next day we went on holiday in the VW for a week to the Isle of Wight. I don't understand why, but they called it honeymoon although I ate no honey, just chocolate wedding cake! We travelled to Southampton then caught the ferry over to the island. We stayed with Dexter the Beagle and Daisy and Shirley Bassett Hounds and their family at Wootton Bridge for a few days, before touring the Island. The weather was dry and there were not too many other people around. We had some lovely long walks in the sunshine and I'm sure I picked up a hint of a few smells that I recognised.

Life returned once more to normal in Devon (although I can't remember what normal is anymore) Mum and I went back to the dog walking and pet sitting and Ian returned to his charity shop maintenance work. Hashing was becoming increasingly more painful for me. I desperately wanted to go and was keen at the start, barking as normal with excitement, but within a few minutes into the run my shoulder joints ached and the pain in my back leg was unrelenting. On a few occasions, we ended up just walking back to the car. I didn't like the circling up of people any more as my hearing was now going and the high pitched laughing made my ears hurt. "What was happening to me?" I was getting old and I couldn't do anything about it! By Christmas the pain in my legs was unbearable and my red eyes gave away the agony I was trying to hide. Mum reluctantly took me to the vets who pushed and pulled my joints then quietly whispered, "No more Hashing".

"What! - Did I hear that right?"

I was given a huge injection and tablets to take, I rested more and more and gradually the pain subsided. Ian slowly walked me down to the river and back each day and on the odd occasion I did go Hashing we only walked gently around the short route. I wore a leg brace on my back left leg which gently warmed my muscles giving support, and I was only allowed in the river in the mornings. Exercise was kept to a minimum and I wore my old brown wax coat if it rained, but it did the trick, and I got better.

As my health improved, poor Vinnie the French Bulldog's health deteriorated. He was experiencing more and more problems with his remaining 'good' eye. Ulcers and swelling were building up behind it causing him unbearable pain. Eventually, after an abundance of different treatments, the vet had to remove it, so now he has no pain - but no eyes! Amazingly he copes so well. Scott and Emma got another French Bulldog called Poppy as a companion for Vinnie and they walk along side by side on a split lead, so that Vinnie can feel her body next to his, guiding him. He has learnt his way around their home and loves and trusts Lottie and Lyla. I'm still not keen on that squashed face breed of dog, but "Grr", if I ever find that Jack Russell that did that to Vinnie, I'll have him!

I was beginning to enjoy retirement life. Just a little gentle stroll each day suited me down to the ground and I could just imagine myself curled up in front of the fire relaxing for the next few years. Unfortunately, the kilos began to pile on and the heavier I got, the more the strain on my poor legs increased. Mum tried to cut down my food a little but I was constantly hungry and forever begging for titbits. I had been well trained as a youngster not to steal food, but one day when Mum and Ian had visitors around for cheese and nibbles, the coffee table in the lounge was just my height and as I walked past I seized the opportunity, swung my head round and grabbed a whole piece of Cheddar cheese! It was delicious and well worth the reprimand, but I was never trusted alone with their food again.

Mum wasn't enjoying the dog walking as much now without me. We had been in partnership for eight years and, although she wouldn't admit to it, I don't think she could cope without me. She was trying to think of other jobs that we could do together, when Ian came up with the bright idea of travelling for a year in the camper van. The more they thought about it the more it seemed possible, but they had to do it soon, before I got too old to enjoy it. Mum needed to complete the year of pet sitting and another Christmas came and went. (Oh and Holly came to stay for a few weeks just while Hannah and her boyfriend moved house again. It was great to have her back for a while and we re-established our love/hate relationship.)

In the New Year Ian started to look at bigger camper vans. The talk was of travelling around Britain for 6 months in the summer, then crossing over to France for the winter for 6 months. As I would be venturing abroad I had to have a passport, and to get a passport I had to have a painful rabies injection. "Ouch!" Luckily, I was already micro chipped, I'd experienced that painful intrusion before I did my walk around Britain.

In the February Ian sold the VW camper to a fellow Hasher and bought a motor home. It was only small but had a bigger fridge and cooker and a lounge area in the back which, with a lot of pushing and shoving turned into a double bed. There was a small bathroom for them to wee (I still had to go outside) and a big storage area over the front seats, where along with other things, my bike trailer and food was kept.

In the March I celebrated my 14th birthday, then 6 weeks later we left. We gave the dog walking business to Scott. He accompanied us for a couple of weeks to meet all my friends and their owners, learning who lived where, who was walked when and who got on with who. He took to it like a 'duck to water' and by the time we left we had no worries handing over the leads. Our house contents were packed into boxes (again) which unsettled me (again), then stored in a huge metal box for the year. The important things we needed for the next twelve months were packed into the motor home. I took my sheepskin rug to sleep

on, my winter coat in case it got cold, a giant sack of my favourite food, (the type that doesn't make me windy) a year's supply of worming tablets, flea drops and Metacam, (I'm allowed 17mls a day to keep me pain free) my bike trailer, oh and my favourite teddy bear (who happens to be a dog).

My second gap year begins.

We left home to start our year-long motor home adventure (I still think of it as a campervan) on May 3rd 2016, but by May 14th we were back! No, they hadn't fallen out, they had a wedding to attend. Hashers Wide Receiver and Tight Lips were getting married in our village, so I was packed off to Anne's again to stay the night (I really thought I'd seen the last of that place) but it was only for one night, so I tried really hard to be good and the time passed quickly.

For our first couple of weeks away we headed east, exploring Kent and Sussex. Of course Mum and I had been there before but it was a first for Ian. We stayed on little campsites that were quiet with friendly hosts and usually child free. The weather was amazing, it was so warm that I could lie outside the van and just let the heat of the sun soak into my old bones. We ventured on some lovely gentle walks around the grounds of National Trust properties and even rode on a steam train through enchanted bluebell woods. I saw oast houses, lighthouses (and public houses) and spent ages reminiscing over trees, lamp posts and walls trying to decipher other dog's calling cards that I'm sure I'd sniffed before. From the tops of the white cliffs of Dover, I looked over the grassy edge and was fascinated by the little cars and lorries below, driving onto the huge ferries waiting in the port about to sail to France and Belgium. I knew I was going to France soon and wondered if my ferry would be as big. As we walked along the white chalky paths I definitely remembered being there before, but it was such a hot day I wasn't feeling brilliant. Luckily, at the lighthouse I found a bowl of water, which I lapped up quickly to refresh my thirst. I must have gulped down air as well, because on my return journey across the top of the cliffs I threw it all back up, complete with my breakfast, and Mum wouldn't let me eat it again. Well at least it marked the spot in case I ever revisit for a third time.

While in Kent I made my pilgrimage to Canterbury. I'd heard of The Canterbury's Tales so took my tail along to compare, but none of the hundreds of visitors seemed suitably impressed. The weather that day was wet and miserable and in fact the only good thing about Canterbury was the sausage rolls that we shared for lunch. That afternoon we drove to the seaside town of Hastings. I did remember passing through there on my walk, as it was where I attacked the Boxer dog 'cos he looked at me funny whilst waiting in the queue for a hog roast. This day though, we went in search of a wedge-shaped house that resembled a piece of cheese. On the wall was an interesting plaque that said Mr and Mrs Michael Mouse had stayed there once on their holiday. We used the bikes for the first time at Rye. My collapsible trailer unfolded and was attached to the back of Mum's bike, then she pedalled and off we went along Rye Harbour towards Cliffend and back, which was only a few miles but a good start and I quite enjoyed all the attention I drew.

On our return journey to Devon we stayed one night in the New Forest where I heard a cuckoo. (I must tell Nanny when I see her on Sunday, because she always likes to know when we hear the first cuckoo of the year.)

After Wide and Tight's wedding, we re-inaugurated our travels on the Sunday morning and headed north, stopping just outside Bath to take Nanny out for lunch, little did I know then that this would be the last time I would see her. Then continued driving northwards heading for Durham and Newcastle to meet up with Ian's grandchildren. We stopped regularly for me to wee and pulled into a carpark to admire the Angel of the North. She was a gigantic steel structure, so tall it hurt my neck when I tried to look at her face, so I weed on her feet instead before getting back in the van in search of Hadrian's Wall. "Just a little stroll along the wall" they said, which ended up about six miles, but we did stop at an old homestead where I found the remains of Hadrian's kitchen. Unfortunately someone had cleared his cupboards long before I got there.

The next day was mega exciting! I went on a little boat packed with people from Seahouses out to the Farne Islands. It was a lovely sunny day and the sea was calm. It took about an hour to get there and I could just make out an Atlantic grey seal floating in the water. As we got closer to the islands I could see more fat seals sunbathing on the rocks, glaring at me with silly smiles on their faces. Our boat slowly chugged around the edge of the island, but OMG the smell of guano was intense making me feel quite sick. It hurt the back of my nose and made my eyes water, but despite this I could just make out the shapes of guillemots nesting on the edges of the white stained rocks and the cheeky little puffins with their brightly coloured, triangular shaped beaks and vibrant webbed feet popping up out of their burrows to see me. There were razorbills, shags and cormorants nesting side by side, screeching and squawking, all jostling for the least smelly place to rear their young amongst the expanse of stinking poo! I wasn't allowed onto the island but Mum and Ian went ashore for a while. I could see them being attacked by terns and was pleased that I had stayed safe on the boat with the captain, trying to gain my sea legs as we bobbed about in the water. By the time Mum returned I had stabilized slightly, but was relieved when we eventually returned to the mainland - what an amazing day I'd had.

Scotland the brave little dog.

At last we reached Scotland. I fondly remembered it from my walk nine years earlier and hoped I would pick up some familiar smells. Apparently, so I heard on the TV once, a dog can pick up scents from up to nine years before. (A couple of years ago, much to Mum's horror, I weed on the floor in a pub, in the same spot where I used to wee when I lived there as a pup, ten years earlier.) We parked the van on a largish site underneath the aeroplane flight path to Edinburgh airport, so it was a bit noisy and there were lots of children running about. Mum did the washing and hung it around outside to dry so we looked like travelling tinkers. The following day we joined Edinburgh Hash on a trail around the grounds of an old stately home. A few of them recognised me from when I ran with them before, but they had had too many showers and baths for me to remember them. I hadn't Hashed for ages but my legs were feeling much stronger from all the walking we had been doing, so despite vet's orders I did a bit of running. I kept up, it didn't hurt and I thoroughly enjoyed it (although I did feel a bit stiff the next day).

There were so many lovely places to see up the eastern side of Scotland. Some I had been to before and some

I hadn't, with the Falkirk wheel being one of the new places I visited. This was another thing I had seen on the TV but in real life it was quite amazing. I was in awe of its size and engineering. I sat with Mum for ages on the bank watching the narrow boats motor into the huge metal cradle from the bottom canal, rotate 180° through the air, then motor out of the cradle and into the top canal. After lunch, we cycled from here along the Forth and Clyde Canal till we reached two gigantic silver horse heads sticking out of the ground. They were statues called The Kelpies. Made from hundreds of tiny pieces of shiny metal they must have been at least as tall as the Angel of the North, but it frightened me a bit to think how big the rest of the horse was underground!

Making our way anti-clockwise around Scotland's coast, (the opposite way to which I had walked, which was confusing) we stopped at Arbroath again to buy Smokies, but they weren't smoking on a Saturday so I had to eat it cold, which was positively disappointing. Travelling for three months in Scotland we had plenty of time to visit the many castles. Of course now I was a nobody, I was never allowed inside, but the gardens and grounds were all I wanted to explore and I got to see more red squirrels. (I must start a tally.)

Aberdeen I remembered clearly, although this time thankfully, we didn't stay in Olymprick's spare flat. Mum had arranged for us to run with Aberdeen Hashers but unfortunately, she got the wrong time and meeting place, so by the time we found Olymprick he was already halfway round the Hash walking through the park to the beer stop. He was so pleased to see me and kept rubbing his hands through my fur saying, "I can't believe you're still here". Well where did he think I would be? We did manage to trot the second half of the Hash, through some college grounds, then joined the pack again for cakes and sandwiches in the circle at the end. Mum and

Ian went into the Rugby Club with them for the evening but guess what? 'No dogs allowed'. This time though I didn't mind, as I was so tired that I curled up in the van and was asleep in minutes.

The next two days and nights I watched continuously out of the van window just in case I caught a glimpse. I saw big dark shadows moving and strange ripples on the water, I heard eerier sounds I'd never heard before, we checked out footpaths, camped the night, and drove for hours on end around the shores of the loch, but I never got to see Nessie. I was so disappointed.

The following day cheered me up though as I got to play in the snow with Mum. It took a bit of getting to as

I had to climb the Cairngorm Mountain to find it! The path was narrow and the steps at the beginning were steep and uneven. Up and up we went, and as we passed the half-way train station I could see patches of white in the distance, Ian said it was snow, so despite my aching legs I tried my hardest to keep going, eventually reaching the top station and the snow line. I ran across to it, did a forward roll landing in the snow and wriggled in ecstasy on my back, like I do in sand on the beach. Mum did butt sledging and I ran alongside her barking. Ian is far too sensible to play in the snow, so just watched and took photos of Mum and I having fun together. For one lovely moment I forgot I was fourteen years old and acted like a pup again. Ian and I took a rest at the top station while Mum walked the last bit to the summit. I watched her disappear into the distance and was secretly glad that I had to stay and look after Ian. On our way down a wider, less steep path I saw a ptarmigan; a little fat bird mottled black and white. She was zig-zagging across the path in front of us, scraping her wings on the floor, encouraging me to chase her and desperately trying to distract us from her chick. I wanted to oblige but Mum wouldn't let me and kept me firmly on my lead until the bird thought it safe enough to fly back to her baby.

We arrived at John O'Groats early in the morning and had breakfast in the carpark. It looked a lot different than when I was last there and was warm and sunny with holiday makers everywhere. People were having their pictures taken by the sign post. Some were starting end to end charity bike rides and others were just wanting a momentous landmark photo, but there were no dogs about to set off on a 5,000 mile walk around the coast.

Ian went up to a lady sitting in a wooden kiosk and asked, "Can we take a dog?"

"How small is it?" She answered.

Well I didn't know what they were about to get me to do but I made myself look as small as possible.

"Ok" she said.

We joined a queue at the side of the quay with a group of 'mature' looking people and within a few minutes along chugged a boat, slightly bigger than the one I went to the Farne islands on, but not huge. Of course, I was the only dog on board again, but I kept the passengers amused for the hour long journey. We landed on the Orkney Islands and I was allowed ashore, but I had hardly enough time to wee before we were ushered straight onto a waiting coach. Now I understand why I had to be small, as Mum shoved me under her seat. The journey took ages. As we crossed Scapa Flow I could hear people talking about old German boats sticking up out of the water, and I would have loved to have seen them but I couldn't get out from under the seat. The driver gave a running commentary about the islands, which didn't interest me, but I do remember him saying they have summer cows there. I thought that was weird till he said, "summer white, summer black and summer brown," and everybody laughed.

At last we arrived in Kirkwall, the capital. I instantly recognised my scent, indicating that I'd been there before and was just trying to work out the exact date, when Ian yanked my lead and dragged me across the road to look at a church (It is so annoying that humans aren't interested in dog history) I spent the whole day on and off the coach, being shoved down and pulled out from under Mum's seat, revisiting all the landmarks that I'd been to before, although I did get some pleasure in trying to work out what breeds of dogs had left their scent between my last visit and now. By the time the little boat came back to pick us up from the Orkneys it was raining hard and I was absolutely shattered so I slept the whole way back. Everybody commented on how well I had behaved throughout the day. (It's not hard when you are the only dog getting all the attention)

Continuing our westward journey along the top coast of Scotland, we cycled to Dunnet Head, the most northerly point on British mainland. At the lighthouse, I remembered from my round-Britain- walk this being the best place in Scotland to spot killer wales. From the comfort of my trailer I feverishly looked out to sea again desperate to start a new mental list, but alas it was not to be. As a consolation Mum took me for a walk in the evening sunshine along the deserted soft white sand of Dunnet beach, which was beautiful.

Apparently, on Thursday 23rd June 2016, we voted to come out of the EU (that is the 'Royal we,' as I do believe I didn't get the opportunity to vote) I don't know what the EU is anyway and I spent far too long thinking of what it possibly could be! The best I could come up with was Elephant's Underwear, and I don't think that was right.

We didn't go to Cape Wrath this time as it was too far to walk there and back in one day and Mum didn't want to sit in a mini-bus with other people which would have been costly and the only alternative. We did walk to Sandwood Bay again though, about nine miles there and back in the drizzle. I struggled a bit this time over the uneven ground but Mum helped me. It is such a special place and I was determined to make it one more time. The rain subsided for a few moments while we sat in the sand dunes looking out to sea and ate our biscuits, it gave enough time for me to have a back wriggle, but rain resumed for our long return walk. Not many dogs have seen this vast remote beach once, let alone twice, and resting there with Mum and Ian made me realise what a lucky little dog I am.

Sitting up high on Mum's lap in the motorhome, I got a completely different view of Scotland than I did when walking the coast. I admit I didn't get to sniff so many of the lovely smells that I did before, but I enjoyed seeing the miles tick away without having to tire my poor old legs. On the Coigach Peninsula I saw black sheep with white faces, white socks and tips to their tails that made them look like cats. I saw red deer with huge antlers that crept out at night and played around our van, completely unaware that I was just feet away inside. I watched the familiar, distinctive black and white Caledonian MacBrayne ferry from Stornoway come in and go out of Loch Broom, right past my window, as I sat in the front of the van parked on the campsite in Ullapool. But I'm glad to say it was a foggy day when we drove through the mountains from Applecross to Loch Carron, so I couldn't see the big drop over the edge! I could tell Ian was concentrating and Mum didn't like it as there was complete silence in the van. The road just kept going up steeper and steeper. I could hear the engine of the camper struggling, big rocks were sticking out making the road narrower, and I dug my claws into Mum's legs trying not to panic. We were up in the clouds over 2,000 feet high. Apparently it is the highest road in Britain and called 'Pass of the Cattle'. I could barely see the road in front let alone any cattle! We all breathed a sigh of relief when we reached the top. However, I couldn't believe my eyes when I saw a man appear out of the mist, lying down peddling on his recumbent bicycle. (Bet he couldn't have done that towing a trailer with me on the back)

The route down the other side was marginally better as the road got wider. As we descended the mist thinned and with the aid of gravity it certainly didn't take a two-ton campervan very long. At last we reached the iconic Eilean Donan Castle, proudly guarding the entrance of Loch Dulch. I was glad to get out of the van and stretch my legs and join the other tourists who were completely unaware of the death defying journey I had just accomplished! To steady her nerves Mum went into the gift shop for some retail therapy and returned with a CD of Scottish songs.

Now accompanied by 'Donald where's your troosers' blaring out of the van speakers, we drove from Kyle of Loch Alsh over the bridge to The Isle of Skye, where I saw seals, a distant otter, red deer, golden eagle, a bull, a ladybird and a frog all in one day. (Not sure if I should make tallies for all of these?) After that, the weather deteriorated during our short stay on the island but Ian thought it would be a good idea if we walked up to The Old Man of Storr. I started off OK but the mist got thicker and drizzle turned to heavy rain; I couldn't see the point and I hate walking up hill anyway. So, I walked slower and slower with a pained, pathetic look on my face, till Mum said "Havoc is really struggling, I'll take him back to the van."

She is such a sucker and my plan worked again. We turned around and my pace immediately quickened and within no time Mum and I were back in our warm, dry camper, eating biscuits. Ian continued without us but never saw the 'Old Man' as the mist was too thick and by the time he returned to the van he was completely drenched (and there were no biscuits left!) I definitely had the right idea.

A ferry record breaker.

We camped the night in the ferry terminal at Uig ready to catch the early morning Cal Mac ferry over to Stornoway. The weather on the Outer Hebrides was similar to when I was there nine years ago and I visited places in the rain, that I had been to before - in the rain. Over the next three days we drove along roads lined with peat bogs to the Butt of Lewis in the north, where we watched gannets diving into the swirling white water, then south through the stony lunar landscape of Harris. Here we caught the tiny ferry across to Uist, which is made up of a multitude of little islands. From North Uist, we drove over connecting causeways through Benbecula to South Uist; each one warning us to be cautious of otters crossing, but even with my neck stretched as long as I could to get the best view out of the front window, try as I might, I never saw one crossing. Here, we stayed on a campsite where I've never seen so many Border Collies in one go; some people had five or six sitting in pens outside their campers. Apparently, they were attending international sheepdog trials the next day. I ignored them as best I could and joined Mum and Ian on a lovely walk before the sun set, through a nature reserve towards the coast. I saw redshanks, ringed plovers, and the pretty black and white oyster catchers with legs that matched their vibrant beaks running around on the shore, all busily feeding before it got too dark. I was off my lead as we walked back along the vast open beach, checking out the piles of seaweed and driftwood just in case there might be anything at all edible for me to eat, when Ian suddenly whispered, "Look, what's that?" In the distance, I could see something the size of a cat, but it obviously wasn't, it had too thick a tail and far too short legs. It was a big male otter walking over the rocks. Mum made me sit, and crouched down beside me as we witnessed it playing and rolling in the seaweed trying to dry its fur. We watched for about fifteen minutes before he curled up and went to sleep in the evening sun. Wow! What a privilege. I was so fascinated that I didn't even feel the urge to chase it.

We slept the night in the car park of Lochboisdale Hotel, as we were catching the ferry from there early next morning. Mum and Ian treated themselves to a meal, so I sat patiently under the table waiting for the occasional hand to emerge containing a chip. The ferry had already docked when we arrived in Lochboisdale and left its engines chugging away on tick-over all night, which was annoying and kept me awake. At the ridiculous hour of 7am we left South Uist, sailing to Malaig back on mainland Scotland. We were well behaved and sat in the 'dog area' on the ferry. Mum took my dried breakfast and I ate it while Ian tucked into a full Scottish fry up (which by the way I was offered none of) and Mum ate porridge from a round cardboard cup-like container, which I allowed to lick clean. As it was a particularly long crossing Ian took me for a walk outside on the deck area for some fresh air. I sensed his excitement as he pointed into the water and to my delight we saw two dolphins swimming just in front of the boat. I was mesmerised by their agility, skilfully leaping out of the water and gliding along in front of us with absolutely no effort at all. From that moment, I immediately scrapped my mental tally of killer whales, on which I had none, and re-started my old list of dolphins onto which I could straight away add two.

After a quick walk around Malaig to stretch our legs and have a wee, we continued down the coast then headed inland, stopping at Glenfinnan to see the viaduct that was used in the filming of Harry Potter, then along the side of Loch Eil to Fort William. We parked in Lidl carpark and while Mum went in to shop, Ian and I witnessed the Hogwarts train pulling out of the station. I'm not sure if it left from Platform 9 ¾, but it actually steamed right past me. With our cupboards packed with food and treats we headed for a camp site in Fort William, which just so happened to have an excellent uninterrupted view of Ben Nevis. All evening walkers were returning to the camp having trekked up to the summit and back.

"We could do that in the morning," Ian said excitedly.

"Barking Hell, No!" I thought

"Oh, I'm not sure about Havoc," Mum hastily answered.

After a lot of deliberation, it was decided that they would see what the weather was like in the morning. Thank God, my prayers were answered and we woke up to drizzle. So instead of climbing the tallest mountain in Great Britain, I climbed high into the camper and we retraced our wheels back to Kinlocheil. We slowly drove along the north side of Loch Linnhe and Loch Sunart, then took the stunning windy coast road along the Ardnamurchan Peninsula. It was even more beautiful than I remembered it before, every bend in the road revealed another clear water cove, so Ian pulled the camper into a lay-by every now and then for me to paddle. I would gaze transfixed into the sparkling water, until Mum bribed me back into the van with a biscuit. The seemingly endless road meandered along the water's edge before heading inland to avoid Beinn Na Seilg, which I still remember clambering up and around nine years previously, as we then tried to stick meticulously to the coast.

The final uphill track led us to Ardnamurchan lighthouse, perched perilously on the edge of the most westerly point of Great Britain's mainland, inhabited only by two mountain goats with their sharp looking horns, who tried to get friendlier than I was comfortable with. Avoiding confrontation with the goats we strolled around the headland, admiring the sea view for a while, then headed back to the camper intending to have tea and stay the night, but large notices prohibiting overnight camping changed our plans. Mum brewed a 'cuppa' as she calls it, then, after offering some of my dried food (without my agreement) to a couple of abandoned Collie dogs, which I did actually feel a bit sorry for as the female one looked quite old and thin, we headed back down the track and found a secluded parking area just off the road, sheltered by some large rocks. After my tea, I nestled down in my usual evening rest area on Mum's front seat, but I could have sworn I saw something move in the bushes across the road. I sat up and fixed my stare onto the shrub land opposite. At first it looked deserted, but as I kept looking things began to stir. No, it wasn't my eyesight playing tricks, definitely a number of brown shapes were moving gradually over the moorland. There was about er?... well, a lot more than five adult red deer slowly sweeping majestically across the hillside right in front of me, leisurely grazing as they went. A deep grumble came from the back of my throat and Mum came over to see what I was complaining about. I was trying to decide whether to start a mental count of deer that I had seen on this trip, but as I see one or two fallow deer fairly regularly near my home in Devon, I decided it was too late to start a tally. (Maybe at Christmas I will start counting reindeer.) She held me reassuringly and we both watched them quietly feeding in what was left of the evening light. Silhouetted on the horizon was an enormous stag, with a fine set of antlers, keeping a close eye on his ladies. I lowered my head, glad to be safely hidden inside the camper and the deer continued their evening ritual blissfully unaware that I was there.

From the Ardnamurchan we boarded yet another Cal Mac ferry across to Tobermory on the Isle of Mull. I remembered the rows of colourful houses that circle the harbour from my walk and recall seeing the two otters eating their fish on the steps. I looked again to see if they were still there, but no. As I was eying up the resident ginger cat, Mum wrote and sent a postcard of Balamory, the children's TV programme that is filmed there, to Lottie and Lyla, but unfortunately out of all the post that we sent on our 'Gap Year' it was the only thing that never arrived. Again, the weather turned on us but we found a nice campsite in the hills, where we stayed for a couple of nights and used as a base to tour the Island. Mum recollected walking around Loch Frisa on our previous

visit, so as it wasn't raining for once, she suggested we take the opportunity to get our bikes out and cycle round the gravel tracks. I even managed to get out of my trailer and walk quite a bit, especially on the hilly parts, to make it easier for Mum pedalling. The sun was just making an appearance through the thick clouds and the rosebay willow herb was at its best, so I nestled down in my trailer beginning to enjoying the ride when suddenly, amongst the towering pine trees, we startled an enormous golden eagle who flew right across our path. I could clearly see his brightly coloured legs (Mum told me they were yellow) and the finger-shaped feathers at the tips of his wings. He was magnificent, although I was just glad he didn't see me, as I'm sure he could have easily picked me up in those huge clawed talons and carried me off.

We woke up to a fine drizzle again the next day so followed the scenic, mainly coastal road south to the bottom tip of Mull. Travelling through a woody stretch I spotted another golden eagle, perched in a pine tree close to the road, I recognised it immediately and thankfully I was safe in the van this time. That's two now I had seen, so I considered starting an eagle tally. The trouble was I had so many different tallies in my head and I had to count in sets of five, (as I can only count to five) I got a bit muddled. So, from that moment I decided to officially stop mentally recording dead mice. (Although out of habit I still can't help spotting them.) I noticed, (but not counted) that lots of empty coaches had been travelling towards us all morning. It puzzled me, as the single road only went as far as a small village called Fionnphort. Literally at the end of the road, we arrived at the wet, windy, dismal village and apart from a big car park full of cars, one shop, a café and a ticket office, there was nothing there except a row of more than five empty coaches. As I wasn't in need of a wee, I saw no reason for getting out of the warm van, but Mum insisted. We battled against the howling wind and made our way to the ticket office, which was full of people with suitcases, hugging cups of warm drink. Ian went to the hatch of the ticket office to make some enquiries, while Mum and I were attracting attention from the other visitors. "Oh isn't he cute, what's his name?" and "How old is he?" The usual questions she gets asked.

Ian returned without tickets, (thank goodness, as I didn't fancy going on yet another ferry) and we left the café and got blown back in the direction of our camper.

"Do you want a couple of free tickets" shouted a jolly coach driver to us as we blew past.

"No, no, please no" I thought.

But Ian, who never refuses anything free, without even consulting me, accepted them! The next minute I was standing on the edge of the quay watching a tiny ferry battling against the wind with waves heaving up and down, crabbing its way across the Sound of Iona towards me. I slid down the wet, greasy gangplank along with the other waiting passengers and onto the boat. Everywhere was slippery and cold. I slithered under Mum's seat but the floor was wet and uncomfortable, luckily not for too long as my tummy was lurching up and down in synchrony with the boat. We landed on Iona in the pouring rain and walked up the single track road in the direction of the Nunnery and Abbey.

I was told that the island hosts a Christian retreat, where people go to think and 'find' themselves, although the island didn't appear to be big enough to get lost on. Maybe it was like a dog pound, (there's one near where I live). Luckily, I've never been lost, but maybe I should start thinking about what I would do if I ever needed to be found. The weather improved slightly and without another thought of losing my mum, I had a quick paddle and wriggle on the beach, before heading for the ferry back to Mull. The little boat, still battling against the waves, moored alongside, lowered its gangplank and a whole swarm of people dragging suitcases spilled off the boat and rushed ashore pushing past me. It was like refugees landing on the Promised Land! I could not believe how many people actually get lost and needed to find themselves on this desolate island. I was first back on the boat and found a dry corner to sleep, so was completely oblivious to the lumpy crossing back across the Sound. As I walked up the street in the drizzle to our van, I looked for that blimmin coach driver, but he had already left, so I was unable to give him one of my 'looks'.

We wild camped that night in a beautiful spot next to a river, in what possibly could have been otter inhabited. It continued to rain all evening. The small puddles joined together and became big puddles, which joined together to make one enormous puddle, with us parked in the middle and still it continued to rain. Ian and I ventured outside a few times to look for otters, but the weather was so bad that the looks soon became just glances, until it got dark. Have I mentioned before that Ian hates the rain? I couldn't keep my eyes open for otter spotting any longer, so hopped up onto Mum's front seat and settled down for the night as the wind continued to batter the van, rocking me to sleep. I woke up with a start in the middle of the night as Ian was starting the van! "Just moving it to higher ground, in case the river floods!" he clarified.

The morning brought an eerie silence, so I had a quick check around the van to see if the others had made it through the night. It had stopped raining, the wind was calm and we were satisfactorily still parked by the river, all be it slightly further up the bank. We had all suffered a restless night so a lie in was in order. After breakfast, we drove up the west coast of Mull, with a stunning view over Loch Keal, rivers were full to the brim and water was shooting out of the rocks above us, spilling across the road. Ian parked the van for our lunch break in the gateway of a forestry drive, but was then impatiently strutting about as if he was waiting for someone. A couple of other cars joined us and eventually a young lady in a forestry van pulled up. We all got out of our vehicles and followed the lady up the gravel drive. I would have liked to run free and sniff around in the trees but Mum kept me firmly on the lead, so I was intrigued as to where we were all going. We eventually arrived at a wooden fence that had strategically cut out spy holes in it; one of which the lady peered through. "There they are, white tailed eagles," she whispered and pointed towards the tall pine trees.

I screwed up my eyes and surveyed the forest opposite. Sure enough, by peering around the side of the wooden fence, (as there wasn't a spy hole cut strategically out at my height) I could just make out one sitting in the top branch of a tree. The lady said that that was the male and the female was sitting on her nest, just below. Mum borrowed the lady's long lens camera thing (telescope I think she called it) to get a closer look, and the female then conveniently moved, revealing her big fluffy chick sitting happily in the nest. I never saw the baby but was content to witness two of these rare spectacular birds and of course start another tally. We stayed at the wooden hide for quite a while and I got bored eventually, so kept myself amused by chewing on a lovely piece of wood while the humans 'ooed' and 'cooed' over the eagle chick.

We departed Mull from Craignure and boarded yet another black and white ferry, on an afternoon crossing to Oban. I remembered Oban from my previous visit as being shabby and noisy, and as we drove through the centre of town it lived up to my expectations. Amidst charity shops and fish and chip shops, holiday makers wearing saggy track suits were dragging screaming kids along dirty streets, away from fairground rides that look like they should have been condemned years ago. In contrast, we camped the night just a few miles down the road in a rosebay willow herb edged layby, on the shore of the beautiful Loch Feochan, where I sat on Ian's front seat watching shags, seals and a heron blissfully fishing in the clear, still water.

The road to Tarbert was stunning. I could see far more from Mum's lap in the camper than I ever did at low level walking. The sky was so clear it blended into the sea which was sporadically dotted with floating islands. We stopped at regular intervals for photos, wees and coffee breaks, which of course included biscuits. (I prefer the chocolate ones but plain digestives will do.) Mum always warns me before she offers me chocolate, that it is bad for dogs and could even kill me, but I love the smooth, rich taste of chocolate, and I've lived this long without being ill, so I'm prepared to take the risk. I reckon, if she has at least given me the choice, if I die it will be my own fault, not hers!

From Tarbert we crossed the Crinan canal, which we returned to the next day and cycled along as far as the wooden lock gates which open out to the sea. We then drove the length of Kintyre down the west coast road with views to the islands of Gigha, Jura and Islay in the distance, to Campbeltown, where, although I knew I'd visited before, I didn't pick up any recognisable scents. A small road took us as far as Southend, then a narrow gravel track led us up and up to a gate that Mum had to get out of the van and open. Up and more up and up again until we reached the top of Beinn Na Lice, where a locked gate prevented the van from going any further. There was a large turning area for vehicles and as no one else was around, we parked in it. We walked over the crest of the hill through the heather, and I lowered my head in respect as I passed a large stone that remembers the officers who died in a Chinook crash in 1994 (a double ended helicopter, Mum said). This reminded me of when I was younger, when I chased a low flying helicopter for about half a mile over Dartmoor, and which too could have ended in a disaster, (for me not them). I always chased and barked at strange things in the sky, except birds of course because they are meant to be there, but hang gliders, paragliders and kites. "Grr", I particularly hate kites. I once nearly tipped three ladies out of a canoe that we were in because I was manically barking at a kite!

Anyway, back to the Mull of Kintyre. From the top of the hill a winding tarmac drive continued from the locked gate to the white painted lighthouse below for about another mile. Going down wouldn't have been a problem as gravity assists me but coming back up would have been very slow and painful on my legs. Ian isn't very patient with me sometimes, so as I'd been there before, I was relieved to give it a miss this time. We spent the night in the parking area at the top of the hill and from the hide of the van I watched red deer leaping the heather and frolicking in the moonlight, just feet from my nose. It was a calm night luckily and I had a lovely, long undisturbed sleep. I don't like it when the van rocks in the wind, I keep thinking we are going to blow over.

We drove back up the peninsula following the painted wooden Kintyre Way markers, stopping at Carradale forest for a long circular walk in the sunshine. At Claonaig there was enough time to play on the beach, so Mum threw pebbles for me to catch while waiting for the afternoon ferry to take us across to Arran. It was a short, calm crossing and as it was a lovely day we went up on deck, just in time to see 'The Waverley', the last working, double funnelled paddle steamer in Great Britain, steam across our bows.

We stayed on a lovely campsite, next to the castle ruin, in the small port town of Lochranza. As I relaxed in the sun while mum went for a shower, three stags with huge antlers strolled regally through the campsite, completely unfazed by my or anyone else's presence. (Maybe I will record stags with antlers after all; they are so impressive.)

Mum needed to find a post office to send some cards back to the family, so we had a wander around the streets of Brodick, Arran's capital. I picked up a few faint smells I vaguely recognised, so added my pee to them, to make my scent mark the highest and strongest. Chores accomplished we took the coast road south through Lamlash and Whiting Bay then clockwise round the bottom of the island to Blackwaterfoot, where we free-camped in the beach car park overlooking the sea towards Kintyre. During an evening stroll along the beach, which was mostly made up of huge flat slippery stones that ran along the edge of the golf course, we got a clear view of a couple of porpoises feeding as they were making their way up the Kilbrannan Sound. After breakfast on the beach we took to the road again and continued up the west coast. Our fleeting visit of Arran over, we caught another ferry from Lochranza back to Tarbert on Kintyre, immediately followed by yet another short ferry ride over to Portavadie. I'm sure, I must hold the record for a dog who has encountered the most different ferry crossings in his life. It's a good job I'm not counting inanimate objects, I would have run out of claws for counting ferries! On the subject of inanimate objects that I'm not counting, since we have been on our gap year Mum and Ian eat four yogurts a day; one each at breakfast and one each after their evening meal. I am allowed to lick the empty containers. Well, we will be travelling for a whole year, so that makes.........? An awful lot of yogurt pots I'm gunna lick clean - that I'm not counting!

With the end of our Scottish venture looming fast, Ian thought it a good idea to squeeze another couple of Cal Mac ferries in before we left. After spending the night in the mountains on a busy wooded campsite near Loch Ridden, we caught the early morning boat with a short crossing that was so quick we didn't even get out of the van, over to Rhubodach on the Isle of Bute. The only road from there took us south to the main town of Rothesay, which once would have been a very grand Victorian holiday haunt that the gentry of Glasgow regularly visited. Unfortunately, time had taken its toll on this once cheerful town, and now it was shabby and neglected with most of the buildings in need of desperate repair and a lick of paint. I was saddened to see the derelict hotels in what was obviously once a popular seaside town. I couldn't think what would attract visitors into coming here now and spend their money, so that the place could be restored to its original elegance. As I wandered along in front of the abandoned shops, adding to the distinguished pee stained pavements, wondering who might be interested in investing money into this potentially vibrant resort, I noticed a faded Micky Mouse tragically looking out from inside the window of a tacky one- man discount shop. "That's it!" I thought, "Disneyland Bute." The name definitely has a ring to it, don't you think? Joking aside, I hope one day somebody rich does invest in this depressed little island and restores it from Bute to beautiful again.

The weather turned drizzly so we returned to the camper and set off around the island to explore. When we reached Ettrick Bay, Mum brewed tea and I sat and gnawed on a hide chew while Ian stared miserably out of the front watching the rivulets of water stream down the windscreen. By early afternoon we had seen as much as we could of Bute in the rain, so returned to Rothesay in time to catch the 5 O'clock departing ferry. I secretly smiled as I passed a big sign in the harbour as we left, that read 'HASTE YE BACK'. As soon as our ferry pulled away from the harbour the weather improved enough for us to go up on deck and sit outside for our slightly longer crossing to Wemyss bay, where I relaxed on the grass for my penultimate Scottish evening, watching the sun go down on a small campsite and enjoying the remainder of my hide chew.

For my last whole day in Scotland we drove the coast road south through Largs to Irvine. I stayed in the van and ate biscuits with Ian while Mum sorted out her phone, then on to Troon where Ian understood we could board a ferry to Ireland. However, after driving round a dockside timber yard three times, realized that the ferries no longer leave from there. They depart now from Cairnryan further on down the coast. As we continued south through Ayr, seated high on Mum's lap looking out of the front window at the curving road, I recognised the undulating hills and was desperate for Ian to notice the Electric Brae, so he could witness the camper van rolling down the uphill slope. I began to fidget and my bony elbows annoyingly dug into Mum's legs as we passed through Dunure, Turnberry, Girvan and Ballantrae. As we finally sped down the hill towards Cairnryan I concluded that we had missed the Electric Brae and Ian had lost his chance of witnessing this fascinating phenomenon. Oblivious to this tragic loss he was more interested in Ailsa Craig, the big mound of rock that protrudes out of the sea, and continually commented on it as he drove down the coast.

Cairnryan was literally just a row of pretty cottages facing the sea, which now have two huge busy Irish ferry terminals built in front of them, obliterating their previously uninterrupted view of the Firth of Clyde. Ian blocked their view furthermore by parking in front while we walked along the pebbly shore, I answered the calls of nature but the cold murky water didn't look inviting enough for a swim. After enquiring about prices and times of the next day's sailings we reserved our place on a P and O ferry to Ireland.

We took our turn to stop at the kiosk to register our booking and Mum confirmed that there was 'a dog' on board. Feeling quite important, I waited for the lady to request to see my passport and check that I was the same dog as in the photo but she wasn't even interested, she just waved us on through. Feeling slightly peeved, I curled up on my sheepskin rug by Mum's feet as we drove into the huge belly of the ship. Dogs are not allowed out of their vehicles on this voyage, so Mum settled me down to sleep for the smooth two hour crossing.

To be sure to be sure.

(I'm not sure why they say it twice but as Ian is half Irish, I understand now why he often repeats what he's just said)

A couple of dreamy rabbit chases later, in what seemed no time at all, Mum and Ian were climbing back into the van and we were driving into Larne, Northern Ireland. What immediately struck me as we drove along the road were the brightly painted houses, Union Jack flags on lamp posts and bunting that festooned the streets. We stayed our first couple of nights just south of Larne at a campsite on the Island of Magee (reached by a bridge not a ferry) to find our paws and explore the area. Next, we drove up and down through the stunning glens of Antrim, stopping at a forest to enjoy the warm sunshine and strolled along a beautiful waterfall walk, with views back across the Irish Sea to the Mull of Kintyre. From here, we drove towards the north coast and visited a famous avenue of twisted trees called 'Dark Hedges', which feature in the TV series 'Game of Thrones'. I've never watched this but have heard it's good. Keeping the sea on our right, we walked over the cliffs at Fairhead, which are quoted to be the highest cliffs in Europe. I must admit they were pretty impressive and I lost my nerve a little when peering over the edge to watch several young men skilfully abseiling down the side. Hairs immediately stood up on the back of my neck as I remembered being strapped into a harness and lowered over an abseiling tower when we worked with the naughty school children.

Further along the cliffs is a rope bridge called Carrick-A-Rede, which crosses over to a small island. We were all looking forward to the thrill of crossing thirty metres over the sea, but as Mum was about to pay she noticed a big sign, 'NO DOGS'. At least the lady in the kiosk was apologetic and politely said I could walk along the cliff walk to the bridge but not go over it. The queue was long as we approached the bridge and I was hot and fidgety waiting. As we got to the front and it was Mum's turn to cross, I held back with Ian and watched the ropes sway as she bravely walked the narrow wooden planks. I could hear Ian's breathing hasten as the beads of sweat gathered on his brow. A few minutes of admiring the flora on the island and Mum was safely back and then it was Ian's turn. He handed my lead to Mum then tentatively made his way down the steps to the start of the bridge. Turning back to force a nervous smile for a photo, slowly he inched his way across trying not to look down. I held my breath in empathy for him and at this point I was quite glad I was 'just a dog' and didn't have to make up an excuse not to cross. I wanted him to turn around and wave to me but his glare was fixed firmly on the other side. He disappeared out of sight on the island, where I was sure he was trying to pluck up enough courage to cross back, but eventually he reappeared, joined the procession of tourists and courageously shuffled back over the bridge. Breathing a huge sigh of relief, my safe little family walked triumphantly back along the cliffs to the camper.

The next day marked the beginning of August and well into the school holiday period and now we were officially classed as tourists, so along with hundreds of others we visited a famous tourist attraction called Giants Causeway. Apparently, the mighty giant Finn McCool carved the 40,000 interlocking hexagonal stone columns (No I didn't count them, they are inanimate) to make a causeway across the Irish Sea and attack Scottish giants. Local people believe that standing on the stones you can feel real magic, so I made a wish but am still waiting for it to come true. It was a very hot day and I was struggling a bit, so Mum walked with me back the short route whilst Ian detoured the long way round.

I'm not sure if it was called Londonderry or Derry as we drove into the city next day, but we managed to park for free behind some riverside houses. I sensed Ian's tentativeness as we walked along the embankment into the town, but I was glad to stretch my legs so trotted happily along beside him, my ears flapping happily with each step. We crossed the newly constructed, pedestrian only 'Peace Bridge' which gently curved over the river, unsure whether it's tall supports were meant to lean to the left or right. I always behave impeccably when I am out in public but I met a family where the ladies were covered in black material from head to toe and they could only just see me through a narrow slit in the front. As I'm wary of new things, I gave them a wide berth but they started panicking when they saw me, shouting at their children and gathering them in. This really upset me as I'm not scary or vicious at all, most people say I'm cute - actually, I was more frightened of them. I composed myself enough to cross the road and squeezed through a hedge into a small park. Surrounded by fat pigeons was a square marble and glass column containing the 'peace flame' and after my incident on the bridge I was relieved to see that it was still flickering. My joints were aching and I wasn't thrilled when Ian suggested we climb a steep flight of stone steps to walk around on top of the city wall. However, from the top I got a pretty good view over the city below and the dramatic murals painted on buildings in the Bogside area. I wasn't sure of the significance of all the peace symbols, or why Ian was a bit twitchy, but I was glad when we were all back in the van and driving towards the sea again.

Not far out of Derry we crossed the imperceptible border into Eire or Southern Ireland, which puzzled me as we were heading north. We tried following signs for the recommended tourist coastal route called the 'Wild Atlantic way', which was also confusing as the direction signpost north had S on it and the direction south had N written on it. So, we just kept the sea on our right and followed the coast road to Malin Head, the most northerly point of mainland Ireland. It is naturally wild and not commercialized, except for a small gift shop trailer that was being towed away as we arrived. It was beautiful, and we 'free' camped the night just below the lighthouse amidst the wild orchids and lucky heather. From Malin Head, as we were now driving south down the west coast, the 'Wild Atlantic Way' signs made more sense, (apart from the ones that had been turned around or removed completely) with regular stopping points to brew tea, have lunch or just stroll along one of the many practically, deserted beautiful sandy beaches.

The weather in Ireland had improved slightly but on one particularly drizzly day we visited a 'famine village'. This concerned me slightly as I was always hungry looking for food, and didn't fancy competing with other starving individuals. Inside the gate was an enclosure of white washed thatched cottages, depicting life in Ireland between 1845 – 1852. Apparently, all they had to eat was potatoes, but the crops failed and thousands of people starved to death. I sympathised with these poor folk, as although I can eat potatoes I don't think I would last long if I had to live on them alone! I didn't like the museum village at all, it smelt weird, and the spooky, skinny mannequins wearing dusty clothes glared down at me from under their wonky hair pieces through squinty glass eyes, making me feel fat and uncomfortable, so again I was glad to retreat to the sanctuary of our camper.

Leaving the Inishowen peninsula and Buncrana where we camped for the night, Mum realised she had postcards to send, still with British stamps on them. So, as we weren't far from another border we popped back into Northern Ireland again, stopped at the first letterbox, posted the cards then returned into Eire to continue our journey south.

The coastal route had stunning scenery and I have always loved looking out of the front window, but with my increasing years I find it harder to stay awake for long, so Mum usually had to wake me when it was time to get out for a leg stretch. The heathers were in full bloom and their smell was intense as we walked over the huge cliffs of Slieve League, reaching 595 metres, and also claiming to be the highest in Europe.

Through Donegal and still driving south, we headed inland and back again over the wiggly border into Northern Ireland, to the town of Enniskillen. The sun was out as we walked across a bridge over the river that protected the castle. Although generally in Ireland dogs don't walk on leads, I stayed on mine and kept close to Mum as we made our way through the busy streets. Suddenly a loud 'boom, boom, boom" hurt my ears as a military style band, complete with standard bearers marched out of the car park behind us. We stopped to look and it was closely followed by another, then another. I didn't like the noise, as the sound of drums, trumpets, accordions and bagpipes vibrated through my head. I tried to run away, but Mum held my lead tight as more and more bands followed, flags and banners carried proudly as they paraded up the road. I 'persuaded' Mum to take me across to the wall for safety and as she crouched down holding me tight, I could just about bear to watch the seemingly endless stream of men, women and children all in their different uniforms, partake in a deafening march that had something to do with oranges. Although, for the hour it continued to stream past me, I never saw one piece of fruit. I have concluded already that Ireland is not quite like England, with signs for 'Frozen grass for sale' and 'Grow your own firewood'. I will take each day as it comes.

From Enniskillen we drove through pine forest mountains and around picturesque lakes towards Sligo, Ballina and onto a small campsite at Crossmolina, where we got the bikes and my trailer out for the first time in Ireland. We cycled along quiet country lanes to the next village and sat outside a pub for Mum and Ian to enjoy a Guinness, a strong dark beer with a rather tasty creamy top, which Mum let me lick from her finger. Thirsts quenched, we sauntered up to the small cemetery to see if any of Ian's distant relatives were there. The area seemed deserted, as we walked up and down the rows between the big slabs of marble, looking at the lettering carved out on each one. I sniffed the ground in the hope of picking up somebody's scent, "Here's one" and "There's one" Mum and Ian called to each other but every time I glanced up nobody was there. I thought they must be playing a game of hide and seek so barked excitedly hoping someone would appear but still the cemetery remained mysteriously empty. Totally confused by their actions I climbed back into my trailer and settled down and waited for Mum to tow me back to the camper.

The Wild Atlantic Way deviates occasionally, giving optional extra view points; one of which that we visited was Achill Island, reached by a long concrete causeway. We stayed on a busy, more commercialised campsite adjacent to a long, sandy beach popular with playing children, surfers and horse riders that cantered up the beach, making the ground tremble as they passed. From the site, we took the bikes out again to explore the island, which was tougher than Mum had expected, as she puffed and panted dragging me up the hills. As we slowed on one particularly steep bit I tried jumping out to make it easier for her, but unfortunately I ended up only half out with my harness painfully twisted around my legs. I learnt never to try that again.

While we were enjoying our halfway rest, the weather deteriorated and thick fog shrouded the tops of the hill. As we cycled on through the fog, a sweet, recognisable smell filled the air. It was peat burning on a cottage fire and comfortingly reminded me of my time on Harris and Lewis. Much of the open land in the Donegal area is peat bog, and as we drove along the roads I could see little piles of peat logs (or turf as the Irish call it) drying next to the recently dug trenches.

Away from the narrow lanes, the countryside was more difficult to explore as the Irish farmers are very territorial and do not encourage walkers on their land. There are no small lay-bys to pull into with footpaths to wander, and only official designated walks that were often long and used the roads. No wonder there are no Hashes in Ireland. (Well there is one in Dublin but they don't venture far from the city.) The country lanes though, at this time of year were bordered by beautiful fuchsia hedges, heather and gorse and an abundance of summer flowers in full bloom.

Despite the unpredictable weather, I was enjoying my Irish tour so far, especially the virtually empty, vast sandy beaches where I visited at least one new one every day.

In one very windy beach car park we stopped for the night, and after an exhausting long walk along the sand and back, I settled down in my usual look-out point on the front seat. I was intrigued by a man in the VW camper next to us, who was unpacking a huge kite and surfboard and marched purposely off towards the sea. Within minutes the kite was in the air and he was charging up and down on his surfboard, jumping the waves and spinning in the air as they broke. I grumbled a little but it was worth watching and far enough away not to make too much of a fuss, but suddenly, as if from nowhere a black and white Collie appeared who could not resist the temptation and charged up and down the beach barking and chasing the kite surfer. From the warmth and comfort of my van I watched this entertainment for over an hour until the surfer eventually came in, but the Collie didn't go home, if he even had a home to go to. He just curled up as tight as he could and spent a very cold and windy night trying to shelter underneath the VW van. At first light, I peeped through the gap in our curtains and the little dog was still there. Occasionally he would get up and walk about but returned immediately to his sheltered spot. I saw the man from the van throw some food down for the dog but then he drove away! However, the dog didn't seem too bothered and just wandered around our van instead. I felt guilty (well only a bit) as I gobbled down my breakfast. Mum didn't want to encourage him too close to us but I did notice as we drove away, she had kindly left him a pile of my food to eat after we had gone.

Continuing south, still following the Wild Atlantic Way through more peat digging and drying areas, we arrived at another over-subscribed campsite at Salthill, a flat but long walk along the sea front from Galway. It was a pleasant walk, and along with everyone else that was ignoring the 'NO DOGS ON BEACH' sign, I walked along the sand. The Irish people seem to ignore all dog signs especially the 'PICK UP POO' ones. The councils are trying hard to educate owners and even provide plastic bags and bins but still people ignore them. I was almost embarrassed to be a dog with the amount of poo that is left in the street by irresponsible owners and as most people don't walk their dog on a lead, they are totally unaware (or blatantly ignore!) when or where their dog 'goes'! (Rant over)

Galway was lively and welcomed us with banners, bunting and buskers and the old town and narrow streets were packed with bustling holiday makers. Every other building was either a pub or a gift shop selling everything Irish from leprechauns to leads, so Mum bought both. A leprechaun each for Lottie and Lyla and a shamrock patterned lead for me, (as I'd mistakenly chewed through the tartan one she bought me in Scotland, when I got it confused with the hide bone I was gnawing.) Outside every gaily decorated pub was a musician or singer. I'm not keen on noisy confined spaces, so was glad when we stopped for a rest outside a pub where the young musician was just packing up to go home. I settled down under the table, fascinated by the strange man opposite who was wearing overly large shoes and a shiny round nose and was cleverly modelling animals out of balloons. Mum had remembered to bring my tea, so after enjoying my al fresco meal I waited eagerly for the occasional chip to fall intentionally on the floor from hers. My legs ached on the long walk back to the campsite, so I was slightly 'pissed off' (sorry, can't think of another way to describe my feelings) when we walked in again the next day, to see something Ian had missed the day before!

We stopped briefly for a leg stretch around the pretty little fishing harbour of Kinavarra, then drove over 'The Burren', described for tourists as a limestone pavement. Basically, it was an extensive, barren, hilly area covered in small, flat boulders with a few wisps of grass and not much else, but strangely intriguing in its nakedness. We camped the night in a rough stony layby and watched some novice climbers attempting to scale the rugged rock face adjacent to the road, as another stunning sunset lit up the sky over the sea. Continuing through this massively rocky area, the next day we drove up an exceptionally steep hill to the top of 'The Cliffs of Moher' which also claim to be the highest in Europe. To me they did seem the tallest but as I'm only two feet high, they all seem enormous. From Kilkee I enjoyed a circular trailer ride around the country lanes, visiting a castle and of course another Guinness pub, before taking an evening stroll around the headland from Loop Head lighthouse on the tip of the peninsula, where I was privileged to witness bottlenose dolphins swimming just off the coast. There must have been at least......five? Which I added to my stagnant mental tally.

We parked up for the night on the opposite side of the carpark to the other campers, with the back of our van to the wind to stop it rocking. Mum cooked tea and I settled down for the evening on the front seat. Suddenly, just for a couple of seconds, the whole van lit up like daylight, then was dark again! Just as I reclosed my eyes the sequence repeated; lit up again and then was dark. It was a peculiar moment and I wasn't sure if I was awake or asleep. With a startled expression on my face I looked across at Mum who was laughing, "It's only the lighthouse," she chuckled.

She closed the front curtains, then pulled down the blinds at the back, and by squeezing my eyes shut tightly I managed to sleep through a night of recurring flashes.

I hadn't been itching, but Mum had decided that today I was due my monthly flea and tick treatment on the back of my neck. I don't like it 'cos its cold, tingly and dribbles down behind my ears, so as usual I made a fuss and she gave me a chew stick as a distraction. Ian had been reading one of his many 'freebie' leaflets that he likes to pick up and announced that there was a Folk Festival called 'The Fleadh' for a week at a town called Ennis, which coincided with our visit to the area. There were no commercial campsites in the town, but the Folk Festival had organised temporary ones at nearby football and rugby grounds, so we followed the signs and headed for the latter. After parking the van on the grass next to the pitch alongside the other campers, I naively headed for the complimentary dog friendly minibus which took us into the town. Feeling flea free for the Fleadh, I enthusiastically jumped off the bus and followed closely behind Mum, straight into the throng of bustling people.

Oh dear! I hadn't done my research into what The Fleadh or Folk Festival was. As soon as I heard the music, I put the anchors on and dug my heels into the ground to resist going any further. The frightening vibrations resounded in my ears, making me feel shaky and sick. Mum had no idea how I was feeling and dragged me on, but in every doorway, in every street was a group of young musicians banging and blowing or squeezing and plucking their instruments, making an unbearable noise! At the top of Ennis, a caterwauling American choir were attracting a big crowd of onlookers but I couldn't endure being near them. Mum wanted to watch but reluctantly took me across the street to a doorway, where we both sat on a step and listened from a bearable distance. Little girls in clogs or trainers flung their legs in the air and tapped their feet while spinning in time to the music, and made me feel dizzy just watching. Eventually, with my legs wobbling like jelly, to my utmost relief we found our way through the back streets out of town to the returning mini bus and with the onset of tinnitus I collapsed under the seat. Once we arrived back at the rugby ground, like a naughty child I was put straight to bed, mentally and physically exhausted and within seconds I was asleep. I didn't even hear Mum and Ian slip out to listen to the evening entertainment in the marquee, I was just glad to be safely 'home'.

By next morning Mum and Ian were talking to me again, but I still felt fragile, so was pleased that we spent most of the day travelling. We did stop for our lunch break at Loch Graney, where I enjoyed a scamper through the tranquil forest and along an overgrown stream and back. We continued driving around the loch and found a quiet overnight stop beside a little stone quayside, tucked away off the main road. As I watched out of the window from my usual evening look out seat, a brazen young fox came out of the bushes and walked down the path, inches from the van. I would have liked to have made his acquaintance – but he was bigger than me! Instead, I awoke my dormant tally of 'live' foxes (I don't count dead ones on the road) and added him to my statistics. I had a restless sleep that night, excited because I knew we were meeting up with Kermit the next day.

From the vet to a Psychoanalyst

From the 9th to 12th of September, Mum had organised for some of our Hash friends from Devon to get together with us for a long weekend on a campsite outside of Dublin. Kermit however, was unable to make these dates and had made his own arrangements to meet up with us for a couple of days, a few weeks earlier than the rest. We eventually found him in a typically Irish little town, with its pretty painted houses, bunting and flowers, called Adare that claimed to have the most picturesque row of thatched cottages in Ireland. However, the central ones had been previously damaged by fire and were boarded up, making it look a bit unsightly. Never-the-less we found a pretty pub with a sheltered garden, where we sat in the sun and caught up on the gossip from home. Kermit had travelled over in his 'Roma home', which was an even smaller camper than ours, so we managed to squeeze both of our vans into an out of town gateway for the night.

I am an old doggie from Devon,
who thinks travelling around is just heaven,
I live in a van,
just eat when I can
and sleep there for 24/7

Kermit took so long deciding what he wanted to do for the day, that we continued into Limerick without him. It was a surprisingly big city, but no leprechauns sat on toadstools chanting poems as I had imagined. We managed to find a parking area without the usual height restriction barrier that many car parks in Ireland have, and walked into the city centre along the river embankment. The shopping area was big, busy and noisy but fortunately we didn't hang around there too long and went off to find St John's castle. On the way, I saw a gruesome mural painted on the side wall of a house. It was the head and shoulders of a one-eyed bearded man with a tattoo of 'Hello Kitty' on his neck, and his other eye was in the ice cream he was holding. Tilting my head to one side then the other I pondered for a while trying to make some sense of it, but couldn't come up with a conclusion - just a poem.

> *I walked into Limerick one morning,*
> *not quite awake and still yawning,*
> *Saw a mural not nice,*
> *A man's eye in his ice,*
> *"Don't eat it" I heeded a warning!*

We didn't go in the castle but enjoyed walking around it, over the bridges and back down the opposite side of the river, where I took great delight in sniffing all the benches and lamp posts and adding my own scent to the already pungent smells. The river was wide and in full flood after all the rain we had been having and I watched the canoeists skilfully paddling down the rapids. After sitting by the river long enough to rest my aching legs, we returned to the van and headed off to meet Kermit at Askeaton, where we stayed on an Aire, next to the public swimming baths. (An Aire is a specially designated area for campervans to park, generally free or at little cost, which usually have facilities for emptying waste and filling with water should you require it.) Kermit had also had a fleeting visit into Limerick, driven around, but couldn't find anywhere to park, so drove on. He had brought his bike with him to Ireland, so despite threatening rain we all went for a short afternoon cycle ride to the Shannon Estuary, then ended in a little pub for the evening where, unusually, I was welcomed in by the landlord and locals. The rain continued all night and the river we were parked by rose higher and higher, until it burst its bank the far side, but luckily not on ours. Still raining in the morning, we drove around various valleys and beaches trying to find something to do, but the weather was awful. As poor Kermit didn't have suitable wet weather gear, he decided he had had enough and headed into town while we headed for a campsite. He went home the next day.

As soon as he had left, the weather improved greatly. We visited Tralee, where I took great delight in scavenging along the pavements around the take away stalls after the 'Rose of Tralee' festival, which I'm relieved to say we had just missed. The Dingle peninsula and Connor Pass, which we drove through next, were a bit fur raising. A narrow road, single track in places with over hanging rocks, took us higher and higher. Unlike when we drove through fog up the 'Pass of Cattle' in Scotland, the weather today was beautiful and the view back down the steep valley across the moor, towards the distant mountains was vertiginous and terrifying. (Mum called it clear and spectacular.) While Ian let the van engine cool down at the top, I got out for a leg stretch and wee, before our roller coaster descent down the other side into the coastal town of Dingle. Brightly painted houses, tourist filled gift shops and pubs oozing traditional music, even a real donkey wearing a sun hat beside the smallest gypsy caravan I've ever seen, depict this popular Irish seaside resort. I submissively trudged through the crowded town on my lead, stopping outside every gift shop then patiently waiting with Ian, while Mum went in to look for pressies to take home for the family. She showed me the fragile glass sun catcher she had bought for Nanny to hang in her room. It was beautiful and I hoped we would get it back to her without it breaking. Another long evening was spent laid under a table on a sticky floor in a dark old pub. A small band started up in the corner of the room playing folk music, but as it was subtle and I was already almost asleep, I barely heard it. We stayed the night in the harbour car park just a few minutes' walk from the pub. It wasn't the most picturesque place for breakfast, so we drove to Inch beach, famous for the filming of Ryan's Daughter (where, although I knew neither Ryan nor his daughter, I still enjoyed an early morning wriggle in their sand.)

Some say the Kerry Ring is best driven anti-clockwise, going in the same direction as the coaches, others recommend clockwise, so that you are not stuck behind them. Ian chose anti-clockwise.

So, with our new Irish CD blaring out of the speakers, we followed the Wild Atlantic Way south with the coaches, so that we didn't come face to face with one on the narrow sections of road. This coastal route certainly lived up to expectation; the uncultivated, natural terrain with views over the sea out to the little islands was unforgettable. Seated high on Mum's lap the whole way and despite my head nodding several times, I was determined not to go to sleep and miss one minute of this stunning scenery. We continued for a second day to complete the Kerry Ring, stopping briefly for a walk around the flag festooned village of Sneem, and then the market town of Kenmare, before driving the long, steep hill to the top of Mull Gap, to take in 'Ladies View', which looked out over Killarney Lakes. I felt a little inferior there, as car loads of pedigree Bernese Mountain Dogs were posing for an official photo shoot and as no one had even bothered to brush me that day, I made sure I kept well out of view from the camera.

I know I keep on about the stunning views, but the drive down through Killarney National Park was so beautiful, with the afternoon sun shimmering on the surface of the lakes. I would have loved to stop for a paddle, but Ian was eager to find our night's campsite on the other side of the town. This campsite too was oversubscribed by dogs; pen loads outside of each caravan and camper, constantly barking and annoying! One cheeky guy squeezed in by us in a Mercedes Van with his three Setters didn't even have a proper camping space. His Gordon Setter reminded me of Bramble (who we pet sit for, and not to argue with) so I didn't like to complain in case she bit my head off! (Literally.) I understood that they were all off to a big dog show in the area; probably the same one the Bernese Mountain dogs were attending. Well, the next day Mr Heinz 57 wasn't going to be belittled by all of these pedigrees and proudly climbed into my trailer, and off we cycled into Killarney Park in search of some fun - not some stuffy humiliating dog show. What a great day I had. I saw Jaunty cars (horse and carts) and red deer, visited Ross Castle and shared Mum's ice cream sitting on the grass in the sun, then a walk and cycle around Lough Leane, stopping for a play and swim before ending the day with the creamy topping from Mum's Guinness and a nap under the pub table. "Oh, what did you do today, Mr pedigree dogs?"

Glaring out of the camper window, feeling so much better about myself, I left all the show dogs in their prison pens as we headed back to the painted houses in Kenmore to re-join the Wild Atlantic Way south. We had been recommended to drive around the Beara peninsula, which is said to be less busy and even prettier than the Kerry Ring. Unfortunately, the weather was not quite as brilliant but there were still spectacularly good views out to sea along the jagged coastline towards Dursey Island.

As when I did my around Britain walk, today we

were again using Grandpa's old map, which had a hand-written sticker indicating 'cable car' at Dursey Island. "Oh, we must go and see that," Mum implored as we drove down a narrow single track, the grass dropping away into the sea over the rocky cliff to my left and sheep seemingly unaware that they were grazing perilously close to the edge. Ian fell silent as we approached the car park, seeing the old rusty looking pylons overhead supporting wires that slung about 400 metres over the sea to the Island, and beneath the wires hung, what I can only describe as 'a garden shed'. "They won't allow dogs on that, so we won't be able to cross," Ian then wishfully retorted. Mum and I were out of the camper as quick as a flash and marched up to the ticket office to enquire whether dogs were allowed in the cable car. "Yes, but they are not allowed to walk around the island or they will be shot!" was the ticket man's hasty reply.

Mum bought two tickets and I was allowed to travel free. She was waving them in the air as we walked back to Ian, and his face was a picture. We waited just a couple of minutes before our 'garden shed' arrived. Ian parted the double sliding doors and we boarded the swaying car. A voice spoke through a loud speaker requesting us to close them behind us and with a sudden lurch, we were launched into the air. I decided lying on the floor would be the safest way to travel and I was fascinated by the view of the sea through the holes in the bottom of our wooden shed. A slow, bumpy ride dangled the three of us approximately 50 metres in the air across the strong current of water to the Island, but as there was nothing actually to do other than observe the sheep and as I wasn't keen on getting shot, we caught the next returning shed to the mainland. I think that was the nearest thing I will ever get to flying, it was great.

To complete our Beara peninsula tour we visited the large harbour of Casteltownbere, then travelled around

Bantry Bay and out towards Mizen Head, the significant opposite end of the country from Malin Head. Unlike its polar, it had a purpose-built gift shop, café, museum and information areas where dogs were allowed. Passing underneath a big metal 'Welcome' sign, Mum carried me over the bridge to the lighthouse. It was a rough, windy day and the waves were crashing noisily into the rocks below, so I did my usual mid-air paw swimming actions to help us across. In the distance, I could make out Fastnet Rock Lighthouse, the famous landmark used in the shipping forecast, and watched a yacht fighting against the wind trying to make its way around it, relieved that I wasn't having to travel anywhere in a boat in those gusts. We parked away from the headland for more protection that night, as sometimes it is difficult to sleep when the van is rocking and a gale is howling around outside. From the furthest south west corner of Ireland, we started making our way along the bottom coast, eastwards. A beautiful clear sky reflected in the still water of Schull harbour and hundreds of little pleasure boats bobbed about, making it look so inviting that I ventured in for a refreshing swim. To dry off, I strolled around the small Farmer's Market and Mum bought a delicious lemon and sugar crepe which she shared with me, then I sat in the sun to warm up while Ian enjoyed his first Guinness of the day.

The campsite book described our next site as quiet and relaxing, I beg to differ! The sunny evening encouraged a barbeque, so Mum cooked chicken pieces and sausages, then out came the table and chairs, followed immediately by blimmin wasps! I do my best to ignore them but when they hover in front staring me directly in the face I just snap. Mum shouts at me and warns me not to, but on this occasion, it was too late. I got him - and bugger, he got me! I didn't dare howl, 'cos Mum would just say it was my own fault, so I crawled quietly under the back of the camper and hid away feeling sorry for myself. Still feeling very swollen around my tongue I was glad when it was bed time. Curling up on the front seat, I shut my eyes and tried to sleep, but thumping loud music was coming from the other side of the hedge, because the neighbouring house was having a party! My mouth was throbbing and now my ears were. This shindig continued until the early hours of the morning; so much for a quiet, relaxing campsite.

Half asleep, I was glad to ride in my trailer the next day as we cycled from the camp to a village called Leap, in the centre of which was a life-sized wooden carving of two men in a boat. Celebratory flags and bunting hung from every house and lamp post as they celebrated two of their lads, who had just won gold and silver medals for rowing in the 2016 Olympic Games. As I was admiring the wooden carving, trying to decide whether to wee on it or not (I decided not), I witnessed a Jack Russell dog struggling up the road. He obviously had no use of his back legs, which were dangling pathetically in a sling from a little two wheeled buggy that he dragged behind. I felt sorry for him and as I climbed back into my trailer, which seemed almost like a royal chariot compared to his, I just hope my poor old legs never give up on me like that.

Rosecarry Bay provided a lovely tranquil dog walk for me, then on into Clonakilty town for a walk for them. This seemed a useless exercise as far as I was concerned, as I was not allowed to sniff the shop doorways in case I weed and they just dawdled aimlessly around, hardly ever going into a shop to actually buy anything. I just don't see the purpose of going into these dirty, man- made places full of noise and fumes when the countryside is full of natural beauty and fresh air

Kinsale marked the end of the Wild Atlantic Way, an impressive scenic route I will never forget, but the town itself was just more hours of wasted energy, trudging around concrete streets, only to end up lying on another pub's sticky floor, listening to humans who thought they could sing.

Our last coastal town visit before heading inland was Cobh, the harbour town of Cork, where the famous ship Titanic had its final port of call before its ultimate ill-fated voyage. There was even a 'Titanic Experience' exhibition which we must have walked past at least five times before Ian decided he wanted to visit. He was surprised to learn, as was I, that some lucky passengers actually got off the Titanic in Cobh, only ever intending to travel from Liverpool to Ireland. The Aire we camped on at the quay was popular but pleasant with a view over the harbour, where a friendly seal popped his head out of the water a few times and passed the time of day with me. The biggest ship I've ever seen, called a cruise liner, was moored alongside us at the Aire and kept me amused for hours, watching the passengers streaming on and off like busy ants up and down the gangplanks. I wonder if they visited the 'Titanic Experience' before their ship left.

As we were due to meet our other Hasher friends in just over a week's time, we started our inland route towards Dublin, with the intention of exploring the last bottom right-hand-corner of Ireland, after our planned Hash weekend. It was a fur-raising journey through the busy roads of Cork to Blarney where we parked on a campsite just outside of the town, proposing to make an early entrance to the Castle the following day. It was a beautiful morning so we were one of the first families in the queue. Dogs were welcome in the grounds but, as the staircase in the castle had narrow spiral stone steps, I realised that it could have been a bit dangerous with dogs amongst the hundreds of visitors, all wanting to kiss the lucky Blarney stone at the top. I waited patiently at the bottom with Ian while Mum clambered up the stairs. Looking up, I could just see her at the top, leaning out backwards to kiss the stone. Within a few minutes, she was back down and it was Ian's turn to climb the tower. I know humans do some weird things but I really couldn't get my head around the 'whys and wherefores' of this one! Still, I enjoyed all the attention I was getting at the bottom from the American tourists who had had to leave their poor pooches at home. It was a great day and the grounds were extensive with different areas to explore, which included a poisonous plant garden growing cannabis! Then feeling light headed and happy, I particularly enjoyed the enchanted wood, with its mystical pools and magical steps.

Recently, I had been licking one of my 'old dog's moles' on the top of my leg, which had made it sore and weep. Mum thought it was a bit infected so from Blarney Castle we drove to a small town called Fermoy to find a vet. The traffic was a nightmare, and we queued for ages before we eventually found a parking space on the outskirts of town, then walked down the hill into the centre. It looked as if there was a huge fire in one of the hotels, as lots of fire engines were parked and ladders were leaning against the building. A big crowd of people had gathered and were watching the firemen running up and down, "Oh, how exciting!" I thought as we drew closer.

I stopped suddenly and blinked to adjust my vision. For one moment, I thought I saw Mickey Mouse, then Minnie in a spotted dress. Yes! They were actually there; human sized and running about in the crowd holding buckets, clapping and cheering the firemen on the ladders. This could only happen in Ireland! Mickey waved across the road at me and I got all embarrassed, as I realised it was just a charitable event, so Mum put some money in their bucket and we continued on to find the vet.

The small waiting room was empty when we arrived and the young lady receptionist was friendly. Within a few minutes I was called into the surgery, where an elderly vet with glasses peered down at me as I cowered on the floor. Mum lifted me gently onto the table so that he could get a better look at my leg, as the fur was now all stuck together with congealed puss. He squeezed my mole which made me yelp, then he tried to shave the area with electric clippers, but it was so painful I screamed loud enough for Ian to hear me in the waiting room. Now I'm not one to make a fuss as you know, but this was excruciating! A lot of muttering went on between him and Mum before he thrust a painful needle in the back of my neck. I couldn't wait to get out of there.

We left with a tub of tablets to take twice a day, some cold liquid to wash the infected area twice a day, and a huge ridiculous plastic cone to wear around my neck, if I didn't stop licking it. Oh yes, and a bill for 80 Euros!

With the 'cone of shame' around my neck, I was now longer than the inside width of the campervan and turning around was almost impossible. So, to stop me licking off the cold liquid, Mum made a 'sleeve' for me to wear on my leg out of an old bandana, which was tied around my neck with an old shoe lace. It looked strange but did the trick. I couldn't lick it but the air could still circulate and my sore place quickly got better.

The next day we drove to Tipperary, which, on the town sign as we entered, said "YOU'VE COME A LONG WAY!" But to be honest, I wished we'd never bothered, because it was another place I had heard about but found disappointing when I got there. Without seeming too rude, I thought it was dirty and run down and typically a working town; not out to impress tourists as you might expect. We had a quick walk up the high street and admired all the flags and support in shop windows for the oncoming hurling match against their local rivals, Kilkenny. Outside a fruit shop an elderly gentleman stopped to talk to me and, as like most people in Ireland, was very chatty and friendly. I sat politely looking interested despite not being able to understand his accent nor a word he said.

Before embarking on our scenic drive through the heather covered Wicklow Mountains, and despite being late afternoon, we stopped for what was intended to be a quick walk around the grounds of Kilkenny Castle. Off my lead and enjoying the open space, I passed many open gateway entrances into the park but only saw a few other people enjoying the grounds. As I sat resting my aching legs by a duck infested pond I noted an official looking guy walking purposefully past. As we reached the gate at the far end of the park, which was the exit nearest to our van, to my dismay we found it was locked! Consequently, we had to walk all the way back through the park to try and find an alternative escape. Unfortunately, the official looking man must have been walking in front of us, locking each gate in turn, just before we arrived there. Looking around for somewhere to sleep, thinking I was going to be locked in all night, Mum quickly clipped my lead on and dragged me across the central lawn and we escaped out of the main entrance just before he got there. Phew!

Instead of sleeping on a park bench we stayed the night in a car park (in the camper), amidst the sheep at the top of the Wicklow Gap, with stunning views down the valley. With only a few days to go until my Hash friends arrived, we had a walking trail to recce that they would hopefully execute on the Saturday. From the carpark, we found a squelchy, muddy path that skirted a pine forest past a herd of red deer, then a small stony path led down to some stepping stones across a babbling brook. A few metres on we were halted at a 'bog of no return', the other side was a big area of piled up stones, which actually was a disused lead mine where our path should continue. All we had to do was try and join the two paths up together. We decided to walk back up to the van, Ian then moved it and parked in the village of Glendalough at the bottom of the valley. We then made our way on paw along 'St Kevin's Way', back up the hill to find the other side of the lead mine. What a great time I had; sniffing every rock, blade of grass and lump of mud, getting left behind, running to catch up, eating sheep's poo and jumping streams and puddles, totally free and independent of my lead. I was exhausted, every muscle in my body ached but I went to sleep contented with our proposed Hash walk, and I'd had a proper doggy day.

From the small town of Rathdrum, we caught the early morning train into Dublin. A smart looking lady seated opposite commented on my age and started up a conversation with Mum. She said she was a dog psychoanalyst and worked with dogs with bad habits. Without thinking, Mum asked her why I constantly lick people, (which was a bit humiliating as it wasn't something I wanted to share with someone I hardly knew) Well! that was it - she reckoned I was stressed, and for almost an hour, off she ranted on a subject that she was obviously very passionate about, but spoke so loudly that the whole train carriage knew I had 'issues' and was suffering from a stress disorder! I was determined not to show her how stressed she had now just made me and pretended to be asleep, laid flat out on the carriage floor. I opened one eye just wide enough to see her get off the train and was glad Mum hadn't parted with 150 Euros, which is what she usually charged for an hour's consultation! Stressed, me? Huh- I'm the least stressed dog I know.

The next stop was the fair city of Dublin, the home of Guinness. I jumped down off the train onto the busy, bustling platform and eagerly followed Mum out into the street, pulling back sharply on my lead to avoid her getting run down by a passing tram. With eyes, ears and nose everywhere we headed towards the river Liffey and followed it along towards an area that Ian was keen to visit. This of course involved beer, and was called Temple Bar area, where we stopped of course for a Guinness and I could rest my legs, as the hard pavements were hurting my joints.

Making our way through streets broad and narrow, (I noted how pretty the girls were) we headed for the busy centre, where we tried to find the famous statue of Molly Malone. Between the usual city retail stores were cafes and brightly lit Irish gift shops with musicians and mime artists busking outside. Trying to give them a wide berth, sniffing lamp posts and hoovering up food from the floor all at the same time, I failed to notice that I had accidentally weed on the bottom of Molly's skirt. Mum gave my lead a tweak and I looked up to see the bronze form of a tiny lady holding the handles of her fish barrow. I noticed the sad expression on her face, probably because her dress was rather on the small size revealing her boobies, which were now shiny from people touching them when having their photo taken. After sandwich crusts in the city park and another stroll along the Liffey to look at the boats, I'd had enough of city life for the day and was glad when we were walking over Half Penny Bridge back to the train station and heading for 'home'.

Havoc Bathard

A visit from my friends.

Annoyed, due to my being refused entry into an almost empty pub in the town of Wicklow on Wednesday, I was cheered up by Buzby and Screech arriving on our site in their campervan on Thursday, and in the pouring rain, the rest of my Hash friends arrived on Friday. They had flown over from Bristol Airport, hired cars when they arrived and were staying on our campsite in two big static caravans, only a couple of minutes' walk from our campervans. I wasn't really allowed in their caravans but as other visitors on the site were ignoring all the anti-dog notices, I decided I would too. I was so excited to see everyone again and I think they were just as pleased to see me, although as soon as they had said "Hello" they headed straight for the onsite bar!

I stayed in our camper for that evening while Mum and the others enjoyed drinking and catching up with news from home. Ian didn't take his phone with him and it rang quite late, while he was out. I thought it might be urgent as it rang again a few minutes later, but having no thumbs I couldn't answer it. At midnight, they eventually returned and I tried everything I could to delay them from going to bed in the hope that Ian would pick up his phone. Eventually he did and noticed two missed calls from Auntie Sally in Bath. Despite being very late Ian returned her call, mumbled a few words then handed the phone to Mum. I couldn't really hear what she was saying but her expression changed and I saw her eyes fill with tears. I sat by her side so that she could twiddle my ears, then as she put the phone down she whispered, "My mum has died!" Suddenly, a huge lump came in my throat and I couldn't swallow, "No! Not Nanny, surely not Nanny". She had looked so happy and healthy when I last saw her. Ian came over and gave Mum a hug then the three of us sat in silence just cuddling on the bed.

It was a restless night, Mum and Ian chatted a lot, keeping me awake. I knew I had to be fit for today's long walk, but was it still going to happen? What was Mum going to do? I knew Mum was a fighter and she wouldn't want to let other people down. We were up early and I walked with her over to the others in their static vans. She tried to be brave but burst out crying as she told them the sad news, insisting that the weekend would go ahead as planned. (As a consolation, they had a whip round and bought her some yummy chocolates, which we shared).

As arranged, a mini bus picked us all up from reception at 11 o'clock and drove us through scenic lanes to the top of the Wicklow Gap, where we were dropped off. It was a lovely sunny day and the view down the valley was amazing, so complete with packed lunches off we set. As it had rained all the previous day, the narrow, muddy path that skirted the pine forest was now a quagmire.

For a few hours, I forgot I was an old dog and enjoyed splashing through the mud, running as best I could up and down the pack of Hashers keeping everyone together. Poor Boggy, with his short legs, was getting left behind and some of the girls found it a bit tiring also, so by the time we got to the brook crossing they were ready for a rest and lunch break, and as I was off my lead, I was able to do the circuit, begging and receiving scraps from everyone. At the stepping stones, most people managed to hop easily from rock to rock but the excessive rainfall had caused the water to be quite deep, therefore Boggy and I, with our little short legs, were unable to balance on the stones. So, with help and guidance from chivalrous Poacher, Boggy took his socks and shoes off and we both wadded across. As we had already lost quite a bit of time, Ian decided that the short section to the disused Lead mines was best to walk on the road and to completely avoid the 'bog of no return'. Crossing a wooden footbridge, we picked up St Kevin's Way through the mine and followed the shimmering brook down a rough, stepped path into Glendaloch. The scenery was stunning. (I never used this word until I met Ian, but there was no other word to describe it) Mum put me back on my lead as the group were spreading further apart, the fitter ones at the front raced on to the pub, some of whom did an extra loop, but I stayed with the slower ones at the back, who chatted, took photos and generally just took their time. We visited the stone Abbey and bell tower on our way and the girls enjoyed looking at the gift stalls. Eventually we all met up again at the pub, where I was pleasantly knackered and collapsed under a table while the others chatted and drank. An hour later, despite my tired legs feeling like jelly, we were off again, over another footbridge and into the forest. We followed the gravel track parallel to the river for about another mile to the village of Largh, where the minibus was due to meet us and return us back to our campsite. On the way, I missed my footing and tumbled into a drainage ditch and could have been washed under the road, if it hadn't been for Buzby's speedy reactions, jumping into the ditch and pulling me out.

As it was Poacher's birthday they all went to the pub for an evening meal, followed by a 'hoolie' in the brewery. I just couldn't face all that noise and merriment, I was shattered, but I'd had a wonderful day with my friends, so was content with curling up in my campervan bed for an early night.

The following day was Sunday so, after a slightly later start, we all set off in our vehicles for a tour of the Wicklow Mountains. Still enjoying Mum's chocolates, we stopped at Roundwood, which claims to be one of the highest villages in Ireland, for a walk about. We also visited an indoor Farmers Market where Mum bought me a new teddy (which was a rabbit) 'cos I hadn't played with my old one - I then carried it proudly in my mouth through the street back to the van, shoved it in the front with my old teddy and now I don't play with either. Our convoy followed us to Sally Gap viewpoint, where it was so windy that when we got out of the vehicles I could hardly walk across the road to admire the view of the lakes below; it literally took my breath away! Then we made our way to Johnny Fox's claiming to be the highest pub in Ireland, which is a popular tourist attraction for eaters and singers, so I was banished to the camper. "Grr!" Finally, we took the coastal route back to the campsite 'cos the ladies and I wanted to see the sea. We stopped for a quick paddle at Greystones beach, then I had another early tea and bedtime so that Mum and Ian could enjoy the Hasher's last evening in the campsite pub.

The reality of Nanny's death was now beginning to sink in as I realised I would never see her again and it saddened me more as we said our goodbyes to the others.

Instead of continuing our tour to explore the bottom left hand corner of Ireland, we were all now returning to England. The Hashers were catching their afternoon plane from Dublin, and we had a long drive to Rosslaire to catch an evening ferry.

Again, I wasn't allowed out of the van for the crossing, it was late and I was tired, so I settled down willingly to sleep. We arrived in Fishguard, South Wales just after midnight, so Ian pulled the camper into a carpark on the quay where we stayed the night.

"Goodbye Nanny"

After a sombre drive along the motorway to Bath in the pouring rain, we arrived at Auntie Sally's in time for tea. I chased her cat and ate its food, then settled down under the table while the others all chatted over my head. I overheard that Nanny had died suddenly from an embolism, and although I didn't know what one was, I knew I didn't want one. The following morning Mum disappeared into town with Auntie Sally and Uncle Andrew to see a solicitor, while Ian and I had a relaxing walk along the lane and caught up with a bit of rugby on TV, which we both enjoy. In the afternoon, the funeral director arrived, she was a lovely, soft spoken lady who I remember came to visit after Grandpa died. They talked

about Nanny a lot, saying what she would want for her funeral, but it upset me, so I curled up back under the table with my paws over my ears and went to sleep.

We travelled back to Devon the following day. As I mentioned previously, Scott had been looking after my doggie friends running the pet sitting business and he was currently minding my Westie friends Alfie and Barnie (or the 'testosterone twins' as I call them). Our own house was being let to someone else and we couldn't go home, so we stayed at Alfie and Barnie's and continued the pet sit for Scott, just for a couple of days until their mum and dad came home from holiday. We stayed in England for just over a month before moving on to France. We used a lovely small campsite quite a bit, which was literally a mile up the road from our home, and we did another pet sit for a week in the house of the two Setters, Bramble and Hector. Otherwise we parked the campervan in pub and public carparks or outside people's houses (that we knew of course). On Monday and Wednesday evenings, we were able to return to Hashing - well apart from the first Monday, when the camper was too wide to fit down the driveway of the meeting pub! I had gotten myself all excited, then we had to abandon the attempt and drive away as there was nowhere else to park - Gutted!

From our little local campsite, it was possible to use the bikes to travel around. We were cycling along the new cycle path from Exeter to Exmouth beach, on one lovely warm day that was going so well, until the return journey. Mum pedalled through a chicane gateway and caught the wheel of my trailer on a wooden stump at the bottom of the gate. The trailer tipped one way, corrected itself, but then as I tried to jump out, it tipped the other. Ian, who wasn't looking where he was going, then crashed into the back of us, landing on top of the trailer and squashing me in it! Mum got off her bike and rescued me from the twisted wreckage. Ian, however, was unable to unclip his feet from his bike pedals and was laid upside down with his bike on top of him, moaning. Some passers-by came to help him back on to his feet, which Mum and I thought was hilarious, but as he had obviously hurt his little finger, we tried not to laugh. With a bit of bending and brute force my trailer was straightened, albeit a bit wonky, so I wobbled nervously along in it back to Exeter and despite Ian's pride being in tatters, no serious damage was done.

Two days before Nanny's funeral we travelled back up to Bath and stayed again at Auntie Sally's house, where Mum spent the whole day filling the kitchen with the tummy rumbling smells of cakes, scones and pies cooking, while Ian, Uncle Andrew and I made ourselves useful by going for walks up to the park and watching TV. I accompanied Mum to the funeral which was held in the same church as Grandpa's, and again sat right in the front on the floor. I was very well behaved and listened intently to Aunty Sally's history of Nanny's life and Mum's funny poem. After the crematorium service, where once more I was allowed to attend, we had a scrummy tea party back in the church hall with all Nanny's friends and family. I didn't feel quite as sad as when Grandpa disappeared, but it is weird not knowing where they have both gone and that I will never see either of them again.

The weekend before we set sail for France, we met up once more with all the family on Exmoor and walked along the river to same remote spot where Mum and Auntie Sally had camped as children. We scattered Nanny's 'Dust' amongst the bracken where we had sprinkled Grandpa's only two years before, but, despite sniffing hard and searching the whole area, there was nothing left and I realised that he had gone forever!

Mon bon vacances

On October 18th 2016, jammed between a growling Doberman in a 4x4 and a metal wall, I was on my way to France!

We arrived the afternoon before at Poole harbour and slept the night in the camper alongside the perimeter fence, next to a porta-cabin and a heap of rusty iron girders. The Brittany Ferry had just pulled into the docks and its bright lights were making my eyes squint. I was mesmerised by the cars, lorries and caravans that were spilling out of it onto the quayside in front of me, all fighting to be the first ones ashore. The constant tick-over of its diesel engine purred throughout the night and lulled me to sleep. A couple of times I awoke and popped my head out between the van curtains, just to check that the view of the departure kiosks and street lights had not changed. Morning started early as cars were already arriving at the port. Mum dressed quickly and walked me over to the small grassy area for a poo and wee. We downed our breakfasts and were ready to join the already queueing ferry traffic. The lady in the kiosk asked to see my passport, then scanned my micro-chip to check that the numbers matched. She apologised for being unable to give it a stamp but did give us a big round sticker for the van windscreen, which said 'pet on board'. She wished us a good journey and minutes later we were driving up the metal ramp and into the belly of the ferry.

I had to stay in the campervan for the crossing and it was beginning to get rocky. I could feel my breakfast swaying up and down in my tummy, so the only thing for it was to go back to bed. Mum did come down to the car deck to check on me once during the four-hour journey to France, but I was fast asleep and totally unaware.

The next thing I knew *"je suis ici"* and we were driving on the wrong side of the road through the streets of Cherbourg. We stopped in a layby for me to have my first French wee, then continued on to our first night's stay in France at St Jean-de-la-Riviere; a holiday ghost town. Rows of eerie empty caravan parks and houses were all battened down with wooden or metal shutters for the winter, and hotels, shops and cafes were all vacant. We went for a walk to find the sea. I've learnt that French for the beach is '*la plage*', and '*la plage*' was huge, so I rolled in the soft sand and it was *magnifique*. The next day we ventured out on the bikes to the nearby village of Barneville-Carteret and found some shops, but nobody waved or smiled at me. The few people that we did see looked old and sad, far too concerned with their own affairs to even notice me sitting in my little trailer.

My French trip begins with us driving down the coast road of Normandy. Ian was adjusting to his new driving position on the road and I was trying to get used to having vehicles zoom past immediately on my left which was a bit scary, and I held my breath when they seemed too close! Mum was doing a grand job of deciphering the French maps, except every now and then I would get shoved off her lap onto the floor if navigating got a bit tricky. Between campsites, we stayed on Aires or Passions, which are generally some kind of farm or vineyard, where you can park the camper at night for free, although it is considered polite if you buy something of their produce. My first Passion experience was a cattle farm that sold smoked beef and sausages and we parked in the corner of the farmyard next to Hugo the hog, who was very friendly. Mum bought some *saucisson*, from the lady who spoke no English, which we shared, *et C'est tres bon*.

My next cycle outing a few days later, was from the campsite in Beauvier to Mont St Michel. It was warm and sunny as we cycled for about four miles along the river, then walked the remaining mile with other pedestrians. Heavy horses pulled carriage loads of people across the bridge to the island but I jumped every time they passed as I couldn't hear them coming up behind me! The streets inside the entrance gates were narrow and packed with excited holiday makers and the smell of freshly cooked crepes and gallettes filled the air. I tried to scrape bits off the floor but I was getting under people's feet and Mum pulled me on. (I was annoyed that I just missed a big piece of *saucisse*!) The stone steps rose steeply, and although I wore my leg support strap I still found it painful climbing. A little girl sitting on her dad's shoulders was singing, Twinkle Twinkle Little Star, which gave me a rhythm to walk with, but nearing the top Mum kindly carried me the last few steps. A friendly lady stopped and spoke to me on the way up. Apparently, I am now "*un chien; tres vieux mais tres mignon*". Despite looking very cute, yes, I did feel very old as I cautiously looked over the wall at the people below, which appeared like tiny ants running about. It made my head feel a little dizzy being so high up and I was glad when we returned to sea level, with gravity's assistance down the steps a lot quicker than I had climbed them! I felt claustrophobic, as there were far too many people crammed into too small a space for comfort on the island, and I almost ran over the bridge and causeway back to the security of my trailer.

The following day we went for a really long walk along the dirty, grey river into Ponterson. As most of it was cycle path I could be off my lead and I just about managed it, but my legs really ached on my return. I slept well that night, although I did start gnawing at another of my 'old dog' skin tags and made it bleed, so Mum bathed it in the cold liquid and tied a bandage around my leg, which stopped me aggravating it.

From the same campsite the following day, despite the misty morning start, we cycled in the opposite direction, exploring the French countryside. A lot of it was old railway track, so I could get out and walk through the crispy autumn leaves where I saw for the first time '*la chasse*' signs, which means hunting. It is very popular in France, which disappointingly meant that I hardly saw any wild animals.

Slightly further west along the north coast we parked the van and walked in the sunshine along the sandy beach into Saint Malo. Lots of dogs came up to play but being *quatorze ans* for heaven sake, I couldn't be bothered. We slowly walked at my pace, around on top of the old city walls, where there were plenty of new scents for me to sniff, although Ian gets a bit agitated if I take too long. I ate the remains of Mum's ham filled baguette, then settled down for a sleep while Ian enjoyed his glass of French beer. We headed back along the beach to the camper or 'camping car' as they call them over there, enjoying my final paddle in the sea before our journey headed south, away from the coast.

The main road followed the estuary inland to an old Tudor town built on a hill, called Dinan. My joints hurt as I walked around the cobbled streets, and each pebble twisted my back- left foot, which hurt my already increasingly twisted leg, so that the pain then shot through my hip. I hobbled faithfully and unquestioningly beside Mum down the hill towards the river, tears welling up in my eyes with each step. At last we reached the old quayside with a view of the old stone bridge, where I could lie down and rest, and was rewarded with some of her ice-cream as the cool breeze eased my pain. My return walk back up the cobbled hill was even slower than my descent, stopping at every opportunity to sniff or wee. Mum admired the window displays of the art studios which gave me a break, and somehow at snails pace, I gradually made it back to the old town. That night my eyes were burning red, so Mum gave me an extra dose of Metacam with my tea which helped me sleep, and by morning I was springing down the camper steps like a two year old again.

As we travelled along, sitting high on Mum's lap I got a brilliant view out of the front window. Northern France was so flat I could see for miles. It is mostly comprised of fields of vegetables and maize, and the farmers work very hard. Once the crops are harvested they spend day and night neatly ploughing, ready to plant again in the spring. Different sized birds of prey sit on the fences and posts, waiting to swoop down on any unsuspecting mouse or vole feeding in the fields. As we travelled further south, the fields changed to grape vines for as far as my eyes could see; row upon row, field after field of them.

The second Passion we stayed at was on a vineyard. We arrived mid-afternoon and the sun was still warm enough to enjoy walking through the avenues of vines and many still had bunches of juicy grapes hanging from them. I tried a few but unlike Ian, I wasn't that impressed. He bought two bottles of wine the next day.

On October 31st, Halloween, I usually dress up in a dog skeleton costume and go for a Hash run, but this year, from our campsite at Heric, I rode in my trusty trailer along the Nantes to Brest canal. We followed a trail of painted marmots on the pavements into the town of Blain, which was decorated with colourful chrysanthemums and the shops were also selling them to celebrate the Day of the Dead. We unexpectedly came across two chateaux, where one was like a stately home and the other more like a castle, so we picnicked on the grass before our long cycle back along the canal to the van. As it was late autumn our campsite was particularly quiet, with only one other campervan and a few residential chalets in use. Mum was cooking tea and I was lazily enjoying the view from our doorway. Suddenly, as bold as brass, around the corner walked a tabby cat! Well, I haven't moved so fast in years. I shot out of the van like a bullet from a gun and I didn't even use the little step. I reached the end of my long lead, then 'snap' went my collar! I had pulled the silver ring right out of the leather but kept on running. Mum shot out of the van door almost as fast as I did and was shouting at me to come back, but my 'selective' deafness meant I couldn't hear her. Three chalets, two gardens, a ditch and one car later she caught up with me. The cat had long gone but I was still wandering about looking. By the scruff of my neck I was escorted back to the camper and made to sit inside with the door firmly shut. Disgruntled, I went to bed but was rudely awakened about 8pm as a car and caravan pulled alongside. Mum commented that it was a bit late and dark to arrive on a site. As I was about to settle back down, another one pulled in, then another and another, followed by at least another five, plus a few big white vans, camper vans and cars! Doors were slamming, lights were shining, dogs were barking, children laughing and grown-ups were talking loudly, (Irish I think, although I couldn't make out what they were saying). Ian reckoned they were Gypsies, probably returning to Great Britain after working in France for the summer. Mum said, "I hope they don't come around 'Trick or Treating', we don't have any sweets!"

They didn't, and soon the noise and excitement died down so I could return to sleep. The next morning, when Ian and I went out for my early constitutional wee there were vans parked everywhere! They were parked at every angle, on every bit of spare grass around us, each one with its little outside dog kennel containing a skinny, yappy dog. We tip-toed past and back trying not to disturb them, and a mutual decision was made from that moment; it was probably best we move on.

From Heric, we drove along small, narrow roads following the Loire River towards Angers, noted on the map as a scenic route. The river Loire splits many times, making smaller narrow rivers that join back together further down, before dividing again. We crossed lots of bridges over and back, but each rivulet had hardly any water in it. We camped on an Aire beside the Loire and I walked along the dry river bed, playing in the sandy banks which would normally be underwater. The Loire Valley was very picturesque, with fields full of grazing cattle, trees laden with huge balls of mistletoe and lots of elegant chateaux that reminded me of enchanted fairy tale castles guarding the little stone villages. Some houses protruded from the rocks and there were even tiny homes built into the caves, where they also cultivated mushrooms. I loved getting out of the van for a quick walk and to stretch my legs every time they stopped to take a photo or make a cup of tea, as there were always lots of new smells to sniff and interpret.

The city of Angers is dwarfed by its huge castle, which I reluctantly trudged around, dragging my feet. A steep flight of stone steps covered in broken glass rose to the Cathedral, which Mum carried me up so as not to cut my pads. Ian went in to look around, while I stayed outside the big wooden door with Mum. I scrutinized the stone gargoyles and eyed up a local beggar, and wondered if I sat there looking pathetic, would people drop things into my bowl? Until we arrived in the centre of the town we had failed to realise that 1st November was a public holiday in France. Luckily for me, most of the shops were closed but we did find a bar open where I could sit in the sun, amused by the long bendy busses manoeuvring clumsily round the sharp corner in the road. I don't enjoy town visits but I realise sometimes I have to compromise in exchange for my lovely paddles in the sea. Our route out of Angers was slightly stressful and I got demoted to the floor, as Ian accidently took the Toll Motorway in the direction of Paris, and although I have always fancied going to the capital, it was not scheduled for this trip! Mum managed to direct him off at the next junction, so luckily this detour only cost us 4.80 Euros and we eventually picked up our correct route towards Saumur.

Now in the region of la Vienne, we were making our way towards our planned overnight stop at 'Lips and Stumpy's' house, (ex-Plymouth Hashers, that I've known for years) who now live at Liglet. We stopped for a leg stretch at a town called Chauvigny, typically built on the side of a hill, and we strolled around the outside of the old castle ruins. At the bottom of the hill, looking back up, Mum asked, "Are they vultures up there?" Knowing that they were huge birds that could strip my flesh from my bones in minutes, I cowered down behind her and slowly peered up, expecting to see a group of them circling overhead. At first, I couldn't see them but as I quickly scanned the top of the crumbling castle wall I noticed a large cage, and in it were two very depressed looking vultures. They looked enormous, even from where I was standing, and although I was relieved that they were behind bars, I did feel strangely sorry for these magnificent creatures that should be soaring freely in the air, not prisoners in a castle. Apparently in the summer months they are allowed out twice a day for a flying display but as it was November, they still had an awfully long time confined in their cage until they could stretch their wings and fly again. I know I get cabin fever when I have been stuck in the van for a few hours, so goodness knows how they must feel! I didn't bother starting a mental tally for vultures as I probably won't ever see another, but if I do then I will always remember this sad pair and add them to my list.

Montmorillion, another old town we stopped at, was once the medieval home of writers. I scanned the streets trying to get some inspiration before we drove the last few miles to Lips and Stumpy's home. They have lived in their lovely, typically French house, with a pretty enclosed garden, for eight years now and are quite an asset to their community; organising the art club, children's Christmas party and a walking group. Unfortunately, the French locals cannot understand the concept of Hashing, they say "Why run from a pub, back to a pub - Why not just stay in the pub?" Mmm? As I'm getting older, I am understanding their logic! It was a nice change to spend the evening in the company of other people. They had a roaring log fire and Lips put a rug down in front of it especially for me to lie on, and then fed me tit bits when she thought no one was looking (including the lamb that was left over from their evening meal. Don't tell Stumpy). Their niece, Laura, was staying for a few weeks, so I let her cuddle and smooth me while I slept. I tried pretending I was older and more fragile than I really was in the hope that I could stay in front of the fire all night, but despite plummeting temperatures Mum insisted that we slept in the van. Luckily, I wore my new fleecy sweatshirt to bed, which looked ridiculous but kept me warm, as it dropped below freezing that night!

I was sad to leave Liglet, as I needed a few home comforts at my age. I gazed despondently out of the side window of the van as they waved us off down the road, but quickly remembered how lucky I was having the opportunity to travel when I thought about the two pathetic vultures trapped in their prison cell.

We stopped at Vivonne for Mum to do some shopping, while Ian and I strolled along the river contemplating the disused canoe slalom course. We then drove through the forest of Sauvant, where we found our Passion for the night on a cheese farm. No-one was about when we arrived so Mum and I got out to look around. I could hear a noise coming from inside one of the huge sheds and the lights were on, so we looked inside. Goodness, I have never seen so many little white goat kids in my life, all jumping and playing in the hay, with not a care in the world, (well not till the big lorry came later that night) A young lad appeared from through the goats but spoke no English, so Mum explained as best she could in French that we wanted to stay the night. He agreed, and after the big lorry had gone it was a relatively quiet night (apart from the customary barking dog and chiming church bell). Next morning, Mum politely bought some cheese from the lady in their farm shop, who questioned her choice on the pyramid shaped one, before quickly popping it into a paper bag. We left the farm and Mum put the cheese into our fridge for later. Although it was a cold, frosty morning the sun was shining and we continued our journey through the towns of Couhe and Civray, stopping for a quick walk around an old stone and wooden market place, before having lunch. Mum opened the fridge, but OMG - I thought someone had been sick in there! The smell was intense and made my tummy heave - It was the blimmin goat's cheese! Mum heroically tried some on a dry cracker then passed a piece to Ian. The look on his face said it all, making me slightly hesitant when some came my way to try. It was better than peanut butter (which I detest) but only slightly, tasting soft and creamy but dry at the same time and it left a sour, bitter aftertaste in my mouth, yuk! Mum reluctantly put the remainder in the bin; she hates throwing food away. Ian did accidently buy goat's cheese again (twice!) but at least they were more edible and not as pungent as the soft pyramid.

We stayed for three nights on a campsite near Ruffec, which was a nice feeling, as if I actually belonged somewhere and could relax in the sun outside the van on the grass. There was a lovely paddling river just below the site with off-lead walks in both directions along it and not far into the town to get shopping.

Friday 11th November was Armistice Day and another public holiday in France. We watched a small Remembrance Parade in St Maixent. Firemen, dignitaries and other villagers stood on parade while they played the French National Anthem over loud speakers and placed flower wreaths around the war memorial. I wanted to back away but Mum insisted I stood and listened in respect for the people that had died in the war. I don't understand what war is but I don't like people dying, so I lowered my head and kept quiet.

Later that afternoon, we drove to the 'Vert Venice', which is an area of canal networks around the small tourist town of Coulon. Rowing boats and punts were moored up along the quay as the sun shimmered on the water. I had been on a punt in Cambridge once, so was excited when Ian suggested we might have a go. We wandered along the canal with the other visitors then chatted about prices with the girl in the booking kiosk, but by then it was getting late, so it was decided (although no one asked my opinion!) that we would go punting the following day. At first light, I shoved my head out through the curtains to check on the weather, only to discover it was pouring with rain, so, as there was no movement from Mum or Ian in the back, I turned around on my chair and settled back down to sleep. By the time they got up, pouring rain had relented to annoying drizzle. I still wanted to go punting but Ian, who loathes the rain (in case you have forgotten), suggested otherwise. We ended up just walking along the boarded cycle path over the marshes and back, which was OK as rain never bothers me and I was off my lead deciphering all the musty smells, but nevertheless I was really disappointed that we didn't go punting.

We headed towards the coast again and found a nice campsite, slightly inland, where we stayed for another three nights. The jovial campsite owner, who enjoyed practicing his English, said that we could find fossils and possibly fool's gold on the nearby beach. I have spent many a happy hour looking for fossils on the beaches of Dorset with Mum, so the next day off we set in search of treasure. We found a small beach just north of La Tranche, full of big stones with a rocky cliff behind; perfect. Mum started searching the water's edge while Ian attempted to destroy the cliff face! I just picked up any stone, carried it in my mouth for a while before swapping it for another. I found a few interestingly shaped pebbles before being distracted by the smell of rotting fish further along the beach. I love spending the day on a beach just poking about between the driftwood and seaweed, checking if there is anything disgusting to eat. Mum did find a few lumps of old volcanic rock and a couple of belemnites but nothing of any interest to a professional geologist. The time passed quickly and it was all too soon to return to the campsite. I gobbled down my tea and waited for scraps from theirs, but my legs were so tired I gave in and curled up on my sheepskin rug in the front of the van. My paws still smelt of the beach, so I curled them over my nose, enabling me to breathe in the aromas and drift off, reliving my lovely day.

The next day we set off in the van, following directions from a leaflet Ian had picked up on the campsite to an enchanting woodland walk. The instructions were sketchy but we eventually found our way to the car park. There was nobody else around and we were not sure in which direction to start the walk. Mum asked a French builder working in a nearby house, who told her in the little English he knew, that it had shut down about four years ago! Disappointed that I was not going to see fairies and pixies sitting around magical pools like in the picture on the leaflet, I climbed back in the van and we set of in search of 'Indian Forest', a woodland activity centre.

Unfortunately, as it was winter, that too was closed. So as not to disappoint me further Ian suggested we walked around the grounds. The first direction we took led us into the garden of a large private house, so we turned around quickly and retraced our steps. We then followed a path which took us behind the activity centre and down a footpath underneath the dormant high ropes course, picking up on a disused nature trail which led us deeper and deeper into the woods. Feeling a little apprehensive, I hoped it would turn a full circle if we kept following the painted markers to the left. So I climbed a few hills, slid down a bank, waded through mud and eventually made it back to the carpark where our trusty little home was waiting.

Rain came with the next day as we left the campsite and headed for the pretty harbour town of La Rochelle. I had to sit on the floor as Mum was concentrating on navigating our way through the busy roads to the Aire. The special Aires book quoted that there were two in the town, but the first one we came to was now just a carpark with no provision for camping cars. Frustrated, we slid back into the heavy traffic and followed signs to the port in search of the second. I had been used to staying on Aires and campsites with only one or two other vans, so was shocked to see that La Rochelle was so popular. There were loads of camper vans (Mum said about 30), all parked side by side along the sea wall next to a marina full of pleasure cruisers and yachts. The rain was sheeting down and it was bitterly cold, everybody was tucked inside their vans and only ventured out if their dog needed to relieve itself. Most of them had done so in the little grassy area at the front of our van, and nobody in France bothers to pick up after their dogs. There is mess everywhere, despite the councils providing plastic poo bags (which Mum took loads of to replenish our stock) and plenty of bins, but no one uses them. I hate it all over the grass, as I can't even walk without standing in someone else's poo! Ian slid our van into a space between two others and battened down for the evening, but the rain hammered on the roof, the wind rocked and shook the van and the masts of the sailing boats 'chinked' all night. By morning it had subsided a little but I had had a restless night and was still bleary eyed when Ian insisted it was time for my morning wee. After breakfast, the weather was still a little 'iffy' and, unable to catch a bus into the Vieux Port, we set off walking in the drizzle along the cycle path around the marina, unsure how far it was or how long it was going to take us. Following the estuary, we soon reached a little ferry that chugged across to the Chain towers on the other side. It only cost a couple of Euros for Mum and Ian and I was free, so we hopped aboard. We walked around the old port and town before being enticed into a covered outdoor restaurant, where the lady welcomed me in and offered a bowl of water. A few other people were sat at tables quietly eating, which encouraged Mum and Ian to have lunch, so I settled down under the table. The trouble was, that pigeons kept walking in and out of the open doorway, and although I tried my best to ignore them by closing my eyes, subconsciously a loud bark came out, which made me and everyone else in the restaurant jump! Mum told me off, although I didn't mean to do it, and I tried settling down again but the blimmin pigeons would not go away, and the more I tried to ignore them, the nearer they got to me. Again, I barked to try and get them to go away, but they took no notice. Everyone was staring at us now. Mum gave me one of her 'looks' and I knew I was in trouble! I didn't get a tit-bit that meal and we promptly left the restaurant. By the time we had walked back to the marina, the wind had really picked up again and was howling around the van, so Ian moved it to a more sheltered position between two massive motor homes further along. That night, the wind blew hard, shaking the van violently and the rain absolutely 'chucked it down', turning to hail. I thought the windscreen was going to break, as each huge hailstone cracked against the glass, and consequently none of us got much sleep!

A few days later I watched tractors collecting oysters from the mud, as I played on the beach in Fouras, before walking along the sea front to look at the castle. It was now mid-November and very few other tourists were about. All the towns in France were preparing for Christmas and putting up decorations and lights, which was exciting as I love Christmas. I do believe this year might be quite different though, as we are due to spend it with Rent Boy, an ex-Hasher from home, who had taken over a dog and cat Boarding Kennels in April, and Mum had offered our services over the busy Christmas period.

Unusually, we had to travel the next few miles on main roads, as Ian wanted to visit Cognac, but I was allowed on Mum's lap as she wasn't struggling with the map. The dual carriageway out of Rochefort took us over a big, new, concrete bridge and as I looked out of the bottom of the side window I could see an old, metal transporter bridge, like the ones on my walk around Britain in Newport and Middlesburgh. I wanted to stop and have a ride on this one so stared hopefully up at Ian, but he was concentrating hard on driving and we were travelling too fast. It soon became just a tiny speck as I looked back. Disappointed I grumbled, settled back down by Mum's feet and reminisced.

There was a rowing regatta taking place in Cognac when we arrived, with lots of people cheering their children racing in boats down the river. While Ian visited the Cognac Chateau Distillery for a tour and tasting (as 'no dogs allowed'), Mum and I wandered along the river, then sat in the sunshine on the grass to watch the entertainment. I wanted to bark at the excited children but caught Mum's eye and thought better of it.

Apart from La Rochelle, all the campsites and Aires we have stayed on so far have been nice and peaceful; disregarding the token annoying barking dog and church bell that rings the hour every hour. We found a lovely quiet Aire on the outskirts of a pretty hillside town called Belac, next to a park which was perfect for my late night wees and near the river, so ideal for paddles and dog walks. During the afternoon, just to keep them happy, I trudged up the steep hill for a look around the town, but as dogs seem to poo where they like in France, I was surprised to see a designated dog toilet next to the big church. It was a sandy area, which I thought was more likely to be used by all the local cats, as further along the street I saw a little garden full of small wooden boxes and shelters with bowls of food for stray local moggies. I tried to get my head through the wire fence to assist with the food eating but Mum was holding the other end of the lead and restrained me. Back at the camper, after eating my own tea, I settled down on my sheepskin rug, looking forward to a peaceful night's sleep. It was not raining and not too windy, so should be perfect. Suddenly, I heard a loud 'Rap!' something hard had just hit the top of the van. At first, I thought someone was throwing a stone at us! Then again 'Rap, Rap'. Each time, just as I settled back down, it would happen again making me jump. It was too dark to go and investigate then, so I had to put up with the constant rapping until the morning, only to discover that we were parked underneath a nut tree!

There was only one other van on our next campsite, at Bignac, which was owned by an English family from Cornwall, alongside their own fishing lake which was lovely to walk around off my lead. From here we took the bikes out for a long cycle into Ruillac, mainly along rough farmer's tracks. The only down-side of being towed behind Mum is, that I get annoying little stones flick up from her back wheel into my face. She has tried to buy a mudguard to prevent me getting a black eye but has been unsuccessful. We wandered around the town, found a café for the mandatory beer stop, and then as it was getting late, made our return journey along a cycle path parallel to the main road. We were doing so well until it deviated away through a village that I didn't recognise. We got off and walked up the hill, as I'm too heavy for Mum to tow up steep inclines, and set every dog in the village off barking one by one as we passed. That night Mum borrowed the film 'Marley and me' on DVD from the site, which is about the funny life story about a naughty Labrador dog and all the tricks he got up to. I was really enjoying it, curled up by Mum's feet, until he got old and died! The ending was so sad, that I wished I'd never started watching it.

Christmas is coming, will Santa?

We eventually made it off the site after another wet night; the camper was stuck in the mud and it took a lot of skidding and grass ruining to move us! The Autumn-coloured forests lined the roads as we continued our windy route into the Dordogne area of France. We visited many old, musty smelling towns on the way and I remember getting quite upset as we walked into St Leonards de Noblat. I thought that there had been a terrible accident. - It looked like Santa had just crash-landed into the village! Branches from pine trees, decorations, lights and 'The big man's' sleigh were strewn across the square. Thankfully, Mum explained that they were only in the process of preparing the village for Christmas and everything had just been dumped in the centre, waiting to be displayed properly.

We drove on to find a tranquil Aire, beneath the falling autumn leaves next to a huge lake, on the outskirts of Bujaleuf. I gently paddled at the water's edge in the evening sun, while Mum tried to take clever artistic photos of the trees reflecting a mirror image in the water. A French campervan pulled in opposite us, whose occupants turned out to be English, and they had an old German Shepherd dog, who I'm proud to say I tolerated quite close to our van without growling. (Probably 'cos she was bigger than me) It was a beautiful location, in complete contrast to our next Aire, spent opposite the busy railway station at Allassac, where instead of the usual barking dog or church bells keeping me awake at night, it was high speed trains zooming past!

With me back on the floor so that Mum could concentrate on navigating, we avoided the toll motorway and skirted around the outskirts of the big city of Brive, towards Souillac. Returning to Mum's lap, I was glad when we finally reached the huge, wide Dordogne River and followed the main road parallel to it, in the direction of Sarlat. Out of the side window, while admiring the river, I noticed a lovely cycle path running adjacent to us. I dug my claws into Mum's legs in the hope that she would see it, so that we could stop and have a break from driving, but she was busy chatting to Ian about our next couple of days staying at Rent Boy's. I was confused as to why we were going there so early, as I knew it was still a month until Christmas. We stopped briefly for a leg stretch and wee at Gourdon, where I saw kiwi fruits growing on a tree in someone's garden!

Rent Boy's 'over-the-phone' directions were brilliant and we managed to find his house without getting lost. As we pulled into their driveway he came out to meet us, followed by his wife 'Desperate Housewife' and their baby boy, who both had stinking colds. I thought they seemed pleased to see me, until our tour of their property, when they showed me a cage in the kennels and suggested I slept there! "NO WAY!" Not in a million years was I going in that! "Come on Rent Boy, it's me - Havoc. You have known me for years. I'm the dog that walked 5,000 miles around Britain and raised £50,000 for charity - I'm better than that!"

Had he forgotten who I was?

Mum sensed my apprehension (or rather disbelief)

and suggested that I stayed in the van. Apparently since moving to the kennels, their own dogs Betty and Spooky, have become very territorial over their home. I was slightly disbelieving of this, as surely, they would remember me, I used to Hash with them back in Devon. Reluctantly I stayed in the van, at least until bedtime, and then by distracting Betty and Spooky in the lounge, I was sneaked in through the back door and upstairs to bed, without them noticing. OMG though, it was so hot in the bedroom that night, we had all been used to plummeting temperatures in the van. It was a very uncomfortable night, as every time I tried to move, my claws slipped on the shiny laminate floor and I was getting myself in a right state! Then Mum was up wandering about and balancing on the bedside table, trying to open the window. By morning, the room had cooled and it was time for me to get up and be sneaked out of the house using the reverse of last night's operation and back to the camper. I got a bit fed up of looking at the same view, but I made up on the sleep I didn't get last night, and Ian visited me plenty of times for leg stretching walks and wees. After Rent Boy had finished his work of walking dogs and cleaning cat trays, we were taken in his car to the local Farmer's Market. I was made to sit in the boot with the baby's pushchair, as apparently in France, dogs are not allowed to travel inside a car unrestrained. (i.e. Not sit on your mum's lap in the front.) The market was full of my two favourite smells; dogs and food. There was a stall selling roasted chickens and one selling raw fish, where I managed to quickly scrape up some squashed bits from off the floor. After a rest at the café, we strolled down to the local park for the baby to play on the swings and me to paddle in the lake, before returning in the boot of the car back to my camper van refuge. In the afternoon, we all went for a walk up the lane and with Betty and Spooky on their leads they were fine; a couple of bottom sniffs and I think they remembered me. I'm pretty sure that when we return at Christmas they will allow me into their house.

Over the last few days my dog food had begun to run low, so Rent Boy kindly gave me a bag of the dry food they use in the kennels to try. I liked it and it was fine in my tummy, so Mum mixed it in with the dry food that I had left. Unfortunately, after a couple of days it made my skin itch. I knew I didn't have fleas as Mum had recently put that horrible cold stuff on the back of my neck, but I kept gnawing myself to relieve the aggravation. She realised straight away that it was the change of food that was causing me to scratch and bite my skin, so then had to sort through the whole bag of kibble, separating my old food piece by piece from the new.

We left Rent Boy's house fairly early the next day. It was a lovely feeling to be back on the road again and in the morning sunshine we headed off towards Rocamador, an old pilgrimage town built into the side of an over-hanging rock. We parked on the Aire behind the big church at the top of the rock. It was still lovely and sunny, so Ian got the chairs out and we sat and relaxed for a couple of hours, watched by a pack of stray cats. After lunch, I set off on my pilgrimage, gravity assisted down hundreds of stone steps, through archways and narrow alleyways, to the old part of town below. The town was 'sympathetically' decorated for Christmas, with branches of pine tree, silver foil bows and decorations cut out of polystyrene. Little Santa figures were climbing ladders, trying to get into people's windows at every opportunity - tacky but fun. I had a rest in a café, while Mum and Ian enjoyed a glass of beer, and prepared myself for the much slower ascent back to the top, where I stopped whenever I could to catch my breath. It wasn't until we got back to the summit that Mum noticed that the funicular railway was actually working – "Cheers Mum!" After tea, Ian wanted to venture out again and look at the rock town lit up by floodlight. I was reluctant as my legs were really aching, but as usual I relented. However, it was a complete waste of time for me as I couldn't see over the wall, but I did manage to grab a mouthful of cat poo on the way - disgusting I know, but irresistible! The sky was so clear that night that the temperature dropped well below freezing, I was so cold in the van and I didn't have my fleecy sweatshirt on. I tried to curl up in as tight a ball as I could, but I could still feel a bitterly cold breeze down the back of my neck. Usually in the mornings the front windows are dripping with condensation, but strangely, not this morning. As Ian opened the front curtains he noticed HIS side window had been left open all night (and probably all day). Then, to add insult to injury he had the audacity to blame me for opening it! "Yes of course Ian, I just started the van in the night without you noticing and opened the electric window!" - I'm clever, but not that clever!

Although I thought I was the only one who had seen the cycle path along the Dordogne the other day, Ian had also spotted it. So, we returned, parked the van outside the Marie in Peyrillac and cycled along the river bank to Carsac-Aillac and back. It was so pretty travelling through an avenue of leaf-moulting trees and overhanging rocks, with plenty of opportunities for me to get out and walk. I was off my lead when I saw a sparrow hawk struggling on the ground in front of me trying to pick up a smaller bird in its talons, but it was too heavy and he couldn't fly off with it. There was a lot of squawking and feather flapping as the smaller bird was putting up a good fight, so after numerous attempts the sparrow hawk had to give up and the little bird managed to get away. I meticulously searched in the long grass where he had run but couldn't find him.

We awoke to morning mist as we continued along the Dordogne to Bergerac, which for me wasn't a very interesting town, except for a wide dirty river that I couldn't paddle in and a couple of highly scented lamp posts. We then drove all afternoon for miles through fields and fields of vineyards, with now completely bare vines, to a campsite just outside Montguyon where we stayed and explored the area for four rather cold days. Each morning I woke to find ice on the inside of windscreen. (Mum said Jack Frost had called – but I must have missed him). The outside water taps were frozen, the washing that had been hung out overnight was as stiff as cardboard on the line and the grass was completely white with frost, which I enjoyed wriggling on. Through the freezing fog on the Saturday morning I could hear dogs barking excitedly and horns blowing, which meant '*La chasse*' were on their way. I could see men wearing fluorescent jackets through the trees close behind our van and reassured that there was a tall wire fence between them and me. I didn't fancy being ripped apart by a pack of frenzied hounds. The campsite owners were Dutch and very helpful. They gave us maps of walks and bike rides in the area, along farmers' tracks and lanes, which we tried but got a bit lost on both. On our return, I saw trickles of fresh blood on the road where the fluorescent jackets had been, meaning some poor creature had lost its life for the so called 'pleasure' of others, which sent an unpleasant shiver down my spine.

Returning to the coast again, we spent a couple of nights on an Aire at Blaye, an old town with a citadel and a tidal river, almost full to the top of the quay with thick mud, which Mum banned me from. We found a brilliant cycle path called '*Velo Vert*', which uses an old disused railway line, and I rode in my trailer but also walked for quite a bit. In the distance I could hear the horns of '*La chasse*', but then all of a sudden, a little deer shot across the path at top speed in front of me, closely followed by hounds running just as fast, and then not quite so closely behind were the men in their fluorescent jackets. I stood motionless and watched them disappear across the field down an avenue of vines and I held my breath as at the end of the vines was a busy main road. It was too far away to see what happened next (luckily), but I just hope the deer made it safely across.

Still in the Dordogne area we headed for another Passion, again on a vineyard, at St Emillion, which is famous for its wine shops. There were cars everywhere in the town. Every parking space was full and vehicles were pulling in on the sides of the road, so we joined them to investigate the attraction. It was a very old medieval town, celebrating its *'Festival de Noel'*. The steep, narrow, stone streets tastefully decorated for Christmas were full of people busily buying presents from all the specialist wine shops and Christmas market stalls. 'Jingle bells' and other festive songs were playing over loud speakers into the street, encouraging us to embrace the Christmas spirit, so despite the loud vibrations hurting my ears I did my best to conform and be cheerful.

The next couple of days were misty as we drove along miles of tree lined roads, stopping regularly to look at yet more old towns. Heading in the direction of Bordeaux, we found a campsite not too far from the city, just outside a little village called Creon, where we stayed for five nights. Creon had a disused railway line converted into a cycle path, so presented a great opportunity to use my trusty trailer again. We passed Chateaux, vineyards and overgrown woodlands, where Mum climbed a bank and picked some holly with berries to add to our already Christmas decorated camper. (We even had a tree called Mary, who now had pretty lights as well.) The following day, we drove from Creon into the busy city of Bordeaux. Ian found a parking space right next to the Garrone River and we leisurely strolled along past cafés and boutiques, where there were lots of lovely French town dog smells on lamp posts and benches.

Now I am older it takes me so long to try and sort out all the different scents, it is easier for me to just join in their 'who can wee the highest game'. We stopped for the mandatory beer break, so I could rest my legs and relax in the sun whilst gazing across the sparkling water, which is apparently the biggest estuary in Europe. As we walked back along the embankment, ginormous lorries with trailers and massive motorhomes pulled into the big gravel area one after the other behind our camper. Mum said it was a circus arriving. I didn't know what a circus was but it looked exciting and very important.

On the Saturday Ian was up and dressed very early. He left Mum and I cuddled up in bed, so that he could walk into Creon to catch an early bus back into Bordeaux. His favourite rugby team, The Exeter Chiefs, were playing against The Bordeaux Beagles and he had managed to get a ticket to watch. (I wanted to go as well, until he explained that they were not dogs.) Mum and I stayed on the campsite writing this book and just generally pottered about. When he returned, (triumphant because the Chiefs had won) he said that the enormous circus tent had been erected, and he had seen their promotion poster describing performing lions, tigers, elephants and horses, plus clowns and a motorbike display team. It sounded so exciting I wanted to go and see it, but then I don't suppose for one minute that they would let me in, unless of course Mum puts shoes on my back feet and I walk in just on my front legs. (They might even offer me a job!)

I decided not to run off and join the circus, and instead I stayed with Mum and Ian and drove for miles through pine forests to Arcachon, where we climbed the Dune of Pilat, over 100 meters high and apparently the highest sand dune in Europe! I don't know who measures all these phenomena, but it was very high and made the neighbouring houses look like models, and the people walking on it looked like minute ants. It was extremely steep and hard to walk as my feet kept sinking in, so we approached the top diagonally to make it a bit easier. I wanted to practice my 'polar bear' sliding on my back down the slope, but it was difficult as Mum kept me firmly on my lead, knowing I would get excited and run off. It was awesome! There was sand as far as I could see and 100 metres below me was the sparkling Atlantic Ocean, inviting me to run down for a paddle, although I realised it would be a hell of a climb back to the top. Mum unfastened my lead briefly so I could enjoy a back wriggle before making our diagonal descent. I was desperate to run down but she held me back, knowing I would probably injure myself in the process, but then just before we reached the bottom, she unclipped my lead and I was off like a bullet. I raced to the bottom, my back legs nearly over taking my front legs, resulting in an undignified roly poly at the bottom. Oh Boy, was I stiff the next day, but it was worth it, and I haven't had so much fun in ages.

Mum navigated us along a quiet road that ran parallel to the canal Midi, crossing several narrow bridges from one side to the other looking for an Aire which was advertised in the book. But when we eventually arrived in the town we found that it no longer existed. We retraced our route back to the last village, where we found an area designated for five camping cars in a car park right next to the canal, sharing facilities with any boats that moor alongside. We parked up and walked into the single street town which had no shops or cafes, just a Marie, (where the mayor lives I think). By half past four we were back at the camper and Mum was brewing her afternoon cup of tea, when Jack pulled up alongside in his fiberglass yacht. He was panicking because the service point which provided electricity, only accepted tokens purchased from the Marie, which closed at 5pm, so he left us in charge of his boat while he dashed up to the village. Mum made him a 'cuppa' on his return and we all stood outside chatting for ages about his travels. He told us he was from Sweden and had sailed around England, across the Channel then down the coast of France and was now in the process of motoring through the Canal Midi heading to the Mediterranean Sea. He was eventually making his way to Italy, before attempting to sail the Atlantic to America with a final destination in the Caribbean. Ian was mesmerized by his adventure, but I took it all with a 'pinch of salt' as he didn't look as if he had two pennies to rub together and his little yacht was broken and it didn't look big enough to cross a huge ocean. Anyway, he kept Mum and Ian amused with his story, although all I could concentrate on was my tummy rumbling, wondering how long he was going to keep talking. It was past my tea time, Mum had just bought a sack of expensive new dog food for me and I couldn't wait to try it.

We were now only a few miles away from Rent Boy's house again and I was getting excited as I knew that meant it would soon be Christmas. 'Desperate Housewife' and their little boy had returned to England for a holiday, so we were going to the kennels to help out for a few days over this busy period. We arrived early afternoon and went straight out for a walk with Betty and Spooky so that we could meet on 'neutral ground'. All was going to plan, and I think they remembered me, so I followed them into the house and as I had predicted, all was fine, they had a good sniff around me but showed no aggression. Ian kept an eye on us during the afternoon while Mum and Rent Boy walked the kennel dogs, fed them and put them to bed.

The smells of Rent Boy cooking tea wafted from the kitchen and smelt delicious, so to be on the safe side I was shut behind the stair gate in the lounge. I stayed there while they ate their meal around the table but I did get agitated and barked several times as Spooky and Betty were hovering for scraps. I was beginning to panic as the dishes were cleared away and stupidly kept barking, making everyone get cross with me, so Mum grabbed my collar and tried to 'persuade' me to go outside. I wasn't keen to go and Betty was trying to trip me up with her big black paws and Spooky was getting excited by her actions, so Mum picked me up.

"Howling shih-tzus!" Suddenly, I was screaming out as pain shot up my leg. Spooky had jumped up and sunk his teeth firmly into my back leg and was hanging on. I was still screaming in pain as Rent Boy was shouting at Spooky, and Mum was trying to get him to release his grip. For a few minutes, it was pandemonium and it really hurt. I think I actually felt his teeth on my bone! He was clamped on and determined not to let go! Eventually, between the three of them, I was lowered to the floor. Ian held me while Mum sat on Spooky and prised his jaws apart, releasing my leg but she was bitten on the finger in the process. She then threw Spooky in the larder and Ian put me outside. I limped about for a bit but my leg wasn't broken. After Mum had calmed down she came out and gave my leg a good examination. I had two nasty puncture wounds either side just below my hock. Luckily there was some ointment from the Irish vet left, so Mum bathed my wounds regularly and they soon healed. Needless to say, we three dogs were never trusted together again, and I have to admit that my judgement was wrong about Spooky and Betty - they didn't like me after all! I guess Christmas wasn't going to be exactly as I had imagined.

After the attack, I stayed in the van during the day. Mum was busy helping in the kennels and cattery so Ian kept up my visits and regularly walked me up the lane and back. In the evenings, with careful juggling in and out of doorways, Betty and Spooky would stay one side of the stair gate in the kitchen, while I got the better deal and enjoyed the log burner in the lounge. Wee times and bed time was a skilful manoeuvring act, and that way we never

came into contact again. Mum worked hard helping the cats and dogs which I occasionally met if Ian was out walking me at the same time. I met Sampson the French Bulldog who, with his sharp canine teeth looked like a devil dog, Charlie the soppy Golden Retriever and a little Shih-tzu cross Poodle called Ted Baker - a great name, but the little shit-poo kept me awake all night barking and whining.

The next day Ian took the camper van into Gourdon for some new front tyres while Rent Boy drove Mum and me into Cazels, where I was due to see the vet. I was a little confused by the visit as I felt fine, and my leg was healing nicely. We mistakenly arrived an hour before they opened because, like most businesses in France, they were closed for a two and a half - three hour lunch break! We wandered round the local lake, which was calming and I sniffed around looking for scraps of bread the ducks may have left, while Mum and Rent Boy chatted on a bench. I reluctantly slouched into the vet's reception area but the nurse didn't even look at me; no weighing, no cold thermometer thrust up my bum, just civilised talking, and she then handed Mum a bottle of Metacam in exchange for 80 Euros. If only things were that easy back home. On the drive back they talked of visiting a Christmas Market the next day in Sarlat.

At last it was Christmas Eve, and only one more day to go. After being sneaked out of the house and returned to the confinement of the van, I had my breakfast and morning ritual walk up the lane with Ian. I was looking forward to my market visit, as it would be a nice change from staring out of the van window for hours on end. I always manage to find something edible to scrape off the floor at a market and a Christmas one would probably have festive music, decorated trees and maybe Santa would be there? The three of them were chatting excitedly as they came out of Rent Boy's house, got in his car and just drove off - I couldn't believe it! Had Mum completely forgotten about me? I slumped back down on the seat and sulked. Apparently, the local police are very vigilant at this time of year and as I didn't have a cage or seat belt, Rent Boy thought it best I didn't travel in the car. (Poor excuse, I thought)

Thankfully, they weren't too long. Mum cooked a turkey roast dinner for them that evening, which is the tradition in France, and brought some out for me in the van. It was delicious, plus I saw Mum put a bit extra in the fridge for tomorrow. I was sneaked upstairs again that night but couldn't settle, because one eye kept popping open to see if 'He' had been.

Eventually I must have drifted off. It was just beginning to get light in the bedroom and I could see across the room. Mum was still in bed, so I looked around for signs of presents, but there was nothing. I'm sure last night was Christmas Eve, and Santa always visits me, but sure enough the room was bare. I knew I had been good, (well as good as I could be) maybe because I was in France he couldn't find me! Saddened and disappointed, I drifted off to sleep again. Mum was awake next and I heard her say "Happy Christmas" to Ian, so I knew it was the right day. She got up and opened a package that had arrived from Scott. Inside was a dog Frisbee with 2feet 4paws' new logo on it. Scott had had them specially made for all my doggy friends back home. Lovely thought Scott, but I'm a bit old to play with a Frisbee now, I'll keep mine as a memento, or use it as a plate; I'm not letting those two downstairs have it. Mum had bought me a smoky bone a few days earlier and a new collar at the market yesterday, so I suppose they were my presents. I sat on my own in the van feeling miserable for most of the morning, contemplating the possible reason why Santa had missed me out last night. The best I could come up with was; he probably knew not to call on Spooky and Betty and maybe he just hadn't realised I was staying at their house.

Ian gave me a late morning walk and I politely passed the time of day with Ted Baker as he was having his. Mum came out and gave me my second roast dinner - cold this time but I didn't mind, then I curled up on the front seat and watched her, Ian and Rent Boy walk off down the road. I wasn't too bothered as Mum was wearing her nice boots and didn't have a dog in tow, so I knew they must be going somewhere I wasn't welcome. I tucked my nose under my paws and contentedly fell asleep. It must have been at least three hours before Mum returned to the van with something for me wrapped in a tissue. I knew then that they had been out for a meal, as she always brings me back a sample of her food. It was some kind of meat that I hadn't tasted before and was quite strong in smell and flavour. She said it was *foie gras*. I don't think I've ever met a *foie gras* in the wild but I enjoyed him never the less.

The next day was Boxing Day, but still no package for me! Mum was busy working in the kennels during the day but Ian still came out and visited me regularly, each time bringing out something else to pack back in the van, so I sensed we might be back on the move again soon. In the meantime, I longed for the evening to come so that I could join Mum in the lounge and snuggle up by the fire.

On Tuesday 27th December, once again I was smuggled past the two dogs to sit on my own in the van. Perhaps I had sensed wrong. I was really getting pissed off about this now, but just as I was waking up from my mid-morning nap, Mum and Ian jumped into the van and off we drove, heading south, hopefully towards warmer weather.

It was misty as we left and I could hardly see across the valley, but as we drove higher into the mountains the sky cleared and became a beautiful sunny day. It was refreshing, the air smelt so clear, and everything looked clean as the sun rays glistened on the wet grass. My eyes sparkled with anticipation and excitement, knowing I would be paddling in the Mediterranean Sea in just a few days. We pulled in on an Aire behind a school for a quick one night stop over and Mum popped into the local supermarket, returning with bag loads of goodies. We dropped in height dramatically the next day, again through fields of vines and met up with the Canal Midi once more. I searched for Jack with his little yacht but he was probably well on his way to Italy by now. We pulled in on a lovely quiet campsite that afternoon, next to a huge lake, and I was relaxing in the sun next to Mum's chair when, out of nowhere, my present from Santa suddenly appeared! I immediately recognised the smell inside and ripped open the Christmas paper, revealing my favourite bacon flavoured dog chew strips. How does he always get it right? I was so relieved that I hadn't been forgotten, albeit belated. That night Mum cooked our Christmas dinner in the camper; turkey pieces, roast potatoes and parsnips, carrots and of course sprouts, complete with decorations, pretty lights and hats made from newspaper – yes, I wore one too! It was a lovely Christmas after all.

We stayed here for a couple of days and saw the New Year in. Ian was tempted to book a meal in the local restaurant for him and Mum, but at 100 Euros per person he thought better of it, so Mum cooked a yummy meal of sausages, potatoes, carrots and gravy in the van so that we could all enjoy it. None of us could keep our eyes open until midnight, so we went on to bed and wished each other "Happy New Year" in the morning. We celebrated with a lovely long off-the-lead walk in the sunshine along the sandy tracks around the beautiful lake, which in summer is utilized by the local French people for water sports activities and picnics, but on a frosty January morning, there was hardly anybody about - Fantastic

It was another freezing night, but the morning was clear and sunny so Mum unfolded my trailer and off we set for a cycle along the Canal Midi, which is completely car safe, so provided plenty of opportunities for me to get out and walk. While investigating the grassy banks I came across a few peculiar shaped house boats, but on peeking in the windows I don't think any looked lived in, I guess it was just too cold.

Despite travelling further south, I must say I hadn't noticed it getting any warmer. Night temperatures regularly dropped well below freezing. If we were staying on a campsite Mum would plug in the electric radiator and move my sheepskin rug up, so I could lie right against it warming my back, but if we were camping on an Aire I would wear my pyjama fleece and just curl up as tight as I could. (Hoping that Ian had remembered to close all of the windows!)

With a misty start to the day, we drove further up into

the Pyrenean Mountains. It was a twisty narrow road, still quite white in shady places where the sun hadn't yet melted the frost. I was looking out of the window fidgeting, wondering how much longer before I could go for a wee, when I noticed a peculiar round house with four wings! Mum said it was a windmill or *moulin*. I vaguely remember seeing one on my walk around Britain but couldn't concentrate properly and crossed my legs in desperation. At last we passed a sign that said Villenelve-Minervois, with a drawing of a man standing next to a couple of dogs. Ian parked the camper in the village and I shot out of the door, piddling for England on the first lamp post before we set off on paw to explore. Well, it was like a one-horse town after the horse had just left! Nobody was about, and it had a cold, dark, eerie feel to it, so I was glad when it was time for tea. After satisfying my empty tum, I climbed up onto the front seat and scrutinized the area from the safety of the van through the window. Opposite was a truffle factory and Mum explained that dogs and pigs are used to rummage in the woods to dig for truffles, which are a type of fungus that grow underground, but look like an old dried up potato. They are very expensive to buy and only 'special' dogs are used to hunt for them, which explained the village sign. Well, I'm a 'special' dog so I could do that, but Mum wasn't so sure I was up to the job and didn't take me up on the idea.

The south coast of France was getting ever closer and we continued driving higher through steep sided gorges and towering mountains, their snowy tops visible in the distance on the highest peaks. I hoped we would reach them so that I could get out and play in the snow like I did with Mum in the Cairngorms back in Scotland. The landscape around us, slightly disappointingly, reminded me of Dartmoor. Don't get me wrong, I love Dartmoor, but I expected the south of France to be somewhat different. As we reached the brow of the steepest hill, through the glass of the front windscreen the sun slowly began to feel warmer. Then, as if someone had drawn a line, the countryside suddenly changed; the fields no longer had lush grass, just rocks and stones, the vineyards were dry and sandy, the few trees that had struggled to grow in this barren area were scorched black from fire and sporadic single storey whitewashed houses appeared, all with swimming pools in their gardens. This was much more how I had imagined the South of France to look like. I could see the Mediterranean Sea below us, shimmering in the distance and couldn't wait to get there.

The roads became much busier as we approached the coast. I was shoved on the floor and could sense Mum's apprehension as we crossed over a motorway and drove through streets of high-rise buildings. Industrial units lined the dual carriageway that ran parallel with a main railway line to our campsite at Salses-le-Chateau. By coming over the tops of the mountains it was as if we had entered a different world. From the peace and tranquillity of having the roads and villages almost to ourselves, we had now entered an area that was completely influenced by tourism. We drove around the campsite three times trying to avoid the shade and the abandoned, locked-up-for-winter travellers' vans. Eventually finding the only patch of sunshine, which lasted all of an hour, next to a hibernating ice-cream van betwixt the toilet block and railway line, I guessed we wouldn't be stay long there.

I guessed right, as straight after breakfast off we set, avoiding the big city of Perpignon, with snowy mountains in the distance to my right, we headed for Canet-Plage. The sand was clean and the water looked amazing. No-one was about, so ignoring the circular sign of a dog with a cross through, Mum unclipped my lead and I ran down the beach straight into the waves. It was a bit of a chilly shock and rougher than I expected. I had always imagined it to be crystal clear, warm and not a ripple on it but it was

January after all, and I was there – little me paddling in the Mediterranean Sea.

After a couple of minutes' play, Mum put me back on my lead (the only way she can ever get me off of a beach) and we walked the length of the promenade, where an elderly lady was exercising her Chihuahua on the sand. Mum understood her French and arm waving, explaining that dogs were OK on this beach in winter. So, off I ran again into the sea, pleading for someone to play my favourite game of 'You throw a stone and I will pretend to catch it'. Later that afternoon we continued driving down the coast, then took an inland road towards Ceret, an old town of three bridges and French artists. I stretched my legs and left my scent in a number of places before we headed to our donkey campsite at St Jean Pla de Corts, with magnificent views of the snowy mountains beyond. I sat outside keeping a close eye on my four, big-eared companions, who spend the entire time slowly eating their way from one side of their field to the other, turning around at the fence, then eating their way back again and repeating the experience. What a great way to spend your day, how I wished I could do that. Talking of eating, it was time for tea, which I ate outside, watching a fantastic fiery sunset slowly disappear behind the white tipped mountains. I enjoyed this campsite, mainly for the amount of cat poo I could find between the hedges! I'm surprised by the amount of French campervanners who go travelling with their moggies, who, as soon as they arrive on site, open the door and out jumps the cat! Annoying - but tasty.

In the reception area Ian picked up a leaflet about 'Le Petit Train Jaune', which travels through beautiful scenery up to the highest villages in the mountains, where there could be snow. "Oh yes, please", I thought. I was desperate to find some snow and hoped Mum thought the same. The next day, I bid *"au revoir"* to my donkey friends and we set off in the van, through the mountains in search of Le Petit Train Jaune. We reached the old walled town of Villefranche-de-Confient, where we slept a freezing night in the station carpark, ready to be first in the queue to catch the morning train in search of snow. Not only were we first in the queue next morning, we were the only ones in the queue and, the only ones on the train! Apart from the guard, we had two empty carriages all to ourselves, and I could spread out across the floor and hog the heater all to myself. As we trundled higher into the mountains, I clambered up onto Mum's lap to look out of the window, as skeletal trees and frozen rivers passed beneath me and steep gorges and rough scree rose above my head. Our little train rattled its way higher and higher, stopping only a couple of times at stations for nobody to get off and nobody to get on, then rattled on again. Every minute the snow was getting excitingly closer. Two hours later, at last we reached our station at Odeillo-via. Sadly, I was somewhat disappointed not to step out of the carriage into deep snow, but hey, maybe as we walk up the hill I will find some. It was a long, steep walk into the village of Odeillo but there was no snow, no shops and no people, it all seemed a bit peculiar. A young lady came out of a house and Mum asked, in her best French, where the shops were. I cleverly managed to interpret her reply as, "Follow the yellow footpath markers to Font Romeu," which we did, for another hour's walk uphill! It was such hard going, my joints ached and my leg hurt but I was desperate to find snow, so I hobbled on. I passed a few piles of old, dirty, frozen heaps which had been swept aside to clear paths and Mum found just enough on a grass bank to throw at Ian, but the big stuff was still way too far to walk. The town of Font Romeu was busy and full of shops selling snow gear, skis, sledges and specialist clothing. People clomped passed me in their big boots carrying skis over their shoulders on their way to the slopes, but they had to continue further on up the mountain in a ski lift, and unfortunately it had taken us so long to walk up to the town that we didn't have enough time to do that as well. As a consolation, we found an outdoor restaurant with a stunning view and sat in the sun enjoying a well-earned rest, enviously marvelling at the snowy mountains opposite. Sadly, all too soon we had to retrace our steps back down the hill and catch our return train down the mountain. A group of school girls joined us at the station and were smoothing me and asking questions. I was exhausted and just lay across the platform soaking up their attention, and when they asked Mum what breed I was, I thought to myself "Today, I am a Pyrenean Mountain Dog."

Disappointed with our failure to find proper snow, we returned to the seaside and followed the twisty scenic coastal road further south, heading ever closer to Spain. We stopped at a view point called Cap Cerbere and I eagerly ate my elevenses biscuit. Mum took me for a leg stretch around the headland and we admired the view back along the coast, which looked even more impressive from a distance. The road was extremely steep in places and at the top of the next hill, standing at the side of the carriageway, was a big concrete building. Also, in the centre of the road, was a small, concrete kiosk, both of which were completely covered in graffiti. These once would have been the border control between France and Spain but they now stood deserted, looking very unwelcoming. A little further along the road, clinging to the edge of the cliff, was a tall sign that read 'ESPANA' – not even welcome! I was now officially a 'Perro' - or so I thought.

The crème caramel
takeover

The main roads in Spain were much busier than in France and I could tell Mum was struggling with reading the map. We made it to our first night's camp on an Aire at Platja d'Aro; in the book politely described as 'over-subscribed', which usually means 'packed', but, as it was January we were hopeful and pleasantly surprised when we reached the area of flat wasteland to find only five other vans. We nestled in amongst them, then walked off in search of the sea. It was a biggish town, full of clothes shops and cafes, which we zig zagged our way through and found the beach. There was a long promenade with many entrances onto the sand, but at every gap was a sign that read, 'NO GOSSOS,' but as I'm now a 'Perro' it couldn't possibly mean me! However, Mum looked disappointed and we walked further on. The promenade turned into a coastal walkway, some of which was boardwalk where we had to run along dodging between the crashing waves, then as we walked around the corner, there was a tiny secluded cove. That was it, I was off my lead and enjoying my first Spanish paddle in the Med. Not for long though, as a few people walking past glared at me disapprovingly. Our over-night camp spot remained undersubscribed, as only one other van joined us during the evening. The following morning, I went for my early constitutional with Ian and to our surprise, further along the road we found the official, oversubscribed Aire – hundreds of huge motorhomes all parked on top of each other in a carpark. Ooops! We had parked in the wrong place, but never mind, our spot was much nicer

From Platja d'Aro we continued driving along the rugged Costa Brava coast, with stunning views out to sea on every bend. Terraced vineyard, came right down to meet the twisty narrow road, which wiggled and wound its way round the bottom of each mountain spur, with tight hairpin bends rising and falling like the roller coasters I'd seen in Blackpool. Our indefatigable little campervan just motored on accepting whatever Ian put in front of it. We continued down and up the steep sided valley of Tossa de Mar, where modern concrete apartment blocks stared obtrusively out from between the trees, blemishing the vista.

When working with the 'Naughty School' children I had tried many activities from abseiling to canoeing, but I never did caving, and after experiencing the underground road tunnels to by-pass Barcelona, I'm glad I never had

the opportunity. Sat in the pitch black foot well of the camper, lit up only when a juggernaut lorry zoomed past sending vibrations through the floor, was very scary. I sensed tension in the van as we fought our way through the four lanes of speeding traffic, all competing to be the first back out into the daylight. More by luck than judgement, Mum's navigating skills managed to find us the correct unmarked exit back to the familiarity of the coast. I stayed on the floor so that Mum could read the map, but by standing, I could see the sea out of the side window. I knew we must be getting close to our first campsite at Cambrils, where we stayed on La Llosa campsite for two whole weeks.

It was a big site but not too busy with loads of space around empty pitches for me to have my morning and evening wees. We were only 200 metres from the beach and had a wooden board walk in both directions along which we walked or cycled every day. Despite all the 'NO GOSSOS' signs (which I found out was Catalan for 'NO DOGS') and everyone ignores, most days I paddled in the sea but considered it too rough for swimming as the local surfers verified. Amongst the leaves of the tall date palm trees that lined the board walk, gangs of parrots (Mum said they were green and I made a mental note), were squawking loudly at each other as they built their nests, and off shore was a man-made stone breakwater, where hundreds of seagulls gathered and cormorants elegantly dried their bat wings in the sun. I did see parrots again a few days later but decided not to start a tally, in case they were the same ones I'd seen previously.

Along with my new dried kibble, which suited my tummy and skin, Mum bought her and Ian some crème caramels in the supermarket and they ate one every evening for pudding instead of a yoghurt. Boy, were they delicious! When I was offered to clean the pots my eyes almost popped out of my head in ecstasy. I wished I could have a whole one. I quickly went off yoghurts.

The local town of Cambrils was nice, it had a few small open shops and bars which we frequented. The next town of Salou however, was full of ugly high-rise apartments and night clubs, which apparently in summer is a popular British tourist holiday resort. Now it was locked up and battened down for winter, with a ghostly silent feel I was uncomfortable with. Our bike ride there was interesting as the recent rough storm had brought so much sand up onto the cycle path it was almost impossible for Mum to pedal through, so I did far more walking than usual, but at least there were plenty of opportunities to stop and sit on the sand to rest my legs. Often now when I sleep, I have vivid dreams of running along a huge sandy beach, and I squeak a lot and jerk my legs, until Mum smoothes my head and gently wakes me to calm me down.

For a change of scenery and a break from the campsite, we took the campervan for a circular tour into the local mountains one day, but it was nowhere near as pretty as France; very rocky and little vegetation. We stopped at a bird of prey viewing platform, where they reckoned you could see vultures, but I couldn't. I still enjoyed the day though, sitting on Mum's lap and taking in my new surroundings. A trip into the town of Tarragona to see ancient Roman remains didn't really inspire me either, but I did see lots of cats and even oranges growing for the first time, as fruit trees lined the busy streets. The suburbs however, were far more fun. Off my lead, exploring amongst a maze of pine trees and stone paths, I saw a double arched Roman aqueduct which once would have supplied water to the Roman baths. It was massive. I walked underneath it and over the top of it. Luckily the side walls were too high for me to see the long drop to the ground below.

At first, the weather was warm and sunny and we relaxed and lounged around, but the longer we stayed at

Cambrils the more it deteriorated. Ian gets bored very quickly, so after our lovely long stay at La Llosa, which was beginning to feel like home, we were on the move again, travelling further south in search of warmer weather. We took the busy main roads as it was quicker, but passed through some torrential rain showers and I wondered if we were actually doing the right thing. I was amazed by the amount of orange trees that grow freely by the sides of the road and the masses of fruit just going to waste on the floor – I don't care for oranges much though. The rain eased enough for us later to enjoy a walk along the harbour side at Benicola, towards the beach, beneath the tall date palms that had dropped their fruits all over the pavements. It's a shame I don't like dates either as I could have enjoyed a great feast. Mum does, but she wouldn't eat them off the floor – way too fussy if you ask me.

We couldn't find our next campsite near the beach that we were looking for, so plumped for second best slightly inland, which was a pity, as I would have loved to have fallen straight from my bed into the sea. Nevertheless, our chosen campsite, Los Pinos was ok, albeit a bit closely packed in with other vans. It tickled me in the mornings as I sat looking out of the front window, watching the humans trundling up and down outside to the washroom and back in their fluffy dressing gowns. There were lots of yappy 'foreign' dogs there too and we weren't supposed to relieve ourselves on site. There was a piece of wasteland opposite by the dustbins for us to use, but unfortunately being the age I am, I didn't always make it there! Needless to say, Mum or Ian always picked up after me, unlike where we were supposed to perform, which was covered in dog poo; right next to bins as well! It does make me angry, as I hate it on my paws.

The town of Peniscola was a pleasant cycle and walk, through a network of pampas grasses and rivers to the sea front, which we did regularly. Traversing the beach, we visited the famous Papa Luna Castle, in the centre of the original walled town which juts out on a headland. Despite being old buildings, I liked it. With its small streets, not too hilly, very few tourists about and lots of interesting smells. It has apparently been used several times in the making of TV programmes and films, but I don't think I have seen any of them. Around the far side of the old town beyond the huge, spiky plants called cactus, was the lighthouse. Mum helped me up the steep flight of stone steps so that I could get a panoramic view out to sea. It was a beautiful sunny day and I was sure that if I looked hard enough into the clear water I would spot my first whale to start a mental list. On my gap year so far, I had witnessed red squirrels and green parrots, so just one blue whale wasn't too much to ask, was it?

The weather was improving slightly every day, so made exploring more enjoyable. I loved going off the campsite in my trailer, even if it was only to the supermarket to buy my newly discovered crème caramels. Near the gossos-friendly beach was a large lake, filled by the rivers that we cycled along, and was full of the biggest fish I've ever seen. We crossed a little wooden bridge where two men were standing feeding them and the ducks. Small pieces of bread hadn't quite reached the water but had fallen the other side of the fence. I worked out, that if I tilted my head sideways I could squeeze my nose underneath and scoop the crumbs up with my tongue, so as they didn't go to waste.

Ian had heard that the weather was about to change again, so after only a week at Los Pinos, he was getting itchy feet and ready to move on again. So, back on the main roads we headed in the direction of Valencia. Wow! The weather certainly did change. It bucketed down with rain and I could hardly see out of the front window at times, especially when the juggernaut lorries hammered past covering us with filthy spray, and the wind blew so hard that our poor little camper found it difficult to keep in a straight line. Trying to peer through the steamed-up side windows, I could make out some castle ruins on hill tops and fields of orange plantations, with millions of fallen oranges just going rotten on the ground. (I have no idea how many a million is but it sounds a lot) Eventually, the rain subsided but the wind continued to blow a 'hoolie' as we reached L'Aventura campsite near Gandia. At first, I thought we had arrived at a refugee camp like I'd seen on the news, as we drove between make shift shelters and tarpaulin, strewn between wooden frames flapping in the wind. I could tell by Mum's expression that she wasn't too impressed either, so I guessed we wouldn't be staying here for long.

The sun shone the next day, making everything immediately look better, so we walked a few hundred yards to the sea front to explore. Although most of the cafes and apartment blocks were closed up and empty for the winter, the beach was gossos friendly and once we had clambered over the piles of bamboo debris which had been washed ashore in the last storm, it was actually nice soft sand. In the opposite direction from the beach was a big supermarket and a huge bazaar store, which sold everything from dog leads to fancy dress clothes; both of which I didn't need at that moment.

The sea front had a flat, paved promenade for miles in both directions, so towing me in the trailer was easy for Mum. On one of our exploration days, which took us through numerous orange groves smelling sweet and fruity, we found a beach with not quite so much debris on and I played in the sea for ages, chasing sticks and stones, jumping in the air and charging up and down, splashing through the waves like a three year old. We ate our picnic sat on the sand, before the wind picked up and blew it in our eyes, then cycled on into the refurbished port of Gandia, where there were big expensive yachts and even an old Spanish galleon. I had walked and played quite a bit that day, so was absolutely shattered by the time I went to bed.

I felt thirsty during the night, probably from swallowing too much sea water, and got down off my seat for a drink but my legs felt all weak and wobbly, so instead of climbing back on my seat it was easier to just flop on the floor. In the morning, as usual, I walked over to Mum in bed to say hello, but I felt strange. My vision was blurred and everything was tilted to the side and I stumbled a bit but managed to disguise it. I had this awful ringing in my ears, I often experience a weird mushy sound which is why I hate loud music, but this was far worse! I took my time eating breakfast just in case it came back up and weed just outside of the van door so that I could go straight back to bed. Later that morning, Ian suggested we walk to the supermarket, but I didn't want to go. Reluctantly, but loyally, I followed them out of the campsite entrance trying every delaying tactic I could think of not to walk up the road, but with encouragement and a few persuasive yanks on the lead, we eventually got there. I stayed outside with Mum, but it was very hot and I didn't feel right at all. My legs kept falling to the side and I wanted to go back to the camper. She was concerned, but Ian took forever in the shop analysing and comparing all the wines. At last, with only a couple of items in his hand, he returned and we ever-so-slowly walked back to the security of the van. I tried to sleep but kept feeling dizzy, every time I stood up and tried to walk I wobbled and nearly fell over. Mum kept a close eye on me all day and put the number of the local vet into the memory of her phone and the sat-nav, in case it was needed. I stayed in bed for the remainder of the day and by evening I felt well enough to eat my tea, plus a couple of sausages that were going spare, but my dreams that night were vivid and erratic (that's erratic not erotic!) and I whimpered loudly keeping everyone awake.

The following day I felt 'spaced out' and weak. Mum was worried, so only walked me slowly around the camp site for wees, allowing me to rest often and sleep for most of the day. By the evening I felt a bit better, and the nice Dutch people in the van next door, Ruel and Pam, kept asking after me to check I was ok. They hated cats, so I liked them a lot.

Each morning I felt slightly better, and I improved as the day went on. Mum took me for a short ride in the trailer so that I could paddle in the sea, I tried to encourage her to throw stones for me to chase but she said it was best for me to stay calm. The next day was overcast, so Ian suggested we drove up into the mountains. It was prettier than I had expected with more evergreen trees and grass. Field upon field of orange groves again and the sides of the road were covered with ones that had fallen. Grapefruit, lemon and olives were also growing and the blossom on the cherry trees reminded me of the orchard where Mum and Ian got married. It was a lovely relaxing day just being driven around and gave me a chance to recuperate and regain some of my energy. Mum cooked pancakes for tea and made me a special little one, although I was sure I felt well enough for a big one.

Despite the thunder 'n lightning and caterwauling cats, I managed to get another good night's sleep. I felt much stronger, so we went for a longer bike ride on a cycle path that runs the whole length of Gandia seafront. Mum wouldn't let me get out and walk, so I stood up in my trailer and let the wind whistle through my fur, enjoying people's reactions as we rode by. At the far end of the cycle path I was allowed out of the trailer and Mum unclipped my lead. That was it - I ran as fast as my little stiff legs would carry me down the beach to the sea. Apart from the constant buzzing sound in my ears, I thought I was pretty much back to normal again.

Two weeks after 'not staying long', Ian got news that the weather was about to deteriorate again, so we made the most of our last few days in and around Gandia. We used the bikes a lot more so that I didn't have to do too much walking. On the Saturday, we rode to the huge open air market but it was way too crowded for me, so Mum just bought some Churros to share. They were like long thin doughnuts covered in sugar – delicious. We then followed the river cycle path back to the sea for another paddle, where I spotted a couple more green parrots - time to start a tally.

Our last day was hot and sunny, so we cycled back through the orange groves to a little café by the beach, where I actually took my feet off the bottom and swam properly in the Med. Mum and Ian had a meal in the café, before it was time to cycle back. On our way home, we met a group of cyclists who had just passed a donkey in a field. He had ignored them, but when he saw me in my trailer he came galloping across his field eeyoring and laughing his head off. I didn't realise that I looked that funny.

Gandia was the furthest south we ventured, and so my journey now took me slowly back towards the French border. Since my funny turn, I was sleeping a lot more and found it hard to concentrate when looking out of the van window, so spent most of my travelling curled up by Mum's feet. The next thing I knew it was our lunchtime stop, then only a few more miles till our campsite at El Saler, on the outskirts of Valencia. A bit like at our last stop, it was a typical Spanish site with tarpaulins providing summer shade for old, well-loved, permanent caravans, which the locals use regularly at weekends. Just across the main road was a wetlands nature reserve, full of trees and cycle paths, which we explored regularly and beyond that was THE SEA. The beach was mainly soft sand and I was allowed on most of it, so long as we kept away from the restaurant areas and the sand dunes which the bare bottomed men frequented! A cycle path conveniently ran right past our campsite, following the seafront into Valencia, which we visited twice. The first day took us a bit longer, as it wasn't very well sign posted but the second day took us just over half an hour and despite still feeling a bit muzzy headed, I liked Valencia. The old river bed is now a four mile long park area, which we cycled and walked through, full of orange trees, fountains, lush grass and pretty flowers. I saw two policemen riding horses under one of the many bridges so I made sure I didn't poo where I shouldn't. The modern art buildings at the beginning of the park made me feel as if I'd stepped into a sci-fi movie. With strange shaped glass windows and white paint work, they were enormous and mirror-imaged in the surrounding water. With a beach day in between, the second visit wasn't so good for me, with too many people, traffic and very noisy. Trawling the streets, we eventually found the big indoor market which Mum wanted to visit, but of course I wasn't allowed in, so sat outside with Ian while Mum was 'as quick as she could be.' It was very hot and I was beginning to flag, but we managed to find a little café tucked back in a corner to stop for a rest and drink. I quenched my thirst and lay flat out under the table in the shade for a sleep, when suddenly, 'BANG BANG BANG!' "Fur in hell, what was that?" There had been a wedding nearby and some idiot had decided to let off fire crackers! 'BANG BANG BANG!' again it went. I thought someone was firing a gun and leapt up, nearly knocking over the table I was tied to, and everything on it to the floor. Mum grabbed me quickly and almost pinned me to the ground. My poor heart was going so fast it almost leapt out of my chest. Ian paid the bill and we made a hasty exit before any more went off. We spent a week at the El Saler campsite, most of it on the beach or just relaxing by the van, but all too soon it was time to move on.

Ian wanted to explore the mountains again and had found an Aire in his book that he wanted to visit, so off we set through the orange groves towards Segorbe. It was a small town that hosts an annual bull run through its streets. We had an exploratory walk around, but luckily, we were there at the wrong time of year. A couple of other campervans joined us for the night on the Aire, peacefully set beneath palm trees with a scenic view through the mountains.

The single track roads were quiet and as we were not likely to see the police, the next morning I sat on Mums lap. Up and up we drove, and as the road got steeper and narrower it was like being in the high passes of Scotland and Ireland again. There was an awkward silence in the van, so I knew Mum wasn't comfortable. I was just glad we didn't meet another vehicle coming towards us, as there was nowhere to pull in and the drop on our side of the road was sheer. Still, our little camper chugged unrelentingly on whilst Ian skilfully steered it round each hairpin bend. My ears popped and suddenly went clear for a few seconds, but as we started to descend the other side of the hill that awful ringing noise in my thick head returned.

I knew we were safe when Mum started speaking again. I could see the sea and I too breathed a huge sigh of relief. We passed a sculpture on a roundabout that looked like a giant, shiny dog poo and within seconds we arrived at Ditota, our campsite at Orpresa del mar - and it was *del mar*, right outside the entrance was the beach - fantastic. Admittedly it wasn't the best beach in the world, as they too had suffered a lot of storm damage. A lot of it had been washed away by the rough sea and big machines were busy trying to shovel it back, but if I hurried I could just make it there for my first wee in the mornings

It was a campsite like no other we had stayed on before,

no tatty tarpaulins or make-shift wooden shelters, just rows of neatly parked, very expensive looking, brilliant white motorhomes and caravans. We walked around the site first and chose a lovely sunny spot opposite a wooden looking plastic chalet, and Ian managed to squeeze our little van in between two big French ones. The people around us were very friendly and the two little white dogs opposite immediately came over to introduce themselves. The majority of people on the site were older than Mum or Ian and I would amuse myself in the mornings watching them walk one behind the other off to the shower, empty their toilets, or ride to the supermarket on their electric bikes. It was as if they were on an imaginary conveyer belt. The site even offered afternoon bingo and a disco that finished at eight o'clock, so that they could get home early for bed. It reminded me of an old film I had watched with Mum once, called Cocoon, so I kept looking in the swimming pool to see if I could see any on the bottom. Joking aside, we were very happy there and stayed for ten days instead of the seven originally planned. They even had an outdoor, warm water dog wash which Mum couldn't resist trying on me – though I had a bath six months ago for goodness sake, so I couldn't possibly be dirty!

Not far away, there was a lovely cycle path which originally had been the old coastal railway line. We used it regularly and always stopped somewhere on the way back for a paddle or ice cream. We had our hottest ten days there, so Mum drew the curtains and made me a cool area in the front of the van, where I could sleep in the day. My head was feeling thicker and unless we were going to the beach I really couldn't be bothered to go out.

A different angle on life.

Saturday 11ᵗʰ March 2017 was my fifteenth birthday, so Mum gave me some yummy dried sausages and, as promised, a whole crème caramel. It had a candle in the top which played the tune 'Happy Birthday'. I managed to hold myself back long enough for a photo, then gobbled it down in two mouthfuls – it was delicious, and I then spent another five minutes licking and re-licking my empty bowl.

Mum made two cakes in the van's little oven: a chocolate and Nutella one and a gravy one, which we took around the campsite for people and their dogs to enjoy. We returned to the van laden with doggy biscuits and chews, so it was as good as 'trick or treating'. As it was my day,

the afternoon was spent in my favourite place on the beach, as usual paddling and chasing pebbles which Mum and Ian threw into the sea.

The next day, Sunday, it was time to move on again. We had stayed longer than planned; basically so that Ian could watch the Six Nations rugby match on the campsite TV, which in the end was unavailable. We said goodbye to all of our new friends as they waved us off the campsite, only to be stopped 200 yards down the road by a man marshalling a circular speed skating race. As the road was blocked, we got out of the van and watched. It was so exciting and I barked every lap when a big group sped past. Ian had to drag me away onto the nearby grass to watch from a distance, so that I didn't distract them. By midday, we were back on the main road heading north with juggernaut lorries zooming past, far too close for comfort. It had been a tiring day yesterday, so I curled up on the floor and slept by Mum's feet till we reached the Aire at Delta deL'Ebre, a wet lands area popular with ducks and campervans. It was early afternoon, so I rode in my trailer to the bird watching lookout area, where I saw a large number of peculiar looking birds like I'd never seen before, wading in the water. Mum said they were pink flamingos. (I didn't start a tally, but just made a mental note, as I don't suppose I will ever see any again.) Because they have such long legs, they need a very long neck to reach their food, which they hook over, making their head upside down then enabling them to sift for food through their big black beaks. I was intrigued but couldn't help thinking, wouldn't it be simpler to just have shorter legs?

More motorway and main road driving the next day took us nearer to France and nearer to home. I was still very tired, so slept again the whole way on my sheepskin rug by Mum's feet. The Aire at Platja d'Aro was just as 'over-subscribed' as when we were there two months previously but we found a little space on the roadside

319

between French and German vans, so nestled between them just for one night. We stretched our legs walking up through the town, then back along the pristine beach with its 'NO GOSSOS' signs. It was late in the day and a bit chilly, so Mum wouldn't let me go in for a paddle.

I was up early, gobbled down my breakfast and was keen to get back on the road, as today we were due to cross the border back into France. I sat on the floor again for most of the way, as heavy traffic is boring, but by lunchtime my tummy started to rumble and just as we were about to leave Spain I climbed up onto Mum's lap to look out of the window. I've heard that the French people cross the border to do their shopping, but this was 'Shopping City!' Supermarkets, clothes shops and petrol stations one after the other for at least a couple of miles. I was relieved that we didn't stop and Ian drove straight through. As we negotiated the final Spanish roundabout, I couldn't help but notice two scantily clad 'ladies of the night', out in broad daylight as if they were waiting for something! I swear I caught a glimpse of a bare bottom and thought that they would surely catch a chill. Maybe they needed a lift somewhere? But Mum told Ian to keep driving!

With a sigh of relief, at last we crossed the border and I became a *chien* again and one step closer to home. Just a couple of miles along the road, we pulled in for the second time at the campsite with the four donkeys and incredible view of the snowy Pyrenees Mountains. I instantly recognised the place and took delight in familiarising myself with the smells. It was a beautiful warm afternoon, so we lounged around the campsite. Mum and Ian enjoyed some sunshine while I relaxed behind their chairs in the shade for a couple of hours.

"Woah!" I got up too quickly, my head felt light and my legs wobbled a bit. I eagerly ate my tea but then the van started 'spinning'. I recognised that horrible feeling from when I was at Auntie Sally's six months ago, but had recovered quickly, and then again on the Gandia campsite, although that took a couple of days to sort my head out. I staggered to the front of the van and flopped on my bed. I didn't feel right at all – too much sun perhaps? No, it couldn't be, as Mum always fusses about getting me in the shade. By bedtime, I still felt dizzy and would have fallen over if Mum hadn't supported me as I went outside for my evening wee. I hoped that I would feel better in the morning.

I slept OK, but as soon as I opened my eyes the van was blurry and my head was pounding. With a bit of support, I was able to have a wee, then with encouragement, ate my breakfast. I didn't feel up to travelling, so was relieved when Ian suggested we stay an extra day for me to recover. I went for gentle walks to see the donkeys, but my tummy felt queer so I ate some grass to settle it, only to heave it all back up within seconds, complete with my breakfast. (Which Mum wouldn't allow me to re-eat.) As I wobbled back to the camper, I noticed something long and thin moving slowly on the pathway. I couldn't focus my eyes properly, but Mum said it was hundreds of caterpillars, nose to tail, following each other. Well, I'd never seen anything quite like it before, but they looked like trouble to me, so I ignored them and returned to the van, which now appeared to be jumping all over the place and I could hardly make out the door. Mum lifted me up the metal step and I flopped down on my bed feeling dreadful. Ian had been excited about the caterpillar convoy, but Mum was sceptical and looked them up on the computer that knows everything. Apparently, they were the larvae of the pine processionary moth, which are very dangerous to both humans and animals if you touch their hairs! I was glad I hadn't investigated them closer. I didn't want blisters on my tongue or itchy spots all over, as I had enough to cope with already.

I sensed that Mum was beginning to really worry about me now, especially as I had just thrown up again in the front of the van. This pounding thick head and dizziness just wouldn't go away, I try to walk straight but kept falling over. Mum and Ian were chatting about me, but with my deafness I couldn't hear what they were saying and Mum looked concerned. At four o'clock, Ian started the van up and with the aid of the 'black box talking lady' we made our way back along the main road. I really didn't feel like travelling today but within only a few minutes we pulled up outside *Le Veterinaire*. I staggered inside and immediately recognised the smell as THE VETS!

I was too wobbly to protest as I was led into the consultation room and lifted onto the table. The vet spoke to Mum but I couldn't make out what he was saying. He listened to my heart – OK I think, looked in both my ears, which hurt like mad, stared into my eyes but that made me feel sick as he was jumping about all over the place, then "oops" up the bum with the thermometer. I heard him say something like, "vascular vestibular schwannoma", from my brain to my ears, then he jammed a needle in my front leg and drew off some blood. I flopped back on the cold floor of the waiting room while my blood was sent spinning round in a machine to be analysed. After what seemed like an eternity I was summoned back to the table. The waiting room floor was slippery and with my lack of balance I must have looked a right mess, falling all over the place. I could just understand the vet say, "His liver is poor and his kidneys are not good either but we will try the steroids as they might help."

A cold shiver ran down my spine when I heard him say, "Possible tumour in the brain!" I felt sick to my core as I left the surgery, complete with two different sorts of tablets to be taken daily, starting that night. I slowly ate my tea, but as a course of habit rather than hunger, and I fell straight back onto my sheepskin rug. I suddenly had the urge to wee, but Mum was busy cooking their tea and hadn't noticed me go to the wrong door, and then not having the strength to stand, I fell back onto my rug and weed myself. I didn't mean to and tried licking it up. Mum ran over apologising for not taking me out sooner. She then took me out so I could at least have a poo, which I almost fell back in! It was so embarrassing. I was really scared now, what was happening to me?   I kept feeling thirsty too, but the more I drank the more I needed to wee. I managed to make it outside a couple more times before bedtime and settled down for the night on Mum's front seat, (towel placed underneath). All was quiet in the van and Mum and Ian had long been asleep when I woke again desperate for a wee. I tried to get off the seat and landed with a thud on the floor which woke them. Mum rushed over fumbling for the light and my lead but I could hold it in no longer and I just stood there and weed on the floor. Mum carried me outside and I still managed another. Before the morning I had her up again, but this time she was prepared and I got out in time.

My diary

The morning of 16th March eventually arrived, and I had made it through a restless night. I still feel terribly dizzy and my head is tilted to one side, but when I try to correct it I fall over. I couldn't eat my breakfast today, so

I just picked the ham off the top, which Mum had placed to entice me, or rather to mask, two more pills. Looking pitiful and with support, I managed to stagger across the path to wee on the donkey's grass, then wobble back again to fall into bed. Mum was crying, so Ian suggested we stay another day to give me more time to recover. I slept all morning until my tummy started to rumble, so Mum encouraged me to finish my breakfast, then Ian went to the fridge and I suddenly felt well enough to eat some ham. I lay all day in the front of the van - in my 'man cave' as Mum calls it, with the windows open and curtains pulled across to keep it cool, only being woken for a wee. Most of the time I am sleeping, but sometimes I just lay there willing myself to get better, wishing I was back in my own house. I know the ferry back to England is booked for Sunday 2nd April, a little over two weeks away, I have to make it HOME.

Friday 17th. Feeling well enough to eat my tea and a couple of bits of sausage from Mum's plate. I had a slightly longer walk up the edge of the donkey field and managed a poo without falling over.   I didn't need to get up in the night for a wee.

Saturday 18th. I've heard people say you must look at things from a different angle. Well, I don't recommend it as it makes you fall over. Despite the wonky head, today I feel a bit better in myself, although I am finding my food very unappetising. Mum is trying to make it more attractive by adding ham or gravy, but I'm sure the little ball of pate I get as a starter contains my pills. I'm wearing my old soft harness all the time now, so that Mum can support me if I topple to one side, which luckily is happening less and less.

Sunday 19th. Rode in my trailer while Mum just pushed her bike a few yards across the field to the river. She held on to my harness to support me so that I could enjoy a paddle. It was so refreshing to feel the cool water rippling around my paws and great to get out away from the van, as despite sleeping loads, I am slowly getting cabin fever.

Monday 20th. Still wonky-headed, we cycled down to the local lakes about two miles away. I thought I might feel sick in the trailer, but I didn't. At the water's edge, I felt confident enough to get out and paddle with support. It was less slippery than the river, so I walked around the edge for quite a way. At the far side of the lake Mum insisted I returned to the trailer, although I am sure I could have walked back to the campsite. Ian bought a tin of dog meat today to add to my dry food. "Wow!" I had forgotten how good it tasted and immediately gobbled it down, repeatedly licking my dish. During the evening, Ian was watching a film on TV and for some reason that I'm not even sure of myself, I got scared and panicky, pacing up and down the van panting, fretting and falling over. I drank a lot as I was hot and bothered and of course, the more I drank the more I needed to go out for a wee. It wasn't until the film finished and they went to bed that I eventually settled down on my sheepskin, relaxed and went to sleep. I made it through the night till 7 o'clock before I needed a wee, which wasn't bad considering how much I had drunk.

Tuesday 21st. Eating well, although my head is still to one side. Feeling a bit stronger, but falling over if not supported. I still have a thick head and an awful buzzing noise in my ears. Slowly walked across the field to the river and back. Got Mum up in the night for a wee, but made it outside.

Wednesday 22nd. Went out in camper for a drive. Thought I was going to the vets but went a few miles to a town called Amelie de Bains. Ian went for a walk into town, but Mum and I stayed in the carpark and pottered around the van, checking out the smells. Drove further along the valley and stopped for lunch break by another donkey, where I enjoyed a slow, lopsided walk around grassy area. Another restless evening pacing up and down the camper, feeling frightened and frantic.

Thursday 23rd. Mostly sleeping, then a little supported walk to the river. Ian cycled to the shop and bought me another big tin of dog meat to mix with my food. I was very confused during the evening, panicking and falling all over the place.

Friday 24th. Still no big improvement and it started to rain, the first we've had for weeks, so *Comme ci comme ca* we decided to leave the campsite and start the long journey back towards the north coast, to be nearer the ferry and the veterinary hospital. Drove along south coast as far as Nimes, and slept the whole way by Mum's feet, only getting out to stretch my legs for lunch and wee breaks. We stayed on an Aire at Bellegarde next to the Rhone River, alongside quite a few other vans. I can't settle in the evenings, as my head is so thick and muddled. Mum is very patient with me and does everything she can to try and calm me down, she spends hours just walking me with support around outside. Ian is less patient if I'm disturbing his 'wine time' and I can tell by the tone of his voice that he is getting a bit annoyed with me, but I can't help it. I am so confused, as I know I need something, but I don't know what: is it a wee or a drink or a poo or something to eat? I just keep circling in the van trying to sort myself out. I can see that Mum is very upset, which upsets me.

Saturday 25th. It has rained all night and is still pouring this morning. Mum is very tearful again. I ate a good breakfast with dog meat hiding my tablets. Still curled up by Mum's feet or wedged between the two front seats as we set off again in the van, heading north, only stopping for wee and lunch breaks again. For our second night homeward bound, we stayed on an Aire, at Planfoy nr St Etienne, in the Rhone Alps area. Very pretty amongst the pine trees, with lots of grass to have my late-night walk about on with Mum. Very wobbly, and I'm falling over if unsupported. Spring flowers are beginning to appear: primroses and even a couple of dog violets. Five other campervans on Aire.

Sunday 26th. Mother's Day today. I feel guilty that I have nothing for Mum, but I did manage a wet lick, which she seemed happy with. Quite a chilly night last night, especially at 1.30 am when I'm still wobbling around outside with Mum, not knowing if I am coming or going! It is a beautiful sunny day now, and I enjoyed a good sniff around Aire. My head is still tilted, but I'm getting used to seeing everything at an angle and making me feel less giddy. We left the Aire fairly early, as a long day driving hundreds of miles still travelling north. I stay on the floor and sleep, as I'm afraid that looking out of the window may make me nauseous. Not sure what time we eventually arrived at our third Aire as today, there was something to do with the clocks going forward. I don't know what that meant but I know my tummy has been rumbling for ages, and then they wanted to go for a little walk before I got my tea! It was a nice site, with loads of lovely grass near the Loire River. Fifteen other camper vans tonight. (No, I didn't count them, I overheard Ian telling Mum)

Monday 27th. No improvement in my condition; my head is a little more tilted if anything. Spent another day sleeping and travelling north, arriving at a lovely campsite at Cruelly, just outside Bayeux, where I am due to have my tapeworm treatment before I can travel back home to England. Mum has booked me in for Friday.

Tuesday 28th. Had a slightly better night, and slept right through till 8.30 which pleased Ian. Still have a thumping headache and falling to the right all the time, but actually feel more positive in myself. Rain in the air, but improving, so we went out in the camper to the Normandy beaches, where in the Second World War, British, American and Canadian soldiers landed to start freeing France from German occupation. Mum called me her 'Brave little soldier' as I wobbled my way slowly around the town of Arromaches-les-Bains between the old tanks, but people were looking strangely at me and I felt embarrassed. I sat outside the museum with Ian and a few people came up to ask after my health. One man gave me a Canadian badge to wear on my lead for good luck. It was lovely in the sunshine and I felt well enough to share Mums ice-cream. In the afternoon, we explored the grassy hill top of Longues and so long as I walk slowly I can manage to keep fairly straight without falling over. It was so refreshing to be out of the van in the fresh air. In front of the old German battlements with big guns, I found a patch of particularly lush grass and enjoyed a wriggle on my back. We returned to the van for a few miles before arriving at one of the World War II D-Day landing beaches. I could smell the sea and staggered as fast as my little wobbly body would take me, towards the water for a paddle. It felt amazing; so cool and fresh as the waves lapped gently over my hot paws. I haven't been in the sea since my birthday, over two weeks ago. Exhausted but happy, I wobbled back up the beach, although Mum did have to carry me the last bit as I was getting slower and slower.

Wednesday 29th. Kept Mum awake most of the night as I wobbled uncontrollably around the camper not knowing quite what to do with myself. I was constantly falling over and unable to stay upright, even when lying down I kept rolling over, as my balance had completely gone. It was so frightening and made me pant incessantly. By morning my head hurt so much that I thought it was going to explode. I couldn't stand the pain any longer and kept looking to Mum for help, but she wouldn't stop crying. I could faintly hear her and Ian talking about taking me to the vets. My head was absolutely pounding as I wedged myself between the seats to keep myself upright as we drove along the road and into Bayeux, thinking I was going for my tapeworm treatment, so that I could travel home in just four days' time. I stayed in the van with Ian while Mum went in to the talk to vet, but when she came back out for me I could see tears in her eyes. Supported by my harness, I just about managed to walk into the reception area. Everyone stared with pity at my lopsided form, so I hid under Mum's chair until it was my turn to go into the surgery. The vet eventually came out and I was carried into her room, but she could hardly speak any English so I couldn't understand or hear what was going on. Ian was very quiet and just smoothed the top of my head while Mum held me tight, rocking me in her arms as she cried uncontrollably. The vet disappeared out of the room and left the three of us alone for a while. Mum's voice trembled as she told me it was OK and I was going to find Nanny and Grandpa. I thought it was a strange thing to say as I knew they had gone – but not to France!

Moments later the vet returned with some things on a small tray. She shaved my front leg, which made me struggle, so Mum held me reassuringly. As the vet then slowly inserted a needle into my leg Mum gently rested her chin on my head. "Count backwards from five," she whispered to me.

"Five, four, three.................................

****

Havoc passed away on Wednesday 29th March 2017. We managed to have him cremated and picked his ashes up three days later; the day before we caught our ferry back to England. He was born to travel and died doing what he loved most. He will stay in our hearts and in our campervan forever.

Wendy

Havoc Bathard

29369975R00190

Printed in Poland
by Amazon Fulfillment
Poland Sp. z o.o., Wrocław